BLACK WOMEN
IN SEQUENCE

Deborah Elizabeth Whaley

BLACK WOMEN IN SEQUENCE

Re-inking Comics,
Graphic Novels,
and Anime

UNIVERSITY OF WASHINGTON PRESS
Seattle and London

This publication was made possible in part by a grant from the College of Liberal Arts and Sciences at the University of Iowa.

© 2016 by the University of Washington Press
Printed and bound in the United States of America
Design by Thomas Eykemans
Composed in Andada, typeface designed by Carolina Giovagnoli for Huerta Tipográfica
19 18 17 16 5 4 3 2 1

UNIVERSITY OF WASHINGTON PRESS
www.washington.edu/uwpress

LIBRARY OF CONGRESS CATALOGING-IN-PUBLICATION DATA
Whaley, Deborah Elizabeth.
  Black women in sequence : re-inking comics, graphic novels, and anime / Deborah Elizabeth Whaley.
    pages   cm
  Includes bibliographical references and index.
  ISBN 978-0-295-99495-6 (hardcover : acid-free paper) —
  ISBN 978-0-295-99496-3 (pbk. : acid-free paper)
  1. Comic books, strips, etc.—History and criticism.   2. African American women in literature.   3. Africans in literature.   4. Women in literature.   5. Graphic novels—History and criticism.   I. Title.
  PN6725.W48 2016
  741.5'973—dc23   2015012083

The paper used in this publication is acid-free and meets the minimum requirements of American National Standard for Information Sciences—Permanence of Paper for Printed Library Materials, ANSI Z39.48–1984. ∞

For my mother
Emma Ruth Whaley

CONTENTS

PREFACE

I would buy comics, but I would take them from the store in a brown
paper bag held close to my stomach sheepishly, as if it were some form
of shameful porn. I had an hour bus ride from the [comic book store],
but I wouldn't take the comics out until I was safely at home. In a neigh-
borhood that was majority white . . . I was surrounded by other brothers. . . . I was comfortable. I was at home. I had a people. And they were,
for all their acne and dandruff, *beautiful*.

—Mat Johnson, "The Geek"

Most scholarly books on comics begin with commentary by the author, who
admits to loving comics in early childhood or young adulthood, immerses
the reader in an ethnographic moment of fans and readers, or establishes
distance by asserting the author's primary role as a scholar. Popular books
on the topic are usually by journalists or writers or artists of comics, who
provide a window into their writing and artistic process, and an analysis
that instructs potential producers, satisfies readers and fans with origin stories, and warns of narrative spoilers. As a scholar and artist who grew up
finding solace in drawing comics, and later in alternative rock subcultures
in close alignment with the broad artistic spectrum of sequential art, my
foray into comics takes both a similar and a different authorial route. Multiple subject positions and interdisciplinary training in American Studies
shape how I position myself in the fantastical world of sequential art.

I am a Black woman in a fanboy world.[1] I did training in cartooning as
a teenager; I maintain the artistic practice of painting and mixed-media

art; I build content in the doppelgänger world of virtual avatars; and I am a teacher and researcher of American history, literature, critical theory, film, and popular culture. Being a racial-ethnic and gender minority as well as an artist and scholar situates me in a position to think and to write about sequential art from multiple frameworks. As an artist and cultural curator, I understand on a personal and a commercial level the compartmentalization and devaluation of Black women's creative work. Indeed, being a participant in and researcher of sequential art subcultures has its challenges.

Despite gains in racial and gender diversity at national events such as Comic-Con, comic book stores and regional comic book conventions remain predominantly white and male domains. Cosplay notwithstanding,[2] these sites are difficult for women of color to penetrate, thus converting the original intent of this book from on-the-ground ethnography into more of a cultural history and netnography of sorts.[3] I have never seen anyone in a comic book store who shares my ethnic *and* gender identity. Further, with little written on the topic to date, researching a book about Black women in comics has been like an ongoing treasure hunt, insofar as there was a derailment of the thrill, anticipation, and reward of discovery by the frustration that emerges when one meets a dead end. Internet fan sites, organizations such as the online Museum of Black Superheroes, Black Girl in Media, the Ormes Society for Black women in comics, the Nerds of Color, the annual East Coast Black Age of Comics Convention, and the Midwest Ethnic Convention for Comics and Arts provide a forum for comic artists and *Afrofans* to find information, fun, and community. Of course, this was not always the case.

Like many in the 1970s, I have fond memories of watching reruns of *Batman* on television, especially episodes with appearances by Batgirl and Eartha Kitt's rendition of Catwoman. The visual images of superheroines (Batgirl) and antiheroes (Catwoman) provided contradictory yet powerful symbols of womanhood to aspire to: Batgirl was a girl-next-door type who sought social justice in a criminal world. Catwoman was a powerful, strong-minded, and sexy woman—a rare example of blackness on 1960s television that did not fit the proverbial stereotypes of Black womanhood in the dominant imagination. For me, the visual medium of sequential art was and is a matter of subjectivity and pleasure; it is also a matter of cultural production and consumption.

Writer Mat Johnson notes the power of comics to obtain a sense of self and subjectivity. As a young Black male raised solely by his mother, Johnson found that the pages of superhero comics filled a magical space left empty by the lack of a masculine figure in his household.[4] Later in life, Johnson would assert his affinity for comic book fandom as the positive essence of geek power on the racially expansive continuum of blackness. In her discussion of Black heroic narratives in comics, cultural critic Rebecca Wanzo tells a similar story in regard to her affinity for Wonder Woman, but, in contrast to Johnson, Wanzo asserts that the preponderance of white comic heroes and villains creates a problematic for readers and viewers of color. She writes that white iconography places Black youth in a position of identifying with "cultural representations unlike them," despite the "vagaries of [identification] practices" that these superheroes and antiheroes represent.[5]

In her book *The Right to Rock*, Maureen Mahon provides an ethnographic or participant-observer and scholarly account of the Black Rock Coalition; she argues that the post-1960s civil rights era gave birth to a growing number of middle-class Black youth who lived in predominantly white suburbs and found in rock and punk music an alternative subculture of resistance.[6] This environment also gave birth to what I explore in the last chapter of this book as the Afropunk movement, as well as what I name and theorize as the Afrofan subculture, that is, an articulation of a dual identification with alternative music subcultures of resistance with being a reader, fan, and in some cases producer of sequential art.[7] This articulation is not particular to the demographic of Afrofans or Black consumers. As studies on the riot grrrl movement assert, the production and consumption of comics and zines was a subcultural practice and extension of young women in alternative rock and punk movements; indeed, membership in the latter creatively fueled the former's mode of production.[8] The coinage of Afrofan, then, does not assume a casual relationship between alternative music and comics. Afrofan as a subculture illuminates a productive coupling that reveals the cultural specificity of representation, production, and consumptive practices within the field of sequential art.

Comic book narratives are an embellishment of real and imaginary worlds, as well as their attendant problems, but more important, comics narrate a metaphoric route out of and illustrate the power to fight and maneuver within the world's problems. *Black Women in Sequence: Re-inking Comics, Graphic Novels, and Anime* is indeed a book of maneuvers. It uses sequential art to remark more broadly on American history, culture, politics, and social relations; it reflects the visual eye of an artist and cultural theorist; and it represents the passion and devotion of Afrofans and consumers of all racial and ethnic compositions. Moreover, like a comic book, it provides an opportunity to think and to see from top to bottom, bottom to top, side-to-side, and front to back, in color and in black and white. This study begins with a Black Butterfly, who is a superheroine in a violent, sexually squalid world, and ends with the voices of a critical mass of Black women artists and writers who experience the world of sequential art and its attendant subcultures as sites of creativity, agency, and power.

ACKNOWLEDGMENTS

I am grateful to all the writers, artists, readers, and scholars who helped to shape this book. My discussions with Leisl Adams, Michelle Billingsly, Afua Richardson, Nara Walker, and Ashley Woods enabled me to see and to argue for the ways Black women work independently and in collaboration to change the face and narrative of sequential art. My colleagues at the University of Iowa and elsewhere allowed me to engage with the world of sequential art at workshops, colloquia, conferences, and informal gatherings. Some introduced me to sources or read and provided written feedback on chapters, while others' support of my scholarly and creative work provided the environment or colleagueship through which *Black Women in Sequence* could thrive.

At Iowa, I thank all of my colleagues in American studies, African American studies, and cognate fields, especially Bluford Adams, Jeffrey Bennett, Venise Berry, Nikolas Dickerson, Claire Fox, Naomi Greyser, Tim Havens, Lena Hill, Michael Hill, Meena Khandelwal, Teresa Mangum, Kimberly Marra, Kristy Nabhan-Warren, Tom Oates, Damani Phillips, Horace Porter, Jacki Rand, Laura Rigal, Harry Stecopoulos, Miriam Thaggert, Richard Turner, Omar Valerio-Jiménez, Travis Vogan, Darryl Wanzer-Serrano, Steve Warren, and Jessica Welburn. I especially thank Horace Porter for his intellectual generosity and mentorship. Of great help were the conversations at Iowa about sequential art with comics scholar Nicholas Yanes. I appreciate the structural and/or financial support of the University of Iowa's College of Liberal Arts and Sciences (CLAS), the Obermann Center for Advanced Studies (OCAS), the Project on the Rhetoric of Inquiry (POROI), the Center for Ethnic Studies and the Arts (CESA), and the Comparative Ethnic Studies Working Group. I am grateful for the research assistance of Jane Munksgaard, Wayne Anderson, and Michael Hetra.

Outside of Iowa, I have benefitted from the generosity and advice of Aimee Carrillo Rowe, Maryemma Graham, Nancy Goldstein, Nicole Hodges Persely, Randal Jelks, David Katzman, Matt Mancini, Beretta Smith Shomade, and Sherrie Tucker. Frances Gateward was kind enough to read and offer advice on an early draft of chapter 3. Herman Gray helped me think through issues of representation during his visit to the University of Iowa in the fall of 2013. Joycelyn Moody introduced me to the work of comic strip artist Barbara Brandon-Croft.

Larin McLaughlin, editor in chief at the University of Washington Press, is an amazing editor and intellectual guide. I am grateful for her advice and enthusiasm for this project, and for the attentive and thorough comments of the anonymous readers. I also thank the comic book publishers for permission to reprint visual images, and Tiffany Charles, collections manager at the DuSable Museum of African American History in Chicago, Illinois, for locating and providing an early sketch by Jackie Ormes.

I especially extend gratitude to DC Comics for use of images from the following publications: "Batman" #197 © DC Comics (available in *Showcase Presents: Batman Volume Three*); "Batman" #1 © DC Comics (available in *The Batman Chronicles: Volume One*); "Batman" #210 © DC Comics (available in *Showcase Presents: Batman Volume Four*); *Catwoman: Her Sister's Keeper* ™ and © DC Comics (cover image); *Catwoman The Movie and Other Cat Tales* ™ and © DC Comics (cover image); "Wonder Woman" #206 © DC Comics; "Final Crisis" #7 ™ and © DC Comics; "Vixen" #1: "Vixen" is ™ and © DC Comics; "Suicide Squad" #11 © DC Comics; *Vixen: Return of the Lion* #1 ™ and © DC Comics (cover image).

I had the privilege to be part of the *Journal of Graphic Novels and Comics* special issue on gender and superheroes in 2011, and I thank editors Joan Ormrod and David Huxley, as well as two anonymous reviewers who helped to sharpen my discussion of Catwoman and blackness. A version of chapter 2, titled "Black Cat Got Your Tongue? Catwoman, Blackness, and the Alchemy of Postracialism," appeared in the *Journal of Graphic Novels and Comics* 2, no. 1 (2011): 3–23.

Finally, I impart special thanks to my family, Emma Whaley, George Whaley, Lisa Whaley, and Twilynn Whaley-Collins, for their love and support.

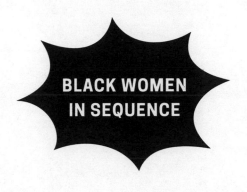

BLACK WOMEN
IN SEQUENCE

INTRODUCTION

> How did I ever get into this superheroine business in the first place?!
> Steady there, baby! This is no time to get into origin stories. We got a
> heavy thing going . . . and I have a hunch it's going to get a lot heavier!
>
> —The Butterfly, *Hell Rider* #1

I N the early 1970s—when mainstream comic books were selling for fifteen cents—adult-themed comic books and graphic novels tapped into a bourgeoning target market. Independent companies such as Skywald Publications upped the comic book ante in violence, nudity, and visual images of simulated sexual activity, and were able to charge nearly five times the going rate of mainstream comic titles. Their prequel to the infamous *Ghost Rider*—a hell-on-wheels character who appears in the two-volume *Hell Rider*—marks a significant moment in the history of Black women in comic books. Created by writer Gary Friedrich in 1971, the hero in *Hell Rider*, Brick Reese, is a white hipster motorcyclist, a Vietnam veteran, a lawyer, and, by night, a vigilante on a fire-flamed motorcycle.[1] Squarely situated in 1970s Black vernacular, the subtitle on the cover of the book includes in bold print: RIGHT ON WITH THE NOW SUPER-HERO. The "now" in italics is as important as the "right on." While "now" represents a break with the silver age of comics (1956 to circa 1970), "right on" signals the title's gesture to multiculturalism, which came in the way of intermittent Black characters and 1970s Black popular culture. *Hell Rider*'s cover features its muscular hero of the same name sporting a helmet with the emblem of a devil's pitchfork and a blue skintight costume that blends the iconography of Captain Marvel's patriotic unitard with the white jumpsuit of Evel Knievel circa 1970. He is drawn hurdling over unsuspecting villains on his motorcycle—just as the daredevil Evel Knievel would hurdle sky-high ramps—while shooting and back-firing flames. In a smaller inlay are two scantily-clad women. One is a woman of African descent in a skimpy minidress, and the other is white, appears nearly topless, and wears tiny bikini bottoms. The two women seductively embrace on a sandy beach. The thrill-riding, violence, patriotism, scant clothing, homoerotic imagery, and cross-racial desire illustrated on this cover were surely meant to entice male readers. Yet *Hell Rider* did notable cultural work by introducing an unlikely metamorphosis in the comic book world: the Butterfly, who is the first Black female comic book superheroine (see plate 1).[2]

The Butterfly ("real" name Marian Michaels) is a nightclub singer by day and a crime avenger in Las Vegas by night. Although the Butterfly is a secondary character in *Hell Rider*, she had a miniseries back-up feature.[3] Butterfly's story line delves into economic and political issues that were at the forefront at that time, for example, the underground economy of drug trafficking and its connection to legal and illegal gambling. On the cover of Butterfly's black-and-white minifeature, Friedrich describes Las Vegas as a "Mecca for organized crime in spite of close scrutiny by the state gaming commission," which had "a stranglehold on the nation's economy." In view of such corruption, the comic's front-page description promises to end such illegal acts with the "flapping of Butterfly's wings." Like many characters in front-cover titles, in her minifeature, Butterfly is scantily clothed in a wraparound body suit that leaves naked more than half of her breasts and her entire abdomen. She wears a mask resembling a bumblebee and thigh-high boots. Her arms open wide to display her sheer butterfly wings, and her legs are spread to make room for the comic book's triangular cursive title. Artist Syd Shore visually represents a consciousness divided between a relatively normal life and a phantasmagorical, adventurous existence: On her left wing we see Marian Michaels in an Afro wig and skintight dress, singing into a microphone. On the right wing we see the Butterfly in costume, fighting masked villains with her superpowers: flying through the air and casting light that blinds.

By today's rating system, *The Butterfly*, a story of heroin trafficking, suggestive sexual content, and violence—far from the innocuous themes that some associate with comic books for children—would earn a Parental

I.1 Gary Friedrich, "The Butterfly," *Hell-Rider* #2, Skywald Publications, October 1971.

Advisory label. We first see the Butterfly as Marian Michaels, at the Vegas nightclub where she sings, reading a letter that demands she leave her go-go boots in her dressing room during her performance so that the letter writer may retrieve the boots without being seen. In a thought balloon, Michaels muses, "Ah, nothing to worry about! Probably just some nutty soul brother trying for a souvenir!" Assuming the letter is the practical joke of a fan with a foot fetish, she performs in the boots that night but later returns to her dressing room, where she faces an attack by villains. Two of the attackers are in bat costumes, and the leader, called the Claw, wears a Ku Klux Klan mask. Michaels struggles with the villains, but they escape with her boots. With the stroke of an inker's pen, Marian Michaels becomes the Butterfly. She flies through the air, flapping her large wings, tracks down the villains, retrieves her boots, and turns the criminals over to the handsome white male biker Animal, who is the leader of a tough-looking multiracial motorcycle gang called the Wild Bunch. The interaction between Marian and Animal, which includes an embrace and enthusiastic kiss, hints that the two are perhaps former lovers, but the story proceeds without any explanation of their past. Butterfly instructs Animal to deliver the boots to her lawyer in Los Angeles, who we find out in the next issue is Brick Reese/Hell Rider.

The Butterfly appears in the next issue of *Hell Rider*, where the reader discovers that Marian Michaels's sought-after boots, given to her by the former junkie Julie Storm, has heroin hidden in the heels. To protect her from harm and to bring the drug traffickers into the arms of justice, Brick Reese/Hell Rider pursues the drug dealers who are after Michaels and her boots. The ending to the second issue of *Hell Rider* raises several questions: Who is the Klan-masked villain known as the Claw? What are we to make of his buddies dressed as bats? Why is Marian Michaels entangled with former junkies, motorcycle gangs, and the sexy Brick Reese? The reader cannot "stay tuned" for the next installment to get answers to these questions because *Hell Rider* lasted only two issues. The reader thus never learns more about the Butterfly, how her boots became transporters for narcotics, or why she immersed herself in the secret life of a superheroine in the nation's Sin City. Following the initial release of *Hell Rider*, creator Gary Friedrich went to Marvel Comics to work as a feature writer; he renamed his main character for Marvel and titled the new iteration *Ghost Rider*.

Hell Rider's Butterfly exemplifies the way cultural production is as dependent on shifts in culture as it is on the legal and financial aspects of the political economy of popular culture.[4] A demand and a desire for exotica and for hip or "right on" characters reflects the popular culture of the 1970s; yet the inability of some independent distributors to survive short-term trends reflects the unpredictability of long-term aspirations of economies of scale.[5] At the time, Skywald Publications had a range of cheaply produced titles featuring adult-themed horror and adventure comics in black and white that initially had impressive sales figures, but in the long run, the company could not compete with mainstream distributors such as Marvel. According to Skywald editor Alan Hewetson, comic conglomerates were powerful enough to discourage newsstands from selling Skywald Publications, helping to precipitate their demise in 1974.[6] More than just a helluva financial and adventurous graphic novel ride, Butterfly's fleeting narrative and the economic obstacles faced by her producers are a befitting beginning for a book about the appearance and disappearance of women of African descent in both independent and mainstream sequential art, and one that argues for the agency of characters, producers, and consumers.

The production and presence of women of African descent in sequential art as a focus for scholarly discussion comes at an auspicious cultural moment. The past decade constitutes a recuperative project in the study of sequential art, in which museum exhibitions, conferences, academic writings, websites, and nonprofit organizations have documented the presence of historically marginalized groups, including Black women as creators and as subjects of comic art. In 2008, curators John Jennings and Damian Duffy gathered the works of underrepresented comic artists for *Out of Sequence: Underrepresented Voices in American Comics*. This exhibition displayed the work of American comic artists who work in the medium of sequential art, that is, newspaper comics, zines, graphic novels, animation, and webcomics. With a cross-cultural focus, *Out of Sequence* and its accompanying exhibition catalogue argued for a representative shift in comic studies. One year earlier, the annual East Coast Black Age of Comics Convention had a feature panel, "Having Our Say: Black Women Discuss Imagery," where cultural critics and comic creators Cheryl Lynn Eaton, Rashida Lewis, and L. A. Banks discussed the production and consumption of Black women in American comics. The panel concluded that the image of Black women in sequential art was stereotyped and deformed, that Black women were represented in comics as being sidekicks or one-dimensional, and that the solution to the problem of such malign depictions was to pressure mainstream comic distributors for complex representations and to support Black women comic creators. In 2007, the Ormes Society formed to serve as a clearinghouse for artists, writers, and fans interested in the Black female image in comics. That same year, a special issue of the journal *MELUS* featured a broad array of cultural critics whose work focused on multiethnic and transnational identities in graphic novels. The issue added to the discussion of sequential art and race as an important and largely underexamined site for the transnational study and circulation of popular literature.[7]

Black Women in Sequence: Re-inking Comics, Graphic Novels, and Anime extends these pivotal moments and interventions in comic book studies by providing a theoretical, historical, and cultural analysis of Black women in sequential art. I present countervisions and problematic aspects of Black women in comic art to address their representations in mainstream comics, and to argue specifically about the complicated and contradictory meanings that one may cull from sequential art. This study pushes beyond a discourse of inclusion, exclusion, representation, and stereotype to ask critical questions about how women of African descent are semiotic referents for social relations and discourses about national and international politics, gender, race, and sexualities. As such, the racial signifier "Black" in this book is not an interpretive monolith. "Black" and "blackness" are terms under constant theoretical explanation and interrogation in speculation about the perception of women of African descent in a historical climate of liberal inclusion and in a contemporary climate of neoliberal, postracial politics. Throughout, I build upon a central argument that reveals sequential art as a viable form for understanding how popular literature and visual culture reflects the real and imagined place of women of African descent in nation making, politics, and cultural production. I describe this process as the making of *sequential subjects*, that is, the various ways fans and Black women as producers of sequential art use this medium to articulate a variety of cultural and political visions from the early twentieth century to the present, which adds credence to my assertion about the cultural work of comics.

Each chapter of the book contains a cultural context of the comic strip, comic books, graphic novels, and anime, as well as the place of characters in a particular historical moment, to help frame the Black female appearance in sequential art. However, this book does not provide an extensive history of the vast field of sequential art or of comics as a whole. Other cultural critics have conducted this work in books published over the past two decades.[8] In contradistinction, *Black Women in Sequence* locates itself within the scholarship that addresses gender, ethnicity, sexuality, and nationality as identities of rupture and suture, rather than as additive to a field focused primarily on writers, artists, characters, and readers in one locale and who are overwhelmingly of the dominant culture (white) and of one gender (male). The production of comic books by Asian Americans, Latinos, Indigenous Peoples, and Black Americans create the necessity of a broader ethnic approach in comic book studies.

Collections such as Jeff Yang's *Secret Identities: The Asian American Superhero Anthology* introduce readers to Asian American characters, story lines, revisionist characters, and superheroes. In this anthology, comic authors Jeff Yang ("Taking Back Troy" and "Driving Steel"), Jonathan Tsuei ("9066"), Parry Shen ("The Hibakusha"), and Naeem Mohaiemen ("No Exit") address the narratives of Asian immigration, the building of the transcontinental railroad, US Japanese internment, the bombings of Hiroshima and Nagasaki, US and Islamic conflict, anti-Asian violence, and broader issues of representation. No explanatory essays or critical analyses accompany the original comics gathered in *Secret Identities*. However, giving such exposure to Asian American artists and writers who historicize and pivot images of Asian and Asian American subjects away from colonialist and Orientalist fantasy is a feat in itself.[9]

Héctor Fernández L'Hoeste and Juan Poblete's *Redrawing the Nation: National Identity in Latin/o American Comics* is a critical and continental mapping of the history, production, and consumption of Latino/a comic images. As the contributors assert, Latin/o comics' strength is in centering cultural narratives while producing politically insurgent messages. Yet for these comics to cast a wider net and continue the democratization and modernizing of Latin/o societies, L'Hoeste and Poblete argue that Latin/o comics must reach beyond the current male-centered popular imaginary.[10] Indeed, several of the essays address this gender disparity in Latin/o comics, most notably Ann Merino's analysis of the alternative comic *Love and Rockets*, which, as she notes, had strong female characters from its inception.[11]

Comics and the U.S. South, edited by Brannon Costello and Qiana J. Whitted, is a multicultural analysis of print comics that demonstrates how region affects characterization and production. Costello and Whitted's anthology is one of the most provocative examples of the geopolitical conditions that birth racial stereotypes in comics, and adds texture to the specificity of local, Southern experiences.[12] Comparatively, Richard King's "Alter/native Heroes: Native Americans, Comic Books, and the Struggle for Self-Definition" is one of few essays to address the historical presence of Indigenous Peoples in mainstream comics and the visual sovereignty demonstrated by Indigenous writers and artists of comic books.[13]

Major texts on Black Americans in sequential art include Jeffery Brown's ethnographic study on the independent comic book franchise Milestone Comics, *Black Superheroes, Milestone Comics, and Their Fans* (2001). Brown's primary concern is the construction of Black comic book masculinity vis-à-vis white comic book masculinity and its impact on young male readers. Christopher Lehman's cultural history of Black representation in mainstream animation, *The Colored Cartoon: Black Representation in American Animated Short Films* (2008), is an interdisciplinary examination of the role that minstrelsy, film, comic strips, sound production, immigration, and social relations have played in the production of Black characters, including anthropomorphic (i.e., "animalized") characters coded as Black. Adilifu Nama's *Super Black: American Pop Culture and Black Superheroes* (2012) surveys the appearance of Black superheroes in mainstream comics, television, and film. Nama's study focuses mostly, though not exclusively, on male Black representation in an impressive number of comics in the superhero genre.[14]

An abundance of intellectual work on white women comic book characters emerged just before World War II. This foundational work has done much to help us understand how writers used white female characters such as Wonder Woman, Liberty Belle, and Black Canary to embody the ideologies of sexuality, nation, and patriotism in the war years and immediately thereafter. Key studies on women in comics include Trina Robbins's comprehensive study *From Girls to Grrlz: A History of Women in Comics from Teens to Zines* (1999), Lillian S. Robinson's work on the activist components of white female characters in *Wonder Women: Feminisms and Superheroes* (2004), and Jeffrey Brown's *Dangerous Curves: Action Heroines, Gender, Fetishism, and Popular Culture* (2011). The latter book lays bare how women's bodies function as an icon of sexual freedom and fetish in comics and action films, but it is also one of the few studies to direct attention to the cross-ethnic representation of white, Black, Latina, and Asian American women in comics and film.[15]

Scholarship on Black male superheroes and white female superheroines thus engages with how writers forge counterrepresentations, new reading publics, and a Black male-centered or white feminist aesthetic from which readers may extract multiple and diverse meanings. Yet none of the aforementioned bodies of scholarship addresses female characters of African descent in a significant way, and, the growing scholarship on manga (i.e., Japanese comics) notwithstanding, few studies examine comics within a transhemipheric, that is to say, a cross-continental, context. *Secret Identities* and *Redrawing the Nation* offer ideal approaches to a critical comic book studies framework in their covert or overt assertion of the ability of artistic productions to explain and illustrate the imperial project of "Americanity,"[16] just as *Black Superheroes*, *Super Black*, *The Colored Cartoon*, and *Action Chicks* push the field toward understanding how the Black and/or gendered subject, object, and, in some cases consumer, pushes back. *Black Women in Sequence*'s focus on production, reception, and the transatlantic dissemination of Black female representation in the various forms of sequential art situates it as complementary to these previous studies but expands upon the existing literature in significant ways.

Black Women in Sequence works out of the tradition of national and transnational scholarly books and journals, insofar as it seeks to pinpoint how comic art has much to say about US culture, its transnational flows, and its history. The book fills a gap and contributes to the scholarship on comics as a whole with its subject focus, American studies methodology, theoretical impetus, explication of past and current titles and artists, and consideration of Black female imagery in US, African, and Asian contexts from popular and independent outlets. Unlike scholarly works that solely explore print comics, I focus on print titles alongside the moving image in television, film, animation, and video games to present a broader analysis of the variety of comic art forms than found in existing case studies in the field. *Black Women in Sequence* therefore provides a cultural history and theoretical interrogation of the various forms of sequential art in which women of African descent appear and, consequently, disappear to contribute to the story of American comics. This study combines several disciplines to view its subject within a spatiotemporal context and across assemblages of race, class, gender, sexuality, and nation in relationship to geographical space and time.

"Spatiotemporal" refers to the placement of an object of analysis within the parameters of a particular historical moment and within a context—historical, social, or geographical—to explain how space and time shape interpretive meaning.[17] The historical periodization and coupling of text, image, context, and Black female representation in print and in moving-image media has much to offer. This book explains why women of African descent as sequential subjects should and do matter to the comic book world, and to writers, artists, fans, and readers, and contributes to the larger fields of literature, history, and visual culture studies by modeling an interdisciplinary and American studies theoretical and methodological approach for sequential art studies. In so doing, I direct attention to change over historical time, how culture works, the uneasy collision between popular culture and history, authorial self-reflexivity, the political economy, and the various modalities of difference. What follows, then, is a pacing through of the language, methods, and theory that inform this study, a preview of arguments about the characters and stories present in each chapter, and an argument for the study of sequential art as a viable avenue of scholarly investigation for American cultural studies.[18]

Semantics in Sequence: Language, Theory, and Method in Sequential Art

In a recent book on theory and methods in comic book studies, cultural critic Henry Jenkins divides comic book studies into two camps: an earlier generation of writers who were mostly journalists, artists, and fans, and a late twentieth-century and early twenty-first-century group of scholars who are a combination of scholars, artists, writers, and readers. As the study of comics continues to expand and grow in academia, Jenkins finds it necessary to ask if the "field of comics should be disciplined." Instead of situating one generation of writing about comics as superior to contemporary studies, Jenkins suggests that comic book studies scholars embrace an undisciplined or interdisciplinary methodology, while remaining self-reflexive; they should be "radically undisciplined, taking its tools and vocabulary where it can find them, expand its borders to allow the broadest possible range of objects of study, inclusive in who it allows to participate and in the sites where critical conversations occur. Academics have significant roles to play in this process."[19] Though he does not name any particular field of study to carry out his methodological advice, Jenkins has outlined the core work of American studies.

Much like the field of American studies, which is an interdisciplinary avenue of scholarly investigation that is continually faced with the question of whether the "American" in American studies is appropriate for twenty-first-century theorizing about the United States, the study of sequential art and comics is facing a similar crisis in naming and meaning. The study of sequential art and the study of comic books, at times confused as being synonymous, are consanguine; the former represents a wider visual terrain than the latter, which is a relational offspring of the former. Sequential art studies constitutes the larger spectrum of work that combines image in sequence to produce a narrative (e.g., comics, anime, cartoons, comic book–to-film adaption, graphic novels, webcomics, and zines), while comic book studies entails the smaller subgenre of image and text (comic strips, gags, graphic novels, and comic books). Both have crossover components, but sequential art is more expansive in its combined object of study.

The idea of image in sequence that sequential art evokes is in actuality a theoretical red herring, as scholars today document the complex, sporadic, and nonlinear way the mind maps and interprets the form. In other words, while sequential art is presented in a particular sequence, usually from left to right and top to bottom (if multiple enclosed panels are involved), a reader will not necessarily read or interpret the art in the order of presentation. A reader may look at a page as a whole, at individual panels, read from top to bottom, left to right, right to left, or back to front, thus disregarding the order intended by the writer and artist. It is quite curious, then, that comic art has a reputation for being an easy interpretive exercise because of its pithy language and explanatory images. Sequential art defies linear interpretation, since the mind must process image and text at the same time, and encode and decode the work based on a litany of extratextual factors and a larger body of intertextual grammars that the genre or title may reference. Comic scholar Neil Cohn provides a cogent explanation of the problems of placing sequential art into the categories of linear cultural production bound by the limits and progression of time and panels, and also refutes the idea that reading and viewing sequential art occurs at a remedial cognitive level. Cohn contends that the pervasive belief in sequential art as a linear and unsophisticated form "stems from a lack of acknowledgement that graphic images represent conceptual information. The images in the visual language of comics follow an *iconic* form of semiotic reference, because they *resemble* their meaning. Because we experience 'reality' on the same terms that we engage iconic images, we forget that they are indeed *representations* that come from—and must be processed by—a human mind: an observation harder to ignore with symbolic phenomena like spoken words."[20]

Given the variety of image making within sequential art and the various time, visual, and language referents open for interpretation, the "sequential" in sequential art assumes that the images are in order but does not presume that the images are linear in form or interpretation. The graphic terrain signaled by moving-image media, avatars, comic strips, graphic novels, comic books, and gags accomplish what I term the "optic cognitive experience" of the form. With no guarantee of one reading experience or interpretation, the eyes and the mind will work through this medium in a deeply engaged, discursive, or multiply deployed way. Pacing through the language and terminology in sequential art is more than hairsplitting between likenesses in meaning, as it helps to specify the constitution and critical interpretation of the form.

There is a similar semantic entanglement of the two related fields of sequential art studies and comic book studies in the terminology war between those scholars who use the term "graphic novel" rather than "comic book." Many argue that preference for the term "graphic novel" is a nod to literary legitimization, and that the "comic book" is the graphic novel's less legitimate stepsister. While there is certainly some slippage of definition, comic books are generally geared toward youth, whereas graphic novels are lengthier works with mature themes of violence and sexuality targeted toward adults. Scholars in comic book studies remain skeptical and aware of the elitist connotations and potential aggrandizing that the increasing popularity of the terms "graphic novel" and "sequential art studies" imply.[21]

However, an increase in technological production substantiates the phraseology of "comic book" as inadequate to describe the vectors drawn between diverse audiences, traditional print comics, computer-generated comics, and moving-image media that draw upon the comic form, which include video games, interactive avatars, film, and television adaptations. The distinction made in this book is a matter of thematic content and audience. Throughout these pages, there is an equal discussion of comic books and graphic novels; each chapter's engagement with the broad spectrum of sequential art aims to add to the literature in ways that existing books singularly focused on one form of sequential art may not. As stated earlier, working from the construct of the spatiotemporal, my engagement with the broad spectrum of sequential art allows a way to think through, in different but related popular art forms, how, as cultural critic Paul Atkinson says of the graphic novel, "the past, present and future coexist."[22] The term "graphic novel" is not a replacement for the term "comic book," nor is it simply a novel with pictures. Graphic novels exist as a form of the comic book, and as a subgenre of sequential art. Their study, then, requires a simultaneous engagement with self-reflexive modes of explanation and textual interrogations, while at the same time giving attention to the historical contexts that place the form in an intertextual conversation with additional forms of popular culture.

If writing about how the field of sequential art is concerned with language and form is necessary for a book that explores visual culture in sequence, so too is it necessary to explain the difficult choices made about language, form, and, in particular, the composition and construction of the arguments in the pages that follow. Each character, writer, and artist discussed at length here is done so strategically; I concentrate on the producers or characters who were the first of their kind to break significant ground in their genre. The arrangement of this book is chronological and thematic, spanning the early twentieth century through the early twenty-first century. Since I cover the four major areas of sequential art—comic strips, comic books, graphic novels, and the moving image (e.g., television, film, and animation)—it is necessary to employ methods relevant to each form. I thus use textual and visual readings of comics, biographical information about writers and artists, and interviews with writers, artists, and readers to construct my arguments. Theories in cultural studies and postcolonial studies are the analytical impetuses for the book.[23]

I maintain a commitment to presenting how sequential art marks broad shifts in culture in a given historical moment. This allows for an articulation of new analytical frameworks that explain how readers might understand such cultural shifts. Although it is a scholarly enterprise, *Black Women in Sequence* defies the assumption that books are either for popular audiences or for a select group of scholars. It instead consists of a balance of narrative and theoretical interpretation that challenges the idea that consumers of sequential art are not intelligent readers or viewers invested in the rigor of thick description of the art form, nor does it assume that scholars cannot see in storytelling a larger, critical analytic at work. At its heart, then, *Black Women in Sequence* tells the story of Black women in comics by allowing this story to take precedence. The historical contexts, interdisciplinary methodology, and critical analytic are an aid to understanding the powerful symbols of representation and aspects of history and culture embedded in various forms of sequential art. Beginning with an array of Black female characters within the context of nation, national culture, and a departure from the Black male image concretizes what readers glean from seeing and experiencing Black women in sequential art.

National Subjects: Black Women in Comics, Graphic Novels, and Anime

Lee Falk created the first character of African descent—Lothar—for his comic strip *Mandrake the Magician* in 1934. In 1966, Dell Comics featured the Black male character Lobo in their title of the same name. Marvel featured the African character Waku in *Jungle Tales* in 1954, but the first Black male superhero was Marvel's Black Panther, who appeared in 1966. The largest influx of Black characters in comic books came about in the 1970s, in congruence with the blaxploitation film era, a time when seductive typifications of Black culture became a cheaply spun yet financially lucrative commodity for the silver screen. Blaxplocomics were compatible with this trend, and writers made Black superspades such as Luke Cage and Black Lightning a mixture of hypersexual bravado, brute, and brawn. A generous amount of critical scholarship explores the Black superspade archetype in comics, as well as the emergence of earlier Black superheroes such as the Black Panther and DC Comics' the Green Lantern (1971). Skywald Publications' *The Butterfly* was thus part of a much larger financial and representative trend, but scholars have been slow to address the Black Panther and the (Black) Green Lantern's female contemporaries.

Black Women in Sequence locates the initial appearance of Black women as subjects in comics through the thematic rubric of gender, blackness, and nation making. The characters in these pages are an integral part of nation making: they may reify ideologies that support American exceptionalism and uphold national order through performing patriotic identities. Comic book nation making can occur in a number of ways, including the writer's structuring of narrative and dialogue and the artist/colorist/inker's creation of visual cues and action sequences. Nation making can take subversive forms, too, as characters come to represent and act upon a national project that is counterhegemonic and serves historically marginalized groups. In some cases, Black women in comics constitute a mixture of national agendas: they are a part of the US national machine and they question and undermine that apparatus for politically progressive ends;

they may also purport to have a "homeland," and claim a Black or African nationalism in opposition to US nation making.[24] As national subjects involved in nation making, Black female characters may choreograph social relations and political operations on a small scale to, in the words of comic book character Martha Washington, *weave the fabric of a new world—and a new society.*"[25]

Frank Miller, the writer of *The Dark Knight Returns* (Batman) and *Sin City*, presents the project of nation making with his patriotic yet subversive freedom fighter Martha Washington in *The Life and Times of Martha Washington in the Twenty-first Century*. In this six-hundred-page beautifully illustrated graphic novel written for the independent distributor Dark Horse Comics, Miller chronicles the experience of Martha, a young woman who lives in a lower-income housing structure in Chicago, which is a depiction of the real-life but now defunct housing structure Cabrini-Green. Cowriter Dave Gibbons and artists Robin Smith, Angus McKie, and Alan Craddock provide a rarity with Martha Washington, a character who eschews predictable dialogue and dialect and an exaggerated sexuality. Washington has a fit as opposed to a sexualized physique, dark brown skin, and is bald or has blonde hair drawn in braids, locks, or a Mohawk. She therefore transgresses what Jeffrey Brown and Adilifu Nama call the popular "white characters dipped in chocolate" aesthetic that mainstream comics at times produce.[26] Washington's mix of ethnic features and brown skin, similar to Marvel's white-haired, blue-eyed, and brown-skinned Storm (*X-Men*), affirms blackness even as it disrupts what the dominant culture imagination has come to see as blackness. The character also has an impressive political legacy. Washington is a freedom fighter battling with white supremacist organizations, disproportionately deployed healthcare, militarism (i.e., the exaltation of military ideals and virtues), and corporate corruption. *The Life and Times of Martha Washington* is therefore a unique title, in which a Black female protagonist combines intellect and education to achieve the desired results, instead of relying upon supernatural powers (voodoo) or superhuman physical strength. Miller avoids an uncomplicated Horatio Alger story as well by avoiding fantasies of the American Dream that class ascension is achieved through hard work, or a bildungsroman wherein a protagonist, after a short-term struggle, succeeds against the odds. To the contrary, *The Life and Times of Martha Washington* depicts the struggle for the equal dispersion of power as an ongoing process that is never complete. The patriotic intonation of Washington's namesake and her identity as a Black female constitute contradictory semiotic referents, and offer an alternative trajectory to imagine an ordinary young Black woman who is capable of transforming the nation's ills and liberating disenfranchised subjects.

Washington's patriotic saga begins with a 1775 quote attributed to Patrick Henry: "I know not what course others may take but—as for me—give me liberty or give me death." Martyrdom is indeed a theme in *The Life and Times of Martha Washington*; Washington will sacrifice herself in the name of collective social justice or choose death over deep-seated oppression. Her father died protesting subsidized housing, which Washington describes as "prison for people who haven't done anything wrong."[27] It is surely no coincidence that Washington's father was born in 1955, a time of civil rights unrest, from the death of the young Black male Emmet Till, who was murdered for allegedly whistling at a white woman, to laws enacted to address racial inequities in education and the desegregation of schools in Topeka, Kansas, such as *Brown v. the Board of Education*. In *The Life and Times of Martha Washington*, such historical injustices are referenced as indirect legacies. In a series of panels at the novel's onset, we see Martha's father being beaten and then arrested by police officers dressed in green, in the same way civil rights protestors were beaten and attacked during civil rights demonstrations of the late 1950s and '60s. In the final panel of the second chapter of the book, a yellow sign reading, "Cabrini-Green: Lower Income Housing Facility, Chicago, Illinois" hangs alongside her father's gravestone, which indicates that he was born in 1955 and died in 1996. This panel depicts Cabrini-Green and Martha's father's corporeality as two opposing forces representing the death of the subject via unfulfilled dreams and the spaces not mended by 1960s civil rights demonstrations, such as the growth of lower-income housing, which may metaphorically kill dreams.

Two speech bubbles below the gravestone, presented as the voice of Martha Washington, explain why her father fought voraciously against a debilitating built environment that was marketed as "progressive": "They call it social welfare, but dad calls it prison. It's got barbed wire like a prison, and they shoot you if you try to get out. Nobody ever gets out. Not even when they're dead. *Dad never got out of the green.*"[28] Her father's tombstone is yellow, splattered with bullet holes and red blood, and the shadow of a green hand with a sword.[29] The collective iconography of Africanist colors and bullet holes signify destruction and ethnic nationalism, death by blood, and hope through armed resistance.

The next installment of the story jumps from the late 1990s to 2001. A new US president has been elected, and Martha is unable to sleep because of the noise of the helicopters flying above her built environment of militarism and terror. The "give me liberty" of one of the chapter titles refers not only to the outward environment of surveillance but also to the intracultural dynamics of the environment, which, Martha says, has particular sexual consequences for young Black women: "There's no streets in [the] green," says Martha, "just sidewalks . . . and the tube if you're too old to walk or if you're crazy enough to take the tube. . . . [I dress] like a boy always. Crazy to dress like a girl."[30]

The consistent themes of patriotism and militarism are illustrated by the armed police force that continually surrounds Martha's building and by the series of relentless commercials she sees on television in which white women and Asian Americans and Black Americans of both genders stand behind an American flag to encourage viewers to enlist in the national defense organization, or "peace force." In one issue, Martha reveals the dark reality behind the patriotic invitation to her social studies teacher when she states, "I hate the peace force because my brother Ken signed up with them and never came home. [He] might be dead."[31] Here *The Life and Times of Martha Washington* makes an indirect reference to the disproportionate number of minority combat deaths in comparison to their percentage in the overall population. It is also here where the political economy of the military, race, and media deployment collide in the ironic, self-referential space of the graphic novel. Departing from standard comic titles with Black characters, *The Life and Times of Martha Washington* does not confine its story line to squalid ghettos and streets. Many scenes show Martha at a computer, in a classroom, or engaged in discussion with her male social studies teacher, who refers to her without paternalism or sexual innuendo as his brightest student. From the character's inception, then, her intellect is as important as the physical agility she later displays while fighting crime.

In 2008, Martha witnesses a murder and her trauma encourages her to leave "the green." In a calculated move, Martha refuses to speak and or to provide details of the murder and is taken to an insane asylum. While at the asylum, she fights for her sanity and to maintain the distinction between reality and fantasy. After breaking out of the asylum, Martha seeks work as an unlikely superhero and crusader for American freedom and democracy. Despite her misgivings, she joins PAX (a faction of the peace force), is quickly deployed to a rainforest region, and saves it from deforestation, but she is not given recognition because a white male soldier in her platoon demands to take credit for Martha's work. "Nobody's going to believe some street Nigger out of a nut house that I'm anything but a war hero; don't give me no shit," the white male combatant warns.[32] Martha concedes, but not without suffering extra psychological trauma. Miller's writing presents the idea that the dominant culture views blackness as untrustworthy and incompetent, which racist aggressors capitalize on by cashing in on the value of their whiteness.[33] The writer and his artistic collaborators, through the medium of comics, make theory legible by showing how being a member of the dominant racial group impacts social relations and contributes to the racialized trauma of historically marginalized groups.

In another installment of the series, a newsprint page ruptures the narrative with headlines declaring the state of the nation: the mentally ill have been neglected by traditional healthcare; a Saudi Arabian leader who was once a US ally is now a foe; Wall Street malfeasance is threatening to take down the American financial system; death clouds caused by environmental waste are spreading across the nation; and indigenous people are fighting for cultural and independent sovereignty. *The Life and Times of Martha Washington* reflects an understanding of emergent politics as it employs a Black female character, whom the reader follows from birth to middle age to death, as a committed freedom fighter. While Washington's name and many aspects of the graphic novel rely on patriotic symbols, they do so to undermine and question those symbols; Washington is not a patsy, nor is she a ventriloquist of American propaganda. To the contrary, her primary role is to remind the reader of the psychological pain, as opposed to the social prospects that have come to define patriotic conceptualizations of the United States. Miller's *The Life and Times of Martha Washington* is an astonishingly insightful and fresh feat. It is a counterpart to other contemporary, independent titles, such as *The Abandoned* (2006) and *Wet Moon* (2005) by white male comic creator Ross Campbell. Miller's and Campbell's work asserts that the creation of powerful Black women characters is not the sole domain of Black women artists and writers.[34]

Like the Butterfly, Martha Washington represents attendant possibilities in independent titles, but, more important, she provides an ideal framework for thinking through the relationship between gender, blackness, and the violent, epistemological aspects of Americanity or US nation making. Yet Washington is not the only significant departure in comic book representations of the counter-narratives of nation making and social justice. Characters in mainstream publications preceded her and served similar purposes, while also depicting problematic typologies of Black womanhood. Monica Rambeau, alias Captain Marvel (*Spiderman*, 1982) and Photon (*Marvel Divas*, 2010), has the ability to channel the power of energy forces and the character is a metonym for the energy crisis of a postindustrial landscape. *Power Man*'s Black Mariah is an antihero who emerges in 1971; she is a grotesque, unapologetic drug trafficker—a morphing of one of the earliest visual images of the welfare queen, but also a parallel narrative to the growing threat of Black enfranchisement during the post-1960s civil rights era.

The character Cecilia Reyes (*X-Men*, 1996) is an example of Afro-Latino diasporic consciousness; she wages critiques of the moralistic and imperialistic attributes of the superhero in her role as a physician and as an accidental and reluctant hero. Misty Knight (*Marvel Team Up* #1, 1972) joins a handful of characters in the early 1970s that deftly depict blaxploitation superheroes' struggle as enforcers of law and national security. Yet Knight is also a cultural critique of the legal apparatus's disproportionate attack on the Black urban masses. Furthermore, her interracial liaisons with white superheroes Spiderman and Power Man serve the purpose of sexual fantasy and racial transgression. As a comparative collective of national (un)belonging, these characters assert how their visual and narrative formations rebel against (Black Mariah and Misty Knight) and remake (Captain Marvel/Photon, Martha Washington, and Cecilia Reyes) the nation.

Through these five characters one can chart a cultural history of representation that connects sequential art to social relations in a given historical moment. The treatment of the Black female subject in sequential art says much about the place of people of African descent in nation making and national ideology within the United States and abroad. A good number of Black female comic book characters exist, and while I do not detail all such characters in chapters 1 through 5, the comparative mention of the ones listed above helps to frame the world of Black female representation in comics. From here on, I argue that from 1930 to contemporary times, writers, illustrators, and readers of sequential art engage in a mutual production of fantasy about Black women and the Black female body and its transhemispheric meaning in the United States, Africa, Asia, and Europe.

Chapter 1 argues that the comic art of Jackie Zelda Ormes is representative of what cultural critics Michael Denning and Bill Mullen describe as a consciousness born from a politically aware, critical mass of artists and cultural workers. "The Popular Front," the term by which this group would come to be known by the mid-1930s, was, in the words of Mullen, a phrase used by "Leftists to connote their insistence on culture as one arm, or front, of a widening campaign for social, political, and racial equality."[35] The cultural leftist ideology that disseminated from the Popular Front made its way to the urban masses via periodicals and a wide range of expressive mediums within the arts. Ormes's propagating of what I call "cultural front comics"—from a Black female perspective—made legible the resistance to Black subjugation in the 1930s, '40s, and '50s. As Ormes became active in the cultural front and her art began to take on a sharper critique of the US government, the FBI began collecting data on the cartoonist.

The Popular Front, the culture of surveillance, and Ormes's dual position as newswoman and comic artist serve as the historical and cultural context for the first chapter. Ormes integrated theories of social change for Black Americans through her comic strips, but she did so in the face of government surveillance at a time when social activism—even at the most banal—might draw suspicion as constituting communist sympathies. I expand on existing work on Ormes through a theorization of cultural front comics as a consistent theme over the span of her career, Ormes's place within the newswoman occupation of the 1930s, the cultural work of Black newspapers, and the way in which visual images and narratives served as forms of resistance at the dawn of the civil rights era.[36]

"Postracialism" describes a politics of purporting not to see race or to see beyond race and racial distinctions. This line of reasoning is congruent with an assumption that dismisses the reality of social injustice and the presence of racism. The idea of a postracial rhetoric constituting postracialism that shapes production, consumption, and material relations in the public sphere is put to the test through a historical and contemporary analysis of Black female comic book characters in television and film via a case study on a particular character's evolvement over historical time. Chapter 2 explores the character Catwoman in the comic book *Batman*, the graphic novel *Catwoman*, as well as in her adaptations in moving-image media, including video games. I examine the sexual connotation of Catwoman, while giving attention to how the framing of her varied racial identities shapes production, perception, and interest among a wide variety of fans. In her television premiere in the 1960s and her feature film premiere in the twenty-first century, Catwoman is a dubious mixture of 1960s civil rights protest and racial inclusion; in her twenty-first-century portrayals, she is co-opted by postracial rhetoric.

To explore these conclusions and the narrative use of Catwoman vis-à-vis the cultural politics of race, chapter 2 begins with a history of the character to situate her in space and time, and proceeds to interpret the various meanings of Catwoman's characterology alongside several interlocking forms of difference. Textual readings and fan commentary of the comic lead me to argue that while the writers of the print, television, and film versions of Catwoman purport to subscribe to a politics of color blindness, the execution of the narrative and the interpretations of Catwoman by fans testify that race matters to the comic book world and audience. There are popular books and scholarly articles about the character, but there is no study of the character in relationship to the production and consumption of "blackness" as a racial signifier.[37] Thus, I intervene in studies on comic book and graphic novel fandom, where Catwoman's racial fluidity from ambiguously Chinese to white to Latina to Black has yet to enter the scholarly discourse.

Chapter 3 engages with the Occidental or Western imagining of the African female character, with how those imaginings predicate themselves on US and Western interpretations of Africa, and with the possible connection between writers' narratives, political ideology, and practice. Hence, I focus on comic book and graphic novel titles that use Africa as a semiotic referent.[38] These significations—both material and imagined—represent the perceived cultural practices, norms, and beliefs of African peoples, as well as the cultural landscape of Africa, as the narrative framing for the actions, powers, and moral authority of Black female characters. Three superheroines or antiheroines in titles with a wide readership are examined in this chapter: Nubia in DC Comics' *Wonder Woman*, Storm in Marvel Comics' *X-Men*, and Vixen in DC Comics' *Vixen*, *Justice League of America* (*JLA*), and *Suicide Squad*.

I argue that *Wonder Woman*'s Nubia engaged with the existing debates spearheaded by the culture wars of the 1970s, that *X-Men*'s Storm rhetorically decentered the advent of colonialism in Africa and the United States, and that *JLA*'s Vixen oscillated between blaxploitation heroine and postcolonial critique of the Reagan-Bush administration's deployment of "constructive engagement" in the 1980s.[39] Although different writers and artists created the titles, a common denominator in all is that Africa exists as a contradictory sign of origins, and that the circulation of these titles are products of what theatre historian Harry Elam calls "black cultural traffic." "Black cultural traffic" refers to the cultural significance and circulation of Black popular culture and blackness for consumption in the global marketplace.[40] Recent articles on comics grapple with the representation and consumption or Black males in the 1970s and '80s; however, these studies do not focus on female representation.[41] Chapter 3 does more than expand upon the gender and racial issues of comics; it also provides an understanding of how ideas of Africa in the popular imagination collide with domestic and international policy.

Travelogue literature uses the literary components and attributes of writing to document an individual or group experience in one or a series of geographical sites. Postcolonial theory shows how this genre reveals the political implications of individual and group constructions of spatial displacement and geographical movement. Chapter 4 provides an analysis of the first and most visible anime character of African descent, Nadia of *Nadia: The Secret of Blue Water* series, and illustrates how the trope of travelogue mitigates spatial constructions for the main protagonist via the political and theoretical lens of postcolonial critique. Produced and directed in the 1990s by Hideaki Anno, the show's narrative concerns an African girl who joins a crew of explorers as they sail in search of a threatening force that may lead to the destruction of the planet. In the series, the articulation of Japanese and African worldviews converge to create a narrative that is liberating in its rhetoric yet colonialist in its sexualization of Nadia's prepubescent body. An aesthetic, textual, and theoretical interrogation of the series shows a literary coding of sea travel, what I term "empire in movement," while pointing out how the visual components of the show provide an experimental and cognitive viewing experience that is particular to the aesthetics of anime. I aim to add to the literature on the transnational circulation of anime, while concluding that the show's pre-teen target market and adult fans increase its effectiveness as a form of cultural and televisual production.

Chapter 5 focuses on the sequential art of Black women writers and illustrators. Its chapter title takes its name from the popular comic strip *Where I'm Coming From* by Barbara Brandon-Croft. *Where I'm Coming From* presents Black female protagonists in dialogue with each other, acting as visual pundits responding to the cultural and political milieu of the 1990s.

While chapter 1 places the work of the first female Black cartoonist to gain wide recognition, chapter 5 begins with the work of Brandon-Croft, the first Black female cartoonist to garner a syndicated column in mainstream newspapers. The strip engaged with issues such as colorism, interracial romances, the neoliberal rhetoric of the Clinton administration, and the Rodney King beating and trial. *Where I'm Coming From* merged comedy with Black vernacular language and experiences to act as a voice of suppressed and interior Black political thought. Brandon-Croft's work is an unacknowledged precursor to the popular work of comic strip writer and artist Aaron McGruder, the writer of the now defunct comic strip *The Boondocks*. A discussion of Brandon-Croft thus unearths a comic legacy of radical Black consciousness in the early to mid-1990s that is often associated with McGruder's later work on *Boondocks*.

Textual and visual readings of contemporary Black women artists and writers who work within the sphere of mainstream and independent comics buttress the discussion of Brandon-Croft. The integration of interviews conducted with writers and artists in 2009–10 continues the work of chapter 4 by establishing the major impact of Japanese popular culture, anime, and manga on Black women in the field of comics. I theorize four key attributes of their works:

1. Afroanime, an articulation of Black American cultural politics and Japanese visual aesthetics
2. Afrofuturism, an articulation of science-fiction narratives of dystopia and utopia with postmodern interpretations of blackness
3. Afrophantasmagoria, an articulation of a mélange of fantasy and dream imagery with hybrid identities that signify blackness and difference more broadly
4. Afropunk, an articulation of Black American cultural politics with punk rock, hip-hop, trip-hop, and Afrofusion subcultural identities

There is a growing amount of literature on the literary and political aspects of Afrofuturism, yet the aesthetic dimensions of Afroanime, Afrophantasmagoria, and Afropunk in sequential art constitute unique contributions that explain the political, social, and cultural implications of contemporary Black women writers and illustrators. A working through of these articulated categories thus highlights the creation of sequential art by those women who posit counter-visions to the dominant episteme of blackness. This new episteme, or "Afrofusion," holds that Black postmodern identity in sequential art constitutes a creative aesthetic mixture that imagines Black female identity in audacious and fresh ways. Chapter 5 will therefore accomplish the work of revealing how Black women comic artists from the 1990s through the twenty-first century, in both mainstream and independent outlets, offer new and innovative ways to see and articulate the cultural work of comic art in a national and transnational context.

A discussion of the cover wars pertaining to the release of *Marvel Divas* serves as the conclusion to this book. There is a long-standing debate about the exploitation of women's anatomy in mainstream comics, especially on comic book covers, which show illustrations meant to entice male readers. Although *Marvel Divas* is reportedly a title marketed to women readers, its cover added fuel to the debate in the public sphere about how far female representation has come in comics, and the danger in presenting hypersexual imagery to young women.[42] *Marvel Divas* features female comic characters Black Cat, Hellcat, Firestar, and Photon—one of which (Photon) is racially marked as a Black. Marvel writers Roberto Aguirre-Sacasa and Tonci Zonjic, in defense of the book's cover, maintain that covers that are "quiet," or not sexually explicit, do not sell, thus they purport to use sexual enticement as a draw to what they argue is a liberating narrative of young women who balance superherodom and boyfriends on their own terms. Admittedly aiming to replicate the narrative of the former HBO series *Sex and the City* in comic form, including an element of strong sexual innuendo, Aguirre-Sacasa and Zonjic make a case for presenting and constructing a sexually progressive title in which the female characters do more than flaunt their sexuality—they own it.

The *Marvel Divas* cover debate presents a critical moment to reiterate the necessity of a shift in comic book studies in particular and in American and popular culture studies in general. Rather than remaining stuck within a discourse about a title or cover being sexist or progressive, a new series of questions about representation and politics is necessary in the study of sequential art, especially questions that look more closely at the political economy and various meanings readers cull from and attach to such imagery and narratives. Much like *The Butterfly*, when one gets beyond the sexy cover of *Marvel Divas*, a more complex central narrative emerges—about feminism, class, living with breast cancer, and interrelationships between women of different ethnicities and representative powers. The concluding chapter thus reasserts that sequential art is a contradictory but viable visual and narrative form to realize the dangers, possibilities, and pleasures in consuming ideas about Black women. Although the visual depictions in *Marvel Divas* may or may not show that old ways of viewing women of African descent do not die hard, I seek to prove that the future and expansion of this work by writers and artists today resist harder. Thus, I move through a discussion of women of African descent in sequential art with a guiding premise: *Black Women in Sequence: Re-inking Comics, Graphic Novels, and Anime* illustrates the malleability of cultural production where writers, artists, and readers coproduce narratives that serve the restrictive and the transformative representational ends that constitute American popular culture. *Black Women in Sequence* also engages with the cultural politics inherent in the practices of everyday life, and in so doing, aims to constitute a multimodal, fantastical ride. I close then with the words of the Butterfly in her fleeting minibook within the pages of *Hell Rider*: "Hang loose baby. We got a heavy thing going . . . and I have a hunch it's going to get a lot heavier."[43]

RE-INKING THE NATION

Jackie Ormes's Black Cultural Front Comics

In the studio of Jackie Ormes, one of the few women cartoonists, the popular comic strip characters of Torchy and Patty-Jo literally spring to life. Syndicated in scores of [Black] newspapers, her cartoons reach more than a million readers each week. Fashion minded youngsters especially like Torchy togs, the cut out section of the comics. [Ormes's most] famous [creation is] the Patty-Jo doll. One of the nation's first, Patty-Jo is . . . favored in America as the ideal Negro-type doll——a cute playmate that has brought happiness to many of youngsters. *Happiness is her trademark.*

—*One Tenth of a Nation*, an American Newsreel film

[Jackie] Ormes was interviewed by Bureau Agents on May 5, 1953, and July 29, 1953. At these times, she was cooperative and furnished information regarding her *front group activities and affiliations*, but denied Communist Party membership.

—"Zelda Jackson Ormes," Federal Bureau of Investigation

I N a 1940 multipanel comic strip, cartoonist Jackie Zelda Ormes illustrates the challenges of Black women artists and the dismissal of their talent by fusing the discourses of elite artistic spheres with the production of sequential art.[1] The comic strip presents a Black woman who bears Ormes's own likeness in a seemingly traditional art class as she faces her white art instructor, Mr. La Gatta. He asks if she is trained or

1.1 Jackie Ormes, "Comic Strip Sketch" (n.d.). Courtesy of the Dusable Museum of African American History, 740 E 56th Pl, Chicago, IL 60637.

"just a natural born artist." She answers with a chipper riposte: "Oh sure, Mr. La Gatta—my folks say I'm positively a 'natural.' Where's my easel?" One might view the phrase "natural born artist" as a compliment, but lack of formal training is often used to deny artistic legitimacy, and for some critics it signifies a lack of sophistication and refinement. Ormes's art student quickly learns this lesson and catches on to the instructor's veiled insult.

In the next panel, a view of the class is illustrated, and the art student sits down at her easel to draw, but she begins to sweat profusely. Ormes writes "scrub" in the interior of the panel. In the final panel, Ormes depicts the protagonist in front of an easel, where she is drawn three times smaller than in previous panels and the chair she sits in is disproportionately large. Ormes relates through self-deprecating humor that the art instructor has sought to make the protagonist "feel small" by belittling her art and therefore belittling her as a creative woman and human being. She uses humor to convey her point about the marginalization of Black female artists, but the implications of her message reflect a serious stance that is echoed in an elitist artistic imaginary, which is ultimately upheld by Mr. La Gatta's final comments. Mr. La Gatta, with a sinister grin, looks down at the Black female student and the cartoon figure she has drawn on her easel, and exclaims condescendingly: "Hm-m-m-m. You may have it, little lady, but for the present I'd say it's still unexpressed!"

Ormes returns to the theme of comic art within traditional art spheres in her *Pittsburgh Courier* gag *Patty-Jo 'n' Ginger* (December 17, 1955). Here, she pictures a finely dressed young girl (Patty-Jo) and her older sister (Ginger) walking through an art museum. On the wall of the museum are a series of abstract paintings, one of which looks strikingly similar to the work of Pablo Picasso in the late 1930s. At the time, Picasso had made a shift in his artwork

PATTY-JO 'n' GINGER

JACKIE ORMES

"LET'S GET OUT OF HERE . . . I DON'T THINK HE
APPROVES OF US!"

from detailed realism to modernist images of fragmentation and the divided psyche.[2] This thematic shift is replicated in the painting in Ormes's gag, in which an abstract male profile hangs on a rectangular, descending wall; the

1.2 Jackie Ormes, *Patty-Jo 'n' Ginger*, "Let's get out of here. I don't think he approves of us!" *Pittsburgh Courier*, December 17, 1955. Courtesy of Nancy Goldstein.

man's face is divided by sharp lines and haphazard doodles. Patty-Jo and Ginger, aesthetically at least, appear to belong in the space they inhabit; their clothing, style, and class performance is congruent with the idea of museums being public spaces of distinguished taste. Yet, the Picasso-esque painting that glares at them disapprovingly signals that despite their assumed class status, the larger art world looks down on the two and questions their presence in the museum. Indeed, while returning the painting's look of disgust, Ginger exclaims, "Let's get out of here . . . I don't think he approves of us!" In these comic strips of the 1930s and 1950s, Ormes expresses an artistic struggle that constitutes more than the exposure of ongoing racism in the art world. She raises the question of whether or not comic strips have a place within the art world as a whole.

To vie for a position within the field of elite art may constitute an ideological intervention for comic artists, but it is ultimately a fool's errand. I thus argue throughout this book that comic art is significant for its ability to appeal to everyday life and culture given its unique ability to combine image, text, space, action, and humor with the intent to communicate a pithy, powerful message to a reader or spectator. As a form of sequential art, comic strips and gags (single-panel comics) inform on culture and sometimes on politics and mediate or complement the content in the newspaper on the pages before and after their appearance. Equally important, comic strips and gags may provoke laughter and visual fun. The strategic insertion of the comics, fondly referred to as "the funny pages," serves as an ancillary component to the dense contents of the rest of the newspaper. While many may find these pages a form of harmless comic relief, cartoonists of the present and past have faced censure and surveillance for the political leanings of their work. Contemporary comic artist Aaron McGruder experienced censure for his political position on 9/11 in his comic strip *The Boondocks* in the aftermath of the 2001 terrorist attacks. After running a series of strips in which he insinuated a connection between the Taliban and the administration of former president Ronald Reagan and his vice president, George H. W. Bush, local and national newspapers pulled the strip from the funny pages.[3]

Eight decades earlier, cartoonist and journalist Ormes had paved the way for McGruder's artistic defiance. Ormes created art that was ostensibly funny, but her activism and her work's focus on social justice seemed to create few laughs among Federal Bureau of Investigation (FBI) operatives, who considered Ormes subversive and a potential threat to the security of the nation. Ormes's early childhood years, her short career as a journalist, her struggle as a comic artist, and her experience of being under surveillance by the FBI—which suspected she was a member of the Communist Party—frame the diverse aspects of her comic art.

Jackie Zelda Ormes (whose birth name is Zelda Mavin Jackson) was born August 1, 1911, in Pittsburgh and raised in Monongahela, Pennsylvania.[4] Government documents claim that after high school, Ormes attended Salem Business College and, later, art school in Pittsburgh, though family members and recent accounts speculate on the veracity of that continued education.[5] Though she had not trained as a cartoonist when she began penciling comics in the late 1930s, Ormes did study at the Commercial Art School in 1945 and the Federal School of Cartooning years later.[6] Ormes's father was a store owner and pastor, and her mother was an expert seamstress. Her solid upper-middle-class background situated Ormes among the Black Professional Managerial Class (BPMC) of the early twentieth century, a class enclave within the Black community that would negotiate the pulls of class ascension with respectability, uplift, and reform efforts in their communities. Ormes married in 1933 at the age of twenty-two and began her career in news media as a proofreader for the *Pittsburgh Courier*. Although she had applied for a position as a reporter, the glass ceiling of the times limited her to subordinate secretarial duties, and only on occasion did the paper's publisher, Robert L. Vann, allow her to report on stories concerning culture, sports, or fashion.[7]

Historian Alice Fahs has written about the prospects for women in journalism at this historical moment: how they faced a glass ceiling, income disparity, and an overall lack of equal opportunity. In the late nineteenth century through the early twentieth, the number of women in big cities making their living as reporters or as journalists increased rapidly, from 2.3 to 7.3 percent. However, compared to their male counterparts, women worked on space rates (i.e., compensation for units of work), rather than on salary, requiring them to strive for extraordinary achievement beyond their male peers' efforts in order to earn a decent wage and remain active in the profession. To assuage the gender-equity discomfort of their male supervisors and peers, and to appear less threatening, female reporters were inventive and strategic about their space rate assignments.

The plight of Black women in newspaper reporting and journalism was, of course, a double form of discrimination that their white working-class sisters did not experience. Despite gender discrimination, there were no "absolute barriers to working-class [white] women on mass circulation newspapers," writes Fahs, but "there were . . . absolute (if unstated) barriers to African American women on the major metropolitan newspapers."[8] Early Black activists and newswomen in the nineteenth and early twentieth centuries, such as Mary Church Terrell, Victoria Earle Matthews, Fannie Barrier Williams, Josephine St. Pierre Ruffin, and Gertrude Bustill Mossell, were shut out of reporting for and sparingly afforded a voice in mainstream metropolitan newspapers, making the emergence of Black newspapers ever more important.[9] Black journalist Clarence Page, who came of age in the 1950s, writes of the role of Black newspapers:

> The Pittsburgh Courier, the Michigan Chronicle, the Chicago Defender, and the Cleveland Call & Post ... offered something the big white newspapers left out: pictures and stories about black doctors, lawyers, politicians, business folk, society ladies, church leaders, and other "Negroes of quality." ... The comments and cartoons in the colored newspapers had a mission to bluntly and reliably ridicule anyone perceived as standing in the way of black progress.... The Negro press gave African Americans something no other media were ready or willing to offer: visibility and a voice.[10]

Ormes had as predecessors women such as the antilynching activist Ida B. Wells, who in 1892 moved from an editorial position at the Black newspaper the Evening Star to co-owner and coeditor of her own newspaper, the Free Speech and Headlight, which reported on the horrors of racism and segregation. Yet Robert L. Vann's assignments to Ormes show that Black newspapers also engaged in gender discrimination in their leadership and the opportunities they offered women for meaningful reporting assignments. Ormes's disappointment and the gender bias of the day ironically led to the birthing of Black women in comics. Her lack of opportunity as a reporter at the Pittsburgh Courier led her to reinvent herself as a newswoman by reporting through the visual and print form of comic strips.

Historian and cartoonist Trina Robbins has traced the work of white women cartoonists, arguing that, initially, white women experienced autonomy in the field. Nell Brinkley worked with success for the Hearst syndicate in 1907. Other established cartoonists, such as Grace Drayton, Kate Carew, and Marjorie Organ, preceded her; they shared an illustrative aesthetic of cartooning young children as innocent, cherub-type caricatures.[11] Brinkley perhaps experienced the most success and broke away from the standard representation of apple-cheeked children with her creation of the independently minded Brinkley Girl, a comic strip counterpart to Charles Dana Gibson's Gibson Girl published in LIFE magazine in the late nineteenth century. The Gibson Girl was a popular pencil illustration of refined, ephemeral womanhood. Art historian Maria Elena Buszek writes that the Gibson Girl was a mixture of contradictory signs: sexual yet not lewd, assertive yet ordinary, masculine yet hyperfeminine, upper-class yet still the personification of the girl next door.[12] By contrast, the Brinkley Girl was working class and headstrong; Brinkley's illustrations influenced young women to draw inspiration from and replicate this New Woman characterization.

World War II offered opportunities for more white women cartoonists as male cartoonists enlisted or were drafted into the military, but by the 1960s, the number of female cartoonists had dwindled significantly in part because of the popularity of superhero comics and the solidification of the field as a male arena. Robbins charts a history of white female comic strip artists and writers that defies a declension narrative and shows their experiences as a fluctuating narrative, like history itself—one moving from progress to mishaps to progress again. In the early twenty-first century there are more female cartoonists and comic book artists and writers than in yesteryear, but their visibility is still lacking in comparison to their male counterparts. It is in the larger context of women cartoonists in the nineteenth century that one might contemplate the significance of the bravery, tenacity, and longevity of Jackie Ormes in the 1930s, '40s, and '50s.

Jackie Ormes and Black Cultural Front Comics

Ormes created four strips throughout her life as a cartoonist. Her gag *Candy* focused on a witty and glamorous domestic who signified on the woman she worked for while bringing a new voice to Black women in domestic service. Ormes's comic strip *Patty-Jo 'n' Ginger* used the voice of a young girl to challenge segregation, sexism, and racism in the late 1940s through the mid-1950s. Ormes's first and last strip, *Torchy Brown*, focused on a young woman who leaves the South to realize her dream career by becoming a showgirl and singer at New York's Cotton Club. Torchy's comic strip life and world are full of cultural and racial roadblocks, economic mishaps, gender politics, and sexual adventures—a daring subject for any woman cartoonist in the 1930s. *Torchy Brown* ended in 1938, but Ormes resurrected it in the 1950s, this time making Torchy a middle-class nurse and environmentalist. The new version of the strip, renamed *Torchy Brown: Heartbeats*, ran until 1954, when Ormes retired from cartooning. Later in her career, her hands became crippled by rheumatoid arthritis and she worked as a doll maker. Both incarnations of *Torchy Brown* seemed closely aligned with the experiences of the real-life Ormes, who left the comforts of a small town to work in the uncertain environment of a metropolis. While working for the *Courier* and the *Chicago Defender*, Ormes became increasingly involved in oppositional political parties and with artists who pursued socialist commitments and ideas. Accordingly, she began to use her strip to convey cultural and social commentary wherein visuality, text, and humor merged to create what I name Black cultural front comics (BCFCs).

Little scholarship locates and analyzes at length Black women's mass-circulated artistic productions within the leftist arts movement of the early to mid-twentieth century. Scholarship to date on the Popular Front does, however, indicate it as a multicultural movement among self-described leftist artists and cultural workers who viewed cultural production as an arm, or front, for progressive politics. In his tracing of the movement from a white-leftist center to its evolution and the possibilities that extended for a leftist political and artistic approach in the Black public sphere, cultural theorist Bill Mullen writes, "The expression of the cultural front . . . dated at least to 1932, when it was used as the title of a column in the mimeographed *Baltimore John Reed Club Bulletin*. By 1938, it was the title of a column in the Popular Front glossy photo magazine *Direction*. . . . Responding to the international crisis of global depression and fascism, the Comintern's 1935 Seventh World Congress had replaced its call for a proletariat-led global revolution with a call for a 'Broad People's Front' coalition of liberals, radicals, trade unionists, farmers, socialists, blacks and whites, anticolonialists and colonized."[13]

The point here is not to define Ormes as a communist; this is a label she rejected—despite admitting to her belief in many aspects of communism in theory and her alliance with the Communist Party USA (CPUSA) and her participation in their meetings. To label Ormes a communist would repeat the mistake of the FBI; that is, it would suggest that she was part of a political party by mere association, because of her human rights activism, belief in equality for the mass populace, and casual, intermittent participation at CPUSA meetings. Still, as historian Erik S. McDuffie asserts about Black women involved to varying degrees in the political and social justice work of the CPUSA and the Popular Front, it makes analytical sense to analyze Black women's work in these terms if that work embodies a desire for broad, mass-circulated social justice and a redistribution of power and wealth.[14]

The Popular Front emanated from the US Left in the 1930s, but it is not synonymous with the CPUSA. Comintern, an international communist coalition, did call for an alliance of artists and activists committed to social justice and viewed culture and cultural production as a primary site of intervention (hence the name "cultural" or "popular" front), but this broad-based alliance did not always translate into CPUSA membership.[15] Not all who operated within the Popular Front were official members of the CPUSA. Yet elements of shared and mass-circulated production via activism and the arts with the aim of social justice for aggrieved communities makes the Popular Front integral to the history of the CPUSA. For the purpose of my arguments then, Black cultural front comics constitute comic strip art that carries a politically progressive message with the intent to contribute to and inform about broad-based social-justice struggles of the early twentieth century, draws on Black vernacular idioms and performance for the strategic purpose of political subversion through humor and signifyin(g) or Black speech patterns, and presents the diverse aspects of Black, everyday life, including gender, sexuality, and class diversity.

Black women in or affiliated with the CPUSA and the US Left are often juxtaposed with their middle-class Black club women counterparts; the former seen as seeking critical sites for intervention, and the latter's activism seen as caught in the stranglehold of respectability. Ormes is a prime case study with which to test the limits of this false political binary, given her straddling of the CPUSA, the US Left, and, later in her life, traditional Black civil rights organizations. It is perhaps because Ormes's work was presented through the comic strip, the gag, and the funny pages that she has not been recognized as an important voice of the Popular Front. Yet it is precisely her work and her activism within these political spheres, which focused on the interconnection of cultural production, the mass circulation of ideas, and public service, that makes her central to the Popular Front. Additionally, the full spectrum of Ormes's comics in the 1930s, '40s, and '50s offers a unique opportunity to consider the historical malleability of the Popular Front as an artistic movement, and offers an opportunity to see remnants of the movement in the artist's work well beyond the 1930s. To relay the breadth of Ormes's comics and their relevance to the study of sequential art in the 1930s, one must think through how Ormes's central characters inked a pathbreaking visual space and voice for Black womanhood and Black cultural politics in the early to mid-twentieth century. Her significance is further bolstered by the presence of Black female comic creators in the twenty-first century who recognize Ormes's legacy as being central to their growth as creative women and to their endeavors to *re*-ink the nation.

"Brass Plus Legs Equals": Torchy Brown's
Cultural Front Migrations in the 1930s

American Studies scholar Steven Loring Jones writes that starting with the nineteenth-century introduction of comic strips in news media (1890), the Black image in comics has been one of grotesque caricature, often taking its cues from white fantasies of slavery and the minstrel stage. *Little Nemo* (1905), *Abie the Agent* (1914), and *Bringing Up Father* (1913) are examples of complex representations of comic strips in which satire and racial puns cross over to overt racist imagery.[16] Early twentieth-century animation followed suit—from *Mickey Mouse* to *Bugs Bunny* features—by using animals (e.g., rats, rabbits, frogs, cats, and bears) as slightly veiled signifiers for stereotyped blackness. Animated features such as *Zoot Cat* (1944), *Uncle Tom's Cabaña* (1947), and *Coal Black and de Sebben Dwarfs* (1944) were obvious extensions of minstrelsy's mayhem, and, when not depicting Blacks as animals, would portray people of African descent as pickaninnies, mammies, or sambos.[17] In response, Black organizations such as the National Association for the Advancement of Colored People and the Universal Negro Improvement Association protested, and Black cartoonists used Black newspapers as a forum for visual refutation, but at times also using the minstrelized form for subversive ends:

> The Black press offered alternative images to the demeaning and
> monotonous stereotypes presented in the white press. The comic
> strips in the Black press depicted a wide diversity of life experiences,
> often in humorous ways. An example is "Bungleton Green," the lon-
> gest running comic strip in the Black press. "Bun" first appeared in
> the *Chicago Defender* November 20, 1920. By the 1940's . . . "Bun" had
> become a zoot-suited "hep cat," who reflected the optimism of the "jazz
> man." In 1968, "Bun" sport[ed] a dashiki . . . to reflect the outward mili-
> tancy of "the brother on the block."[18]

In contrast, American and popular culture studies scholar Angela M. Nelson writes that post–World War II Black comic strips reflect Black middle-class ideology. Nelson provides a deft analysis of how the comic strips *Barry Jordan* (1954) by Jimmy Dixon, *Little Magnolia* (1949) by Alan Hart, and *Swing Papa* (1948) by David Quinn "exalted African American urban life as a major cultural narrative."[19] *Magnolia* and *Swing Papa* presented segregated spheres in which Black characters upheld respectable images of blackness and the sanctity of heterosexual marriage and consumption, while *Barry Jordan* provided alternative versions of Black masculinity to the caricatures drawn by white comic artists. As Nelson asserts, Dixon's *Barry Jordan*, through its lead protagonist of the same name, "protested earlier portrayals of African American males by creating one who was not feckless, jet black, lazy, dumb, and dishonest."[20] From the mid to late 1930s until the 1950s, the comic art of Jackie Ormes complemented these earlier representations created by Black men. Ormes's work centered on working- and middle-class characters and provided radical commentary on race relations, gender politics, and Black cultural displacement. In all of Ormes's art, a Black female protagonist was the vehicle for this commentary.

Three consistent themes constitute Ormes's cultural-front comics: class, gender, and race relations in regard to 1930s Black migration, the working-class consciousness and subversive sexuality of a Black domestic worker in the 1940s, and racial-ethnic rights in the 1950s. With these themes Ormes rustled the bones of the comic world, not only by becoming the first and for many decades the only recognized Black female cartoonist, but also by becoming part of a small critical mass of Black cartoonists in general who seized upon the opportunity to use comic strips as an arm of social justice philosophy. Her commitment to the cultural work of comics is seen in a December 25, 1937, installment of *Torchy Brown: Dixie to Harlem*. In *Torchy*'s "Orders Is Orders," the top panel shows the character Torchy taking a phone call while in the shower. The next panel shows Torchy, a bath towel covering her buttocks, approaching a bed in which two women are sitting fully clothed in fine dresses. The caption at the bottom reads, "Rustle your bones, honey lambs—that was the dizzy dame who draws us, invitin' us to *Courier Headquarters* for a reunion party, an we gotta fly!" In a self-mocking and self-referential move, the comic artist uses the voice of her main protagonist in this strip, Torchy Brown, to "call" for the lives of Black women to take visual and narrative form on the funny pages of the Black *Pittsburgh Courier*. As *Dixie to Harlem* suggests, Ormes's Torchy pictured the everyday lives of the Black women who navigated the crossroads of region, gender, race, sexuality, and class as they moved from the rural South to Northern cities in the late 1930s. In so doing, *Torchy Brown* served as an example of the contradictions that Black cultural front comics would pose in the field of representation.

1.3 Jackie Ormes, *Torchy Brown: From Dixie to Harlem,* "Orders Is Orders," *Pittsburgh Courier,* December 25, 1937.

Some characters in *Torchy Brown* speak with an exaggerated and forced Black Southern dialect; Ormes used misspellings to replicate the voice inflection of a Southern drawl. Her representation of female characters' physiques was also controversial. Ormes's comic strip women of the North have light skin tones, small waists, perfectly coiffed hair, pouty mouths, and thickly lined eyes; they are half pinup and half Bubbling Brown Sugar. In contrast, her Black Southern characters have big eyes, wide mouths, and hefty physiques; they are half minstrel and half *Amos 'n' Andy* caricature. Ormes's troubling and at times erroneous characterizations of an imagined rogue Southern Black American and an imagined refined Northern Black American led her male peers to initially dismiss her as a comic artist.[21] This denouncement did not take life until Ormes's strip began to leave ruminations on the South behind to concentrate on the prospects of her characters' uncertain Northern futures.

Ormes's narrative and aesthetic mixture, proposes literary critic Edward Brunner, has led historians of comics to describe *Torchy Brown* as a stereotypical fantasy of Black migration, and some Black cultural critics have gone so far as to call the strip a slightly political version of *Amos 'n' Andy* in drag.[22] This latter critique is ironic, given that the first publication in which *Torchy Brown* appeared was the *Pittsburg Courier,* a Black newspaper that started, in part, as a response to the defamation of Black Americans in the media in general and in the *Amos 'n' Andy* radio show in particular.[23]

Even so, Ormes's aesthetic and narrative contradiction is apparent in her earliest strips, including "A Letter t' Home" (January 29, 1938), in which Ormes depicts the struggle of young, single Black women who leave the South for the North. Torchy fears that her relatives back home will view her with derision and suspicion because of her migration to New York

City's Harlem. Nevertheless, she asserts her independence and moves to the East Coast despite the possibility that, as she remarks in the panel, her extended family may no longer hold her in high regard. As she sits down at a desk to write from her Northern location, Torchy tells the imagined reader, "Oh gee—I'm scared. Maybe Aunt Clemme is still mad at me for running away like I did. But honest and true I've been a good girl. I gotta write." The next panel shows Torchy's Aunt Clemme in the South, who retrieves Torchy's letter from her mailbox, holds it high in the air, and declares with enthusiasm, "Well, glory be. A letta fom ma baby at last!" In this strip, Ormes's narrative moves back and forth in time between panels, characters, and locations, creating a fluid and dialogical narrative rather than containing characters' ideas and conversations within individual panels. This spatiotemporal and performative aesthetic illustrates that migration is not simply a movement from one location to another but also exists as a betwixt and between experience for a character wherein the community they left behind and the site at which they reside become inextricable parts of their identity.

Ormes shapes Torchy's narrative within the larger context of gender, movement, and the onset of cosmopolitanism in New York City. As historian Christine Stansell observes of laboring women in New York City a century earlier, workingwomen in cities demonstrate a particular set of social conflicts and familial pressures.[24] Their geographical movement challenged the gender norms held by society and by individuals, including the women's relatives, and clarified the gendered nature of class struggle and work in urban environments. In a society in which single, laboring, and freely moving women caused gender norm confusion, fear of their financial independence, and a variety of sexual suspicions (e.g., promiscuity, deviance, and lesbianism) among the populace at large, any narrative of migrating and laboring women in the 1930s was a valiant endeavor. Cultural critic Angela Davis argues that for Black laboring women during the mass migration of Black Americans from the South to the North in the 1930s and thereafter, the ability to travel and migrate represented an easing of the racial restrictions imposed by the former Reconstruction Era, but also threatened physical consequences for such movement.[25] Put simply, extricated from the proverbial pedestal of white womanhood, Black women as travelers and workers would face increasing gender and sexual discrimination because of their race—a historical and contemporary reality recognized by the women and by those in their larger familial networks. *Torchy Brown: Dixie to Harlem* illustrates this gendering of migration with a refreshing wittiness and intelligence that became the artistic core of Ormes's Black cultural front comics.

The migration narratives in Ormes's comic strip *Torchy Brown: Dixie to Harlem* challenged the idea that the North was a safe haven from oppressive social relations in the South, but her "Brass Plus Legs Equals" installment (April 16, 1938) is also an indirect critique of Black women's marginalization in the workforce. In this strip, when Torchy arrives at a talent agency and asks for representation as an entertainer, the white male who sits behind the desk—an object that one might also interpret as a social barrier—replies that she is not on his waiting list. He then goes on to say that she has "a lot of guts, but not one leg to stand on." Torchy quickly realizes that the agency's "waiting list" is representative of a prolonged wait for equality, and responds to the talent scout's condescension by proclaiming, "Never mind then. You're not the man I'm looking for anyway." The caption responds to the agent's direct discrimination with the phrase "brass plus legs equals." Here, as in most of her comics, Ormes's caption underscores the significant role that titles in comics can play, going beyond mere descriptions of the interior panel. Ormes innovates the use of captions by making them dialogic instead of literal. "Brass plus legs equals" anticipates and remarks upon a larger context of racial and gender discrimination and the various discourses that circulate and define such discrimination. With this caption Ormes also conveys that Torchy has "brass" (a masculinist signifier of strength in popular vernacular) "plus" stronger "legs" than the agent realizes (a feminine countersignifier of strength). The dialogic aspect of the caption does more than answer, invoke, and participate in a larger conversation of discrimination; it is also a fluid, relational, and engaged response that addresses the agent's wrongdoing with an assertive new cultural politics of resistance.

In matters of the heart, Torchy set the rules for her romantic relationships and was adept at making sure men did not take advantage of her in work or in love, as seen in the comic installment "Well Sorta" (April 2, 1938). Here, Torchy exclaims, "Listen, I tell ya, I hate men. Cause if I didn't hate them, I'd love them. And I hate em." Torchy's direct speech refers to a larger range of emotions, and her disaffected stance masks the fear of pain and rejection. Though Torchy claimed the upper hand in engagements with the opposite sex, her hyperfemininity remained the main vehicle through which she would negotiate the rules of gender and sexuality. Sexuality as it intersects with race and gender permeates other aspects of Ormes's work, including a comic strip drawing she did as a freelance artist for Best Yet Hair Products Cosmetics Company in 1947. The ad features a young Black woman, pictured as beautiful in every way, except, apparently, for her short Afro hairstyle. The woman knocks on a door, calling out to her boyfriend Richard, who the spectator sees on the other side of the panel cuddling with a long-and-straight-haired vixen. The seductively dressed woman affectionately holds Richard's chin to bring him close in for a kiss as Richard tells the spectator that he is "practically dreaming" in the arms of his perfectly coiffed lover. The text of the ad, which was written by Ormes, reads, "Don't blame Richard for not opening the door. Just look at the beautiful girl in his arms. Notice her LONG, LOVELY hair. Then look at the girl crying to come in. Can you blame Richard if he prefers the luscious lass with the BEST HAIR ATTACHMENT?"[26]

The ad's subscribing to a European aesthetic may have aimed to provide Black women access to a sphere of glamour with which they were rarely associated. Nevertheless, this access remained squarely situated within hegemonic and damaging (even if historically accurate) ideas of beauty. To achieve the aesthetic of white womanhood, the ad insinuated, was to assure Black male partnership. This visual and textual advertising ploy preyed upon the insecurities of Black women while reinscribing masculinist expectations about feminine appearance. Ormes's melodramatic scenario is as much humorous as it is a reminder of the racialized pecking order. The intersection of sexuality and romance with beauty in this ad as well as in Ormes's comic strip "Well Sorta" may seem to steer away from the aims of the Popular Front, but the type of sexuality that Torchy exhibited, of glamour and confidence, and the misguided depiction of female attractiveness in Ormes's advertisement is political, for it reveals the representative ruptures and sexual contradictions in a range of her comic art.

"Run Along Now, Meester Conductor" (September 4, 1937) presents a train ride from the South to the North as a figurative representation of the struggles of migration and the cultural and political paradox of "racial passing." In this comic, Ormes shows Torchy packed and ready to leave the country atmosphere of the South. Wearing a sleek dress with a neck bow, a checkered cropped blazer, and a fancy feathered hat, Torchy approaches the train, where she sees "white" and "colored only" signs. Torchy tells the reader in a speech balloon, "I'll just pretend I can't read that well." She

takes a seat in the "white only" sitting area, and when the fair-skinned protagonist is questioned by a train conductor, the white male passenger sitting next to her vouches for her whiteness and tells the conductor to run along because he has "reading to do." Torchy's newfound friend is indeed aware of her blackness, as before the conductor entered the car he had asked her if she had heard the "Joe Louis news," to which Torchy replied with a vernacular "You betcha!" Boxer Joe Louis won the heavyweight championship in 1937, a title that elevated him to the status of hero among the Black masses, but Louis was also an icon of desegregation, having fought the tides of racial discrimination in boxing, and later in golf.[27] Segregation on trains and streetcars is a well-documented aspect of the humiliation and degradation of Black Americans, and referencing Joe Louis's victory connects him to the shared struggle of everyday Black Americans who were gaining space in public accommodations and organized sports at this time.

Racial passing in this comic is presented as the identity act of the viewer as much as it is a quest for equal accommodations by the object of the viewer's racialized gaze. In other words, in order for a Black person to "pass" as white, the viewer must hold myopic and essentialist ideas about what constitutes and "looks" like blackness. Ormes's comic strip suggests that the language and grammar of passing require interrogation, as aesthetically moving from one identity descriptor to another highlights the slippage in discourses and material manifestations of difference, challenging one to see the passing act as something that the viewer, rather than the object of the gaze, performs. Put simply, it is the viewer who is "passing" the object or questioning the object's ability to straddle and expose the arbitrary and essentialist lines of racial distinction as social constructions. Torchy's declaration that she will pretend she cannot read the segregation sign is a defiant act against racial exclusion, and her new friend's dismissal of the conductor with his claim of having reading to do intercepts that authority's ability to enforce racial segregation. Rather than abetting and advocating racial passing, Ormes presents a scenario where the Black object who is acted upon transitions to a subject with agency who successfully circumvents exclusion through her jocularity and by forming alliances with whites. Ormes's "wink" at literacy, passing, and resistance therefore frames the trajectory of Torchy's experiences in the North as a continual battle to intellectually mediate her memories and experiences of the social relations of Mississippi's segregated Dixie with the unfulfilled promises of New York's Harlem. Coalition building between Blacks and whites against injustice, and intertextual references to larger civil rights struggles situate Ormes's desegregation and passing narrative as representative of the historical and cultural work that Black cultural front comics had the potential to perform.

Ormes's captions were often clues to her political intentions, and they cause the reader to pause and consider the situation illustrated within the panel and its contradictory meanings for social and economic justice. This is true in "All Is Well That Ends Well" (January 1, 1938), where Ormes depicts Torchy's challenging economic times. In the strip, Torchy contemplates her financial woes as a worker at a restaurant, and then appears to cry in response to her hard financial times in New York. In the last panel, customers finally come knocking, thereby providing hope to what appears as a hopeless situation. Though the working-class intents of the panel are encouraging—even if overly melodramatic—Ormes's conclusion in the caption "All is well that ends well" does the double work of resisting and assuaging classism at the same time. Class struggle is real, asserts Ormes, but the idea that a miracle would bring an end to economic misfortune underserved a more trenchant class critique. "All Is Well That Ends Well" presents the reader with a happy ending and an unlikely economic resolution. Yet, in the midst of an economic depression, such narratives could also serve as the psychological equipment of resilience and tenacity against economic odds.

During the Great Depression of the 1930s, Black unemployment was two to three times higher than that of the dominant culture. Blacks were often the last hired and the first fired, and they were barred from the mainstream charitable organizations with which a white poor citizen might find refuge.[28] In this way, "All Is Well That Ends Well" was as naïve about overturning hard economic times as it was encouraging to Black readers to persevere and to invest in and patronize Black businesses. Torchy's misfortune in this comic strip makes working-class struggle legible, a theme that Ormes would continue to play on when she began work at the *Chicago Defender* and created the mammy's antithesis, a sexy and audacious maid named Candy, whose wartime consciousness and biting critiques of racial surveillance and domestic labor were sweetened by a cheeky smile, a svelte figure, the rolling of cigarettes, and signifyin(g) on her employer.

"Course, Mrs. Goldrocks, You Realize These First Few Weeks You'll Be on Probation!": *Candy* and the Making of Black Cultural Front Comics in the 1940s

Historian Erik S. McDuffie has called attention to the popular and cultural front activities among Black women that continued in the World War II era. He describes Black women's Popular Front, or what by the early 1940s was known as the Democratic Front, as constituting "internationalism, anti-racism, and anti-fascism." Quoting the essential work of Penny Von Eschen, McDuffie writes that Black women's activities challenged "European hegemony and the domestic upheavals of war."[29] Similarly, cultural critic James Smethurst reminds us that while Comitern's call for a broad popular or cultural front against fascism and for the working classes waned by the late 1930s, and was disbanded in 1943, Black women's "style of political and cultural work [within the movement] remained the same."[30] It should therefore not be surprising that the cultural work and activism among Black women in the US Left at that time would focus on giving voice to them and helping them to improve the work they so often did as minimally paid domestic labor. Scholarship on Black women domestics is abundant, and historians such as Robin D. G. Kelley and Angela Davis have in their separate works established capitalism's dependence on domestic work, and pointed out the grassroots organizing among working-class and mainstream civil rights organizations for the rights of domestic workers. While Kelley described coalitions between domestic workers and middle-class clubwomen, Davis maps how Black women's domestic work maintained the foundation of capitalism by exploiting labor for the profit of the ruling class.[31]

Leftist activist Alice Childress's 1954 novel *Like One in the Family* highlighted Black women's exploitation in domestic work and imagined the ways that they asserted their agency.[32] *Like One in the Family* began as a series of short pieces in the leftist newspapers *Freedom* and the *Baltimore Afro-American*. Working within African American literature, Trudier Harris and Mary Helen Washington credit Childress's participation in the US Left with having a significant effect on how her domestic protagonist, Madge, uses dialogicism to place readers in the position of eavesdroppers and witnesses to the racism, surveillance, and condescending treatment Madge endures at the hands of her white employers.[33] Though championed as a trailblazer in politically leftist literature, Childress's fictitious domestic had a radical predecessor nearly a decade before the publication of *Like One in the Family*. Childress's metafiction gave voice to Black domestic workers through Madge, but Ormes's *Candy* merged defiant cultural politics with a "pin-up" aesthetic. In so doing, Ormes artfully subverted the idea of the matronly and asexual domestic without conjuring its sarcastic, wisecracking, emasculating counterpart proverbially known as the Sapphire stereotype, as seen with the depiction of Florence Johnston, a domestic in the television show *The Jeffersons* (1975–85).

In contrast to these former domestic caricatures, Candy exudes sex but is not hypersexual; she espouses politics but is not preachy with her puns; and she speaks through comedic one-liners that use signifyin(g) to invert the power hierarchy inherent in domestic work. The *Chicago Defender* was an ideal site for Ormes's Black cultural front comics (BCFCs) narrative and visual aesthetic; while it was less than perfect in respect to the race question, it was decidedly leftist and political. Bill Mullen writes, "The [*Chicago*] *Defender* was both redder and more profitable than any other newspaper in the country outside of the Communist press, and had easily overtaken the *Pittsburgh Courier* as the most militant voice for black racial reform."[34] Though Ormes did do general reporting work for the *Defender* for pay, she was not paid for her gag *Candy*.[35] Nevertheless, not being paid for the comic, I argue, highlights the artist's commitment to the production of BCFCs and their potential to answer Comitern's call for social justice. Ormes layered her visual representation with a mixture of politics and wit from a Black female perspective and in the Black vernacular tradition. Her use of signifyin(g)—that is, an indirect, satirical Black speech form that utilizes sounding (verbal dueling), loud talking (a direct critique forged with indirect speech), cutting (direct insult), marking (mimicry), and taunting—made *Candy* and her later comics representative of Black vernacular culture.[36]

The Sutherland Hotel, where Ormes and her husband took up residence after moving to the South Side of Chicago, was host to a creative and political cornucopia, and jazz artists such as Louis Armstrong, Dizzy Gillepsie, John Coltrane, and Miles Davis stayed and performed there. It also became a meeting ground for cultural front activists, and one of the few places where whites and Blacks could and did commingle. *Candy* was a product of this environment, as it made direct use of signifyin(g) as a performative and oral tradition and became a discreet deployment of what had by the 1940s become the solid Black cultural front of which the *Defender* was a tool. Nancy Goldstein places Ormes within what is often dubbed the artistic counterpart to the Harlem Renaissance in the Midwest, that is, the Chicago Renaissance. I want to place a finer point on Goldstein's keen observation to agree with Bill Mullen, who posits that what some historians define as a "renaissance" in Chicago represents an articulation of artistic production with Black "cultural radicalism."[37] This was particularly the case for artists and quasijournalists such as Ormes, who were participants in cultural front and CPUSA activities.

Asserting the way that cultural radicalism can manifest through the arts, within the confines of the capitalist state, and in seemingly innocuous forms, Mullen writes, "Historians of the Popular Front have . . . not taken under close study the ambitions of the U.S. interracial Left to foster a separate Companion 'front' for African Americans: the Negro People's Front. Indeed, as a *Defender* editorial suggests . . . the Popular Front 'survived' notably . . . beyond its tenure as official Communist Party policy as a nascent model and inspiration for cultural insurrection created and led by African Americans."[38] In Chicago, Ormes took art classes, became a board member of the Works Progress Administration–funded South Side Community Art Center, and attended and participated in meetings at which front activists and CPUSA members commingled. When *Candy* emerged on the pages of the *Defender* in March 1945, the comic, in what soon became Ormes's transition to the gag or singular panel form, would place a Black voice within the discourse of late World War II leftist culture and the Negro People's Front.

Candy defied the popular idea of the docile domestic, and on a weekly basis, Candy critiqued her employer, Mrs. G, for her racism, as well as for her cultural ineptness. In Candy's first appearance, on March 24, 1945, she is drawn in a figure-flattering black dress with bloused sleeves, a small white apron adorned with ruffles, and high heels with ankle straps. Candy's make-up is pronounced: she wears black eyeliner dark lipstick, and her eyebrows are groomed. She stands with one foot resting on a pedestal, revealing her legs, and her hand rests on her hip. A smiling "Asianesque" statue is pictured besides her, in a similar pose. Looking more like a pin-up than a domestic, Candy remarks, "Course, Mrs. Goldrocks, you realize these first few weeks you'll be on probation!" Ormes immediately frames the series as an autonomous and resistant space. She inverts the labor hierarchy while speaking to the surveillance that many domestics—as historians and ethnographers of twentieth-century Black domestic work affirm—were subjected to, and the statue placed next to her suggests an international alliance with Asia.[39] The statue is included for more than adornment, and is likely not a visual sign of Orientalism. Instead, it speaks to a larger discourse about the United States' persistent practice of what cultural critic Jodi Kim refers to as "Asia watching." Kim defines Asia watching as a relentless discourse and practice of keeping tabs on the military and political practices of countries within the continent of Asia, especially those with socialist or communist regimes.[40] Together, Candy and the statue perform the international solidarity that the Black cultural front sought to nurture. Rather than Candy being on probation as low-paid labor, she declares that Mrs. Goldrocks (whom she often refers to as "Mrs. G") had best treat her with respect or Candy will terminate her employment.

In a July 14, 1945, installment of Ormes's gag, Candy resists the asexuality of the Black domestic in the popular imagination. She poses to the side with her hands on her hips and remarks, "I sold Mrs. Goldrocks on spending the evening out. . . . My date's kinda sensitive when she's around." However, Candy does more than look attractive and brag of male partners; she taunts and brings attention to her own physique while mocking her larger-sized employer in a March 31, 1945, gag. "Gee," says Candy, "I hope Mrs. Goldrocks doesn't gain any more weight. I can't possibly wear a size larger." Critiquing Mrs. G's ineptness at raising her children, but also boasting of her own rich social life, Candy uses the vernacular of sounding or "calling out" when she remarks in a May 5, 1945, gag, "I'm passing up a swell party tonight. I just couldn't trust those poor kids with their mother." Though at that time there was a tendency in popular culture to confine images of domestics to household spaces which they needed to clean or where they tended to family members, as seen in 1950s television sitcom *Beulah*, Candy inhabits various rooms in her employer's home and claims

"CANDY" – – – – – By Jackie Ormes

"Course, Mrs. Goldrocks, you realize these first few weeks you'll be on probation!"

1.5 Jackie Ormes, *Candy*, "Course, Mrs. Goldrocks, you realize these first few weeks you'll be on probation!" *Chicago Defender*, March 24, 1945.

those spaces as her own terrain. Such is the case in an April 7, 1945, gag in which Ormes pictures Candy on a balcony, looking down on a gathering of Mrs. G and her friends, remarking in what seems like a critique of the bourgeois class, "This job's good for me. . . . The more I see of her friends, the more I appreciate my own!"

From the 1939 film *Gone with the Wind* to the aforementioned television show *Beulah*, depictions of domestics in the cinema and in popular culture insinuated that a Black domestic's life was solely in service to her white employer. Her own social life was an impoverished one, and her own family was invisible to viewers. The film *Imitation of Life* (1959) intervenes in this portrayal, in which a Black female domestic, Annie, tells her employer, Laura, that she has many friends, after Laura has expressed that she assumed that Annie had no life outside of her domestic service. Candy's employer is never visible within the single frame that constitutes the gag

"CANDY" – – – – – By Jackie Ormes

"This job's good for me . . . The more I see of her friends, the more I appreciate my own!"

1.6 Jackie Ormes, *Candy*, "This job's good for me. . . . The more I see of her friends, the more I appreciate my own!" *Chicago Defender*, April 7, 1945.

form. However, Candy's consistent reference to Mrs. G, whom the spectator assumes is white, given the historical moment, is a persistent reminder of the kindly assertive point made by Annie in *Imitation of Life* in regard to her robust social life. Attributing autonomy and giving a voice to an arena of labor wherein Black women were exploited as laborers made *Candy* an artistic arm of Popular Front resistance. Readers thereby had an opportunity to relate to, gain strength from, or learn from such comic images. They also had an opportunity to laugh. Ormes's *Candy* was adept at sexual, labor, spatial, and familial subversion, but another persistent theme in *Candy* was the contemplation of Black US patriotism in the last months leading up to the end of World War II and in the few months after "victory."

In a May 26, 1945, gag, Candy, dressed in evening attire instead of her domestic uniform, pulls her dress up to reveal her leg. She looks at an imagined spectator with a concerned expression, in contradistinction

"CANDY" – – – – – By Jackie Ormes

1.7 Jackie Ormes, *Candy*, "Mrs. G is telling all her friends about my Victory garden. Wait till she sees the meat balls I planted last week." *Chicago Defender*, June 30, 1945.

"Mrs. G. is telling all her friends about my Victory garden. Wait till she sees the meat balls I planted last week."

to her sexual posture. The caption reads, "Mrs. Goldrocks is still in a V-E daze. . . . Imagine giving me the evening off, then taking the car on a binge of her own." Such quick references became a way for Ormes to narrate history as it occurred, a staple of newspaper comics in general. V-E Day refers to the public holiday celebrated in Europe on May 8, 1945, to mark Germany's concession to the Allies, which brought an end to World War II. In the context of Ormes's historical moment, Candy is an illustrative news reporter in comedic form; in our contemporary historical moment, one might recognize *Candy* as documenting Black Americans' engagement with the discourses and materiality of World War II on the domestic front.

Ormes addresses wartime patriotism a June 30, 1945, gag in which she shows Candy raking her garden while wearing high heels, a miniskirt, and a tight striped shirt. Abstract doodles represent the garden, whereas Candy's outfit is detailed and shading defines the contours of Candy's phy-

"CANDY" – – – – By Jackie Ormes

"I'm getting fed up with rolling her cigarettes. It's enough
to make me break down and share my tailor-mades!"

1.8 Jackie Ormes, *Candy*, "I'm getting fed up
with rolling her cigarettes. It's enough to make
me break down and share my tailor-mades!"
Chicago Defender, June 2, 1945.

sique. This is one of few gags where Candy is not in Mrs. G's house, which
supports her assertion of having a life outside of her low-paid job. Candy
boasts, "Mrs. G is telling all her friends about my Victory garden. Wait till
she sees the meat balls I planted last week." During the war years main-
taining a garden added to the war effort by producing and rationing food
supplies. A Victory garden allowed people at home to feel that they were
contributing to the war effort. Such depictions show Candy as a multifaceted sequential subject, that is, as one who is conversant with world affairs
and a Black patriot, as well as a voice of political and class defiance.

A June 2, 1945, gag presents Candy in the kitchen rolling homemade
cigarettes. In the caption, Candy exclaims disdainfully, "I'm getting fed up
with rolling her cigarettes. It's enough to make me break down and share
my tailor-mades!" This reference to rolling tobacco may seem like a mis-
cellaneous mundane task, but it is also a comedic nod to the difficulty of

getting prerolled or mass-manufactured cigarettes during World War II. Candy's complaint also suggests that she is a smoker, which, like Torchy's migration narratives, was a daring move at that time. Art historian Maria Elena Buszek, in her assessment of an *Esquire* calendar pin-up in 1942, writes that such implied imagery of women smoking was seen as a sign of masculine confidence, sexuality and oral sexual acts, and audacious femininity. The image Buszek refers to depicts a fair-skinned blonde who stares daringly at an imagined spectator; she wears a white suit, painted red lips, long, feminine curls, and she holds a cigarette defiantly near her lips between carefully positioned fingers. Buszek calls this aesthetic mix "monster beauty," referring to the definition of the term offered by performance artist and scholar Joanna Frueh, who explains that "monster beauty is artifice," as well as "pleasure/discipline," and "cultural invention."[41] Candy's monster beauty, or hyperfeminine appearance, posture, and audacious stance, positioned Black women in the tradition of the defiant pin-up aesthetic usually associated with white pin-up femininity. Additionally, in the comic or gag form, Candy had the added capability of being an example of visual and narrative defiance.

Instead of portraying Candy as a "down-and-out" pink-collar laborer, Ormes uses her as an example of how some working-class Black Americans invested in material items or entertainments that allowed them access to the world of the class-advantaged even as they critiqued it. In so doing, Ormes engages in a larger class discourse aimed at solidifying the dignity and pride that fine adornments might bring to those disadvantaged by color and class. In addition to intervening in depictions and assumptions about socioeconomic class, Candy showed that domestic work was "thinking" labor and not the labor of the feeble-minded or inarticulate. When drawn within the household in which she works, Candy "poses" more than she appears to do household work, though at times she is pictured dangling hangers, or sitting at a kitchen counter, suggesting that she does perform labor. Her portrayal does not glamorize housework. To the contrary, the house interior that Candy inhabits is drawn with sharp, clean lines and a minimalist aesthetic, representing an immaculate atmosphere. In this way, *Candy* affronts the depiction of Black women as being dumb and lazy, as mammies who solve the problems of white families yet have no family or romantic life of their own, as wise-cracking Sapphires oblivious to larger historical and social circumstances. Continuing to use the gag form to impart social messages,

Ormes's next comic, *Patty-Jo 'n' Ginger*, pushed political barriers even further while also edging Ormes further into the suspicions of the Federal Bureau of Investigation.

"One Naked Individual, with Liberty and Justice for All": *Patty-Jo 'n' Ginger*'s Popular Front Performances at the Dawn of the Civil Rights Era

Candy's short run was followed by *Patty-Jo 'n' Ginger*, a comic appearing in and contracted to the *Pittsburgh Courier*, even as Ormes continued to reside in Chicago. On November 1, 1947, Ormes defiantly remarked on the pressure, surveillance, and witch hunt that openly progressive intellectuals, activists, and artists were being subjected to by the state. In the gag, Ormes pictures Patty-Jo, the strip's pint-sized lead protagonist, and her sister Ginger, in long black dresses and rimmed cone hats. Patty-Jo carries a small broom, and Ginger, a cat. Apparently, the two are at a Halloween costume party; Ormes draws jack-o'-lanterns along the top of the panel to signify the holiday. With an impish grin, Patty-Jo tells her sister, "You'll be GLAD we came as witches—wait an' see! I understand some Hollywood scouts are simply HUNTING them down these days!" A surprised Ginger gasps at Patty-Jo's remark, and raises her hand to her mouth. Ginger's reaction confirms the fearlessness and danger in Patty-Jo's inadvertent innuendo, and indeed, such signifyin(g) commentary, even in comic form, garnered unsmiling notice from the office of the FBI. The gag was thus more than a tongue-in-cheek observation about McCarthy's Hollywood witch hunt for Communist sympathizers. By this time, Ormes's interaction with socialist groups who convened on Chicago's South Side made her a person of interest to the US government as a potential subversive.

Patty-Jo 'n' Ginger included segments about Ginger's dating life and Patty-Jo's interest in playing football despite it being deemed, much to her chagrin, a "boys" sport, and made use of a full spectrum of Black signifyin(g) comedy. However, indirect political speech and moments of brave defiance are what *Patty-Jo 'n' Ginger* became known for by the early 1950s. Moreover, Ormes's own political activities became an invisible hand through which she would "ink" what had by that time become an extensive canon of BCFCs in independent newspapers, and this increased use of her political voice did not go unnoticed. On December 29, 1951, an anonymous source reported to the FBI that Jackie Ormes was a member of the Commu-

1.9 Jackie Ormes, *Patty-Jo 'n' Ginger,* "You'll be GLAD we came as witches—wait an' see! I understand some Hollywood scouts are simply HUNTING them down these days!" November 1, 1947.

nist Party. This informant, and other unnamed informants cited as "reliable" in Ormes's FBI file, claim that Ormes "attended several meetings of the South Side section of the Communist Party in 1945 or 1946, and that she spoke at several of these meetings; that she attended a Communist Party meeting on November 28, 1948."[42] By 1953, the FBI had assembled a hefty file on Ormes's activities, especially during the 1940s, chronicling everything from her financial donations to her daily activities. In the 250-page report, the FBI noted the following activities that they deemed suspicious: Ormes had sponsored the Civil Rights Congress (CRC) on November 8, 1948; she had donated money to the Du Bois defense fund; she had attended American Peace Crusade activities and Chicago Council of the Arts performances; and, she held a position of leadership in the Progressive Party of Illinois in 1950.

Detailing each of her affiliations one by one, the report declared that the Civil Rights Congress was a Communist organization and the American Peace Crusade was "an organic part" of the Communist "peace" offensive by the House Un-American Activities Committee. The report claims that Ormes was more than an attendee at political functions, and that she was sent to several fund-raisers as a representative of the CRC. Such a detailed list of activities indicates that the FBI had access to all of Ormes's financial transactions and comings and goings; Ormes had likely been under government surveillance since the late 1930s, even though her FBI case is dated 1948–58. Seemingly innocent trips to the local bookstore became the subject of detailed documentation; FBI operatives wrote of her ongoing visits to the Modern Book Store in Chicago, which, according to the FBI report, was a "propaganda outlet for the Communist Party." Ormes's husband, Earl Ormes, the FBI reported, was not a member of CPUSA, nor was he involved in the meetings Ormes attended. Unlike Jackie Ormes, the report said, "[Earl] has not participated in Communist Front organizations." During her interrogation by the FBI Ormes herself declared that her husband, though a general manager and bookkeeper at Sutherland Hotel, where Popular Front activists often stayed, "had no interest in politics." The FBI labeled Ormes a "security subject," necessitating that the government ascertain her "present sympathies."

When Ormes was interviewed by the FBI at her studio and residence in 1953, operatives described her as being pleasant and compliant as they explained to her that "the Bureau has no concern with an individual's ideals, desires for reform, or with ideas a person may have to see a change in government through constitutional methods." Agents did insist, however, that they needed to identify those persons and organizations that sought to make changes to the current government under "unlawful and unconstitutional means." Operatives thus asked Ormes questions to determine her loyalties to the United States, including queries about "Korea, Russia, The Smith Act,[43] the Communist Party, and the Negro Question." In regard to questioning about Korea, Ormes remarked that US troops should withdraw, that the Korean War was one best fought between the direct parties involved, and that Russia was right in supplying China and North Korea. Of particular importance to the FBI was Ormes's position on Russia; the interviewers claimed that Ormes felt that Russia's intent was generally that of peace keeping, and Ormes criticized the current environment of hysteria in which the US government accused some American activists of being communists. The FBI report also lists people affiliated with the CPUSA that Ormes admitted to being acquainted with, including Claude and Geraldine Lightfoot, Paul Robeson, and W. E. B. Du Bois. In regard to Ormes's possible affiliation with the Communist Party, the agents record, "The subject stated that on many occasions she has aligned herself, theoretically, with the Communist Party because they, the Communist Party, had offered humanistic, social, and economic advantages to the Negro people. Ormes stated that on those occasions which she had aligned herself with the CP[USA], she found herself in accord with the benefits offered by the CP[USA] for the Negro people but this did not necessarily mean that she subscribed to all of the Communist beliefs."[44]

Beyond admitting to having a theoretical congruency with the CPUSA, Ormes represented herself in the interview as a member of the "upper strata of Negro society." Some FBI interviewers praised her intelligence, and commented that she was "well read" and "socially conscious," but wrote with sarcasm that she was "noticeably pleased to be classified as an intellectual and leader among the Negro people." Other agents directly insulted Ormes by saying she was "not very well informed or intelligent but rather a pseudo-intellectual . . . flighty in temperament, and not inclined . . . to seriously consider what the agents were attempting to clarify." At the end of the FBI report, operatives concluded that Ormes was either "confused as to the actual Communist position concerning the Negro, or she has been deliberately misled concerning some of these basic issues." After subjecting Ormes to two separate interviews, FBI agents took no further action, but it would take an additional five years to close her case. Ormes thus remained a "person of interest" to the FBI, and she was certainly not alone in her maltreatment. "Facing relentless government persecution during the McCarthy period," writes Erik S. McDuffie, "state repression isolated some of the most committed black activists for a brief but crucial moment from the emergent civil rights movement and the global political stage."[45] It is within this insidious and stressful context of surveillance, then, in which guilt was assumed and radical politics incited insecurity and fear among the larger society and those invested in upholding the ideological state apparatuses (ISAs) mandate and rhetoric of conservative nation making, that Ormes continued to create her comics and maintain her sense of humor.[46] The government's tactics notwithstanding, there was an increase in the political aspect of her comics after the FBI's inquiry into her affiliations.

Nearing the mid-1950s, the Popular Front coalition would fragment, but the BCFC elements in Ormes's gags were sharpened. *Patty-Jo 'n' Ginger* dealt with segregation and traditional civil rights concerns, but the vexed question of Black American patriotism and political boldness remained a core narrative device. An October 16, 1954, installment of *Patty-Jo 'n'*

1.10 Jackie Ormes, *Patty-Jo 'n' Ginger*, "One Naked Individual, with Liberty, and Justice for All," *Pittsburgh Courier*, October 16, 1954.

Ginger, for example, shows an impish Patty-Jo in a classroom looking up angrily at an American flag and refusing to salute it, while her integrated classroom pledges allegiance. Patty-Jo's noncooperation is deliberate. She does more than refuse to pledge alliance here; her proximity to the flag, which curls around a pole twice her size, and her courage to look up at its tip, demonstrates that a small voice can still assert agency at the local level. A chalkboard behind the children serves as a written explanation and contradiction to the classroom exercise of the pledge ritual. It reads, "De-segregation Progress:" followed by a list of four locations with accompanying symbols. Delaware and Maryland have a minus sign, "Our Town" a plus sign, and the South is given a question mark. Ormes's caption reads, "One Naked Individual, with Liberty and Justice for All." This gag shows how, with words and images, a comic strip may exhibit political defiance. Patty-Jo's refusal to pledge alliance to a nation that does not allow people of African descent the full rights of citizenship leaves her, as the caption suggests, "naked," or vulnerable, but in this gag she aligns with the *Brown v. Board of Education of Topeka Kansas* desegregation decision in May of that year.

Biographer Nancy Goldstein writes that Ormes's young characters in *Patty-Jo 'n' Ginger* could not possibly have understood the politics that they espoused, owing their representation to the literary and stage traditions of *Topsy* and *Shirley Temple*.[47] Patty-Jo's mixture of intellectual and stump speech, writes Goldstein, added a touch of comedy to the series, resulting in "sly puns." In a Black, everyday context, I argue that one might also see Patty-Jo's puns and slide from standard speech to vernacular as a process of signifyin(g) performance, in particular, Ormes's decision to employ vernacular language, code switching, and code meshing.[48] Patty-Jo's impish expressions and slightly awkward performative stance, which is almost doll-like, has some crossover characteristics in common with the child star Shirley Temple in movies such as *Bright Eyes* (1934), *Curly Top* (1935), and *Heidi* (1938). Yet Patty-Jo's performance seems scarcely congruent with *Topsy*'s minstrelsy from the book *Uncle Tom's Cabin* (1852), nor with the subsequent film based on the book, *Topsy and Eva* (1927), nor do the complexity and totality of her character seem best described by Temple's precocious and sometimes unconsciously racist filmic naïveté. To the contrary, Patty-Jo is likely a product of Ormes's invention and a grounded representation of how a young, middle-class, educated Black child in the throes of the civil rights era would express herself.

Jay David's anthology *Growing Up Black* (1971) gives voice to the intelligent young Black children in the late twentieth century, and chronicles their struggles with slavery and Reconstruction, and civil rights. David's compilation underscores how Black youth, who would later become prominent activists (e.g., Frederick Douglass, Gordon Parks, Anne Moody, Maya Angelou, and Angela Davis), were from a very young age aware of and affected by the racial politics and discrimination of the times. Their autobiographies reveal that the disparate culture in which they lived, that they were subjected to, and that they had to maneuver within made oblivion and racial naïveté impossible.[49] It is the children of Patty-Jo's generation that were being bullied and taunted in schools during Jim Crow segregation, and who were also the subjects of some of the landmark judicial cases that concerned them as young Black Americans, such as 1954's *Brown v. Board of Education*. Attributing words and acts of political rebellion to children and young adults allows artists to deflect the responsibility they might face for representing adults using the same words and actions. Their approach thus inadvertently serves to radicalize Black youth. Charles Schultz's *Peanuts* and Aaron McGruder's *The Boondocks* are only two examples of this common approach by comic strip artists, that is, using the witty voices of children to expose and comment upon the cognitive sophistication or mental abilities that they hold. Young people's knowledge is at times hidden within simplistic language structures, but they are equally skilled at problem solving and observation, and the cultural and societal problems and contradictions that adults hash out in the public sphere are of equal concern to the adults of the future.

Comparing Patty-Jo to Topsy, Goldstein observes that Topsy's "words and actions pricked the consciousness of the nation."[50] In contradistinction, literary and film scholars argue that Topsy's exaggerated dialect and features, and her fumbling, foolish performances greatly diminished her subversive characteristics.[51] Both camps are correct; stereotypes can serve subversive ends, especially through comedy, but the comedic form coupled with crude representations can also limit the transformative effect for spectators and readers in the long-term. Patty-Jo is fun and funny, but she does not fumble, nor is she foolish; her neat appearance and assertive demeanor were exactly the ammunition that Black American parents needed to arm their children with to face the wads of saliva, baseball bats, police dogs, epithet hurling, and overall brutality they encountered in the white public school system while trying to obtain an education in the initial years of desegregation. In Ormes's comic strip world, all aspects of Black life, including the voices of children, can act as the voice of the Popular Front that activists were calling for at meeting houses, bookstores, civil rights speeches and rallies, and in their mass-circulated literature. Of course, alternative political communities were not the only sites for engaging in activism.

Championing more traditional modes of activism, a November 2, 1946, *Patty-Jo 'n' Ginger* gag shows Patty-Jo and Ginger carrying voting rights signs as they walk through the streets in respectable attire. Ormes uses motion doodles beneath their feet, and (as was characteristic of the gag), the two characters step outside of the box frame of the panel. This technique was a carryover from Ormes's *Torchy Brown* and increased the performative aesthetic and connection with readers. Patty-Jo and Ginger's placement outside of the box panel in Ormes's gag relays that they are venturing outside of their comic strip world and into the "real" world of the civil rights struggle.

Ginger, though the older of the two, appears more like Patty-Jo's sidekick, and all of the most trenchant political critiques and observations come from the young Patty. In an April 5, 1947, gag Patty-Jo is drawn with great detail and pictured in an attic, dusting a sewing form while speak-

1.11 Jackie Ormes, *Patty-Jo 'n' Ginger*, "X-er-cise your ballot—weather or not," *Pittsburgh Courier*, November 2, 1946.

ing of US foreign policy: "I always figured this thing was a world map from the DARK AGES, but the way Daddy talks about Truman's new foreign policy it must be shapin' up again." Questioning the definition of Americanism and, indirectly, Southern segregation, in a February 8, 1947, gag, Patty-Jo holds a pen in her hand as pages of a letter fall to the ground and outside the purview of the panel. She says to Ginger with an angry frown, "It's a letter to my Congressman. . . . I wanta get it straight from Washington. . . . Just which is the 'American way' of life, New York or Georgia?" Everyday activities were presented as opportunities for Patty-Jo's political commentary, as in a July 12, 1947, gag where she approaches a street salesman peddling roses and remarks as Ginger stands on the sideline, annoyed and embarrassed by Patty-Jo's forthrightness, "You're stocked pretty heavy, Leo . . . Ain'cha scared they'll be viewed with alarm by that new committee an tagged un-American beauties?"

A gag from December 22, 1951 (listed in Ormes's FBI report as the year anonymous sources began coming forward about her front group activities), spoke directly to FBI agents' suspicions of the artist's communist loyalties. It was perhaps an indication of her position on the Korean

War, the Soviet Union's support of North Korea, and her opinion that the United States should not intervene in North and South Korea's military conflict. Here, Patty-Jo and Ginger are praying beneath Christmas holly and resting their hands upon an earth globe that contains the wording "Peace on earth, goodwill toward men." At first glance, the gag appears to portray no more than holiday cheer and goodwill, but the caption indirectly signifies on foreign policy and warmongering: "An' please God . . . if we can't have PEACE all over, let's at least limit the fightin' to the few folks who are Mad at Each Other!" The most forthrightly political gag that featured Black girls and women during the latter years of the Popular Front, *Patty-Jo 'n' Ginger* defined an era and a space in which civil and human rights intersected with vernacular comedy and visual performances of multifaceted blackness.

Carrying a Torch: The Ormes Society
and the Reincarnation of Torchy Brown

Torchy Brown, Ormes's first female protagonist, was featured in her new romance-themed strip for the *Courier* in 1950: *Torchy Brown: Heartbeats.* Chronicling love interests and ongoing flirtations, most of the strip was a soap opera narrative about Torchy and her male suitors. For younger readers, at the end of the strip Ormes included a Torchy paper doll with outfits that one could cut out. At a time when realistic Black imagery in relation to womanhood often escaped doll manufactures, Ormes's paper doll and her Patty-Jo doll,[52] in the likeness of the character in *Patty-Jo 'n' Ginger* in 1947, gave young Black girls representative options. Moreover, a free paper doll in a Black newspaper might have been poor girls' only paper doll, and Ormes's dolls would have given them the gift of an image of themselves in contrast to the debased images of Black women and girls as pickaninnies, mammies, and Sapphires (see plate 2). In view of the infamous Clark doll test, which sought to show how the larger racist culture shapes the attitudes, perceptions, and racial preferences of Black youth through their interpretations of dolls, the magnitude of such material images and material play is culturally significant.[53]

Ormes passed away in 1985, but Black women comic artists continue to carry the torch of the ideas and iconography she created through the medium of comics and, later, through her doll making. The formation of the Ormes Society, an organization of young Black female comic artists and writers, is testament to the reverence many feel for Ormes. It is no coincidence that visual reproductions of Torchy Brown adorned an early iteration of the organization's website.

Like the riot grrrl appropriation of the pin-up as a sexual icon of liberation, Black female comic artists have resituated the visual iconography of the first Black comic strip heroine—Torchy Brown—as a powerful symbol of sexuality and Black cultural politics. In her book on the genre of the pin-up and its feminist appropriation by the female punk rock and riot grrrl movements, Maria Elena Buszek argues that young feminists in the twenty-first century find in pin-up imagery a celebration of sexual awareness and an embrace of the female form.[54] An engagement with nonnormative sexualities, emancipatory heterosexuality, and artistic alteration of the pin-up form, Buszek argues, has provided an avenue for young feminists to merge the aggression of punk rock music with the aggressive display of a myriad of pro-sex images found in the modern and postmodern pin-up. Buszek's analysis is useful for thinking through why Black female artists use Torchy Brown iconography in a similar way. Given the historical specificity of race and Torchy Brown's aesthetic and narrative defiance, young Black women seem drawn to Torchy Brown because of Ormes's explicit narrative of social justice in view of racism, classism, sexism, and government surveillance.

The Ormes Society encourages Black women comic artists to reimagine Torchy Brown as a sign of Black women's efforts to gain visibility and voice in a male-defined and -controlled field. Ormes's comic art, with its progressive themes of race, class, sexuality, and gender, immediately began to break down barriers in the late 1930s. Contemporary Black female comic artists have taken the roots of Ormes's work and replanted it; they are growing and nurturing new visions of change in their own comics—a topic I take up in the final chapter. Comic artist and writer Nara Walker's haunting sketch of Torchy Brown from 2007 is, however, an instructive preview. Walker keeps some of Torchy's core features—the chiseled bone structure, pouty mouth, and short, wavy curls—but replaces Torchy's thickly lined eyes with eyes that have an introspective expression, a mix of manga and a unique aesthetic Walker has coined "prettyism" (see chapter 5 for more on this aesthetic). Dangling from Torchy's ear, and adding contrast to the black-and-white sketch, is an earring with a burning torch in yellow, orange, and red. Such reinterpretations of Torchy Brown suggest that however imperfect, the advocacy that defined cultural front comics

1.12 Nara Walker, "Torchy Brown Sketch," 2007. Courtesy of Nara Walker.

from a Black and female perspective began, but did not end, with Jackie Zelda Ormes's illustration of defiant Black womanhood.

Ormes, as did other Black comic artists of the early twentieth century, laid the groundwork for late twentieth-century Black comic artists in mainstream newspapers, most notably Robert Armstrong's *Jump Start* (1989), Barbara Brandon-Croft's *Where I'm Coming From* (1991), and Aaron McGruder's *The Boondocks* (1996). *Jump Start* championed the middle-class narratives made popular by *Barry Jordan* in the 1950s by using bold color and simple lines to illustrate the lives of an upwardly mobile Black family. *Where I'm Coming From* used black-and-white drawings of talking heads with detailed cultural features to re-create Ormes's dialogicism; Brandon-Croft's drawings would place readers in the position of eavesdroppers to the political, social, and cultural conversations of young Black women in the 1990s. *The Boondocks* created an Afromanga and Afroanime aesthetic to question US militarism, the Iraq War, and the commodification of Black culture, and to position the hip-hop generation as an essential voice of political critique. Contemporary comic strips by Black women pay tribute to Ormes with their organized artist society, but one also sees the transnational influences that have sparked this aesthetic direction: Japanese comics, animation, and video games have been aesthetically wed to the cultural and political issues that concerned Ormes in the 1930s, '40s, and '50s.

Despite Ormes's diverse work spanning three decades, her comics are absent in anthologies on women in cartooning. Only a few books mention Ormes, and these refer to her later volumes of the 1950s that focused on romance or environmental racism.[55] The early years of her work, recently chronicled by doll collector and Ormes biographer Nancy Goldstein, and literary scholar Edward Brunner, unearth essential aspects of Ormes's legacy. My cultural and historical analysis of Ormes's comics and interpretation of the strips and gags discussed, lesser or not, accompanies this previous scholarship. Additionally, I move the work of Ormes from a cultural project of inclusion to the emergent, theoretical possibilities of what I have described throughout this chapter as Black cultural front comics. As a Black newswoman, artist, and leftist activist, Ormes's comics could not help but reflect the spheres within which she operated and her commitment to community art and world politics enacted in the Black public sphere. For Black communities, the Popular Front was not dependent upon all aspects of the CPUSA; Black newspapers and broad united fronts were equally concerned, as Bill Mullen writes, with "the U.S. culture industry [and] its negative and stereotypical images of blacks, radicals, and other racial minorities."[56] Given their concerns, Ormes's "refined" female characters—young and old, and with militant and sometimes vernacular or stump speech—did double ideological work. Her characters undermined parochial ideas about Black females in the dominant and in the male imagination while engaging in trenchant political critiques that re-inked the nation or redefined the role of blackness within US nation making.

Domestic workers, showgirls, children, society girls, and nurses carry powerful political messages in Ormes's work, and their pretty looks are secondary to the political potency and efficacy of their words. Ormes's romance comic strips were no doubt important predecessors to later syndicated comic strips that would feature an attractive Black female lead, such as Jim Lawrence's early 1970s strip *Friday Foster* in the *Chicago Tribune*.[57] As the 1950s came to a close and Ormes stopped writing comics and began to focus full-time on doll making, actor Eartha Kitt picked up the representative torch in the 1960s, as did actor Halle Berry later. In their different and historically disparate portrayals of Catwoman in comic books, graphic novels, television, and film, Eartha Kitt and Halle Berry contributed to the Black female image in sequential art, and spectators were challenged to decide whether their roles could keep the fire of Ormes's political fight lit. Catwoman as Asian, Black, white, and Latino in comics, graphic novels, animation, and video games provide a comparative opportunity to assess how readers and producers dealt with the conundrum of blackness and embraced postracialism in the later twentieth and early twenty-first centuries—what had in Ormes's times been referred to as the proverbial "Negro question" and its attendant practice of color blindness.

PLATE 1 Gary Friedrich, *Hell-Rider* #1, Skywald Publications, August 1971.

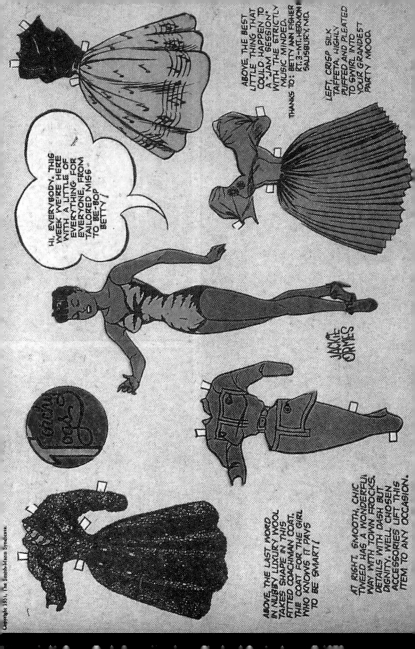

PLATE 4 Gardner Fox, *Batman* #197, December 1967. © DC COMICS.
Available in *Showcase Presents: Batman Volume Three*. All rights reserved.

PLATE 5 Frank Robbins, "The Case of the Purr-Loined Pearl," *Batman* #210, March 1969.
© DC COMICS. Available in *Showcase Presents: Batman Volume Four*. All rights reserved.

PLATE 6 Mindy Newell, "Her Sister's Keeper," *Catwoman*, May 1991.

PLATE 7 Chuck Austin, *Catwoman: The Movie and Other Cat Tales* (2004).

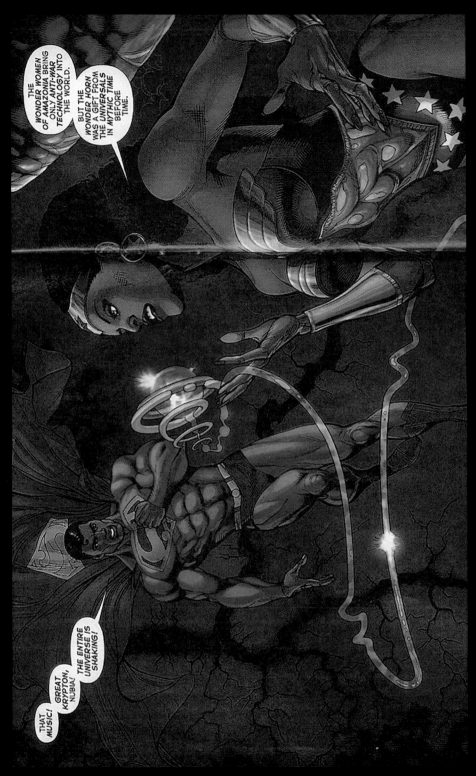

PLATE 8 Grant Morrison, *Final Crisis* 1, #7, Mar. 2009, 2–3.

Final Crisis™ © DC COMICS. All rights reserved.

PLATE 11 Willow Wilson, "Predators," *Vixen Return of the Lion* #1.

BLACK CAT GOT YOUR TONGUE?

Catwoman, Blackness, and Postracialism

Catwoman is a unique breed. Never taking the same form twice, but whatever form she takes, she'll always reign supreme.

Eartha Kitt, *The Many Faces of Catwoman*

When I first saw Eartha [as Catwoman], I didn't know what it meant, but I knew it was important and that I connected to it and felt good about myself after watching her.... I'm reviving something she originated.

—Halle Berry, *Jet*

N 2013, the independent label Blue Water Comics contributed to the coupling of blackness and female representation in sequential art with their release of the comic book *Eartha Kitt: Femme Fatale*.[1] Writer Marc Shapiro presents the character Catwoman as bearing a likeness to a teenage version of the actor Eartha Kitt, who played Catwoman for a short time during the 1960s television series *Batman*. The audience for Shapiro's Catwoman is preteen; she is an Afropunk and surfing riot grrrl who, while catching waves in Honolulu, combats the dinosaur Gorgon (see plate 3). Wearing black goggles and a black-and-gold wet suit, Catwoman sweeps across the ocean on her surfboard while hitting Gorgon from the left and the right, effortlessly balancing recreation and the task of defending beach goers. At the end of volume 1, she defeats Gorgon and tells readers, "Catch a wave and you're sitting on top of the world!"

This newer Catwoman is young, fun, cool, and audacious; writers rely on historical signs of Eartha Kitt as Catwoman to offer an alternative to the racial representation of the character as seen in contemporary graphic novels and as seen in the film *The Dark Knight Rises* (2012). Yet, while Shapiro presents Catwoman within the framing of de-essentialized blackness and resurrects the character's legacy and contribution to the framing of Black women in comics, the "white" Catwoman has come under scrutiny for her depiction in the video game *Arkham City*, which incessantly refers to Catwoman as a bothersome bitch. Journalists, bloggers, and news media made note of the repetitive, aggressive, and sexualized dialogue in *Arkham City* soon after its release in 2011, pointing out the troubling gender politics of a form of sequential art media that engages users through interactive role-playing. When a user navigates through the game and plays the role of the male villain or superhero, he or she embodies characters that the game has programmed to speak to or of Catwoman in the following way:

> "That'll teach the bitch to screw with Two-Face."
> "Bitch deserves it ... it was only a matter of time before she got a little payback."
> "I'll make you meow, bitch."
> "He sent Paulie B over to blow that bitch's secret hideout sky-high."
> "I want you guys to blow that bitch apart!"
> "He had her just where he wanted her and that bitch broke free."
> "I win, bitch!"
> "Help us decide if we should kill the bitch who tried to steal from us."
> "Two guns, bitch!"
> "Don't come any closer or this bitch gets a hole where her head used to be!"
> "That crazy bitch!"
> "She scares me. Fortunately, I saw the crazy bitch leaving!"
> "I don't know what Joker sees in that crazy bitch."
> "Yeah, the boss had the Cat all chained up, but that bitch broke free."

Fan and comics critic Laura Hudson reveals the gender trouble of Catwoman in *Arkham City* succinctly: "The game holds a mirror up to [an] unpleasant truth, and is . . . [a] reflection of people's innate inclinations to do and say these things. And it's very easy, particularly as throwaway dialogue in a video game, for it to fade away into the background as something ambient, unexamined or even accepted as normal, rather than something worthy of notice or reaction."[2]

In contrast to *Arkham City*'s bitchiness, a 2004 release of *Catwoman: The Game* bears the likeness of the Black actor Halle Berry as Catwoman; players perform as a problem-solving and physically strong woman who navigates difficult missions in urban locations. *Catwoman: The Game* accompanied the film *Catwoman* released the same year, and it is one of the few video games to feature a Black female character as autonomous and as the primary subject. Do these seemingly transformative Black Catwomen in recent children's comics and in video games affirm that the field of sequential art has gone postracial? Given these wildly different versions of Catwoman in contemporary times, in print and in moving-image media, a mapping of the gender, race, and sexuality of the character from her inception to modern times shows the dynamic cultural uses of one of the most visible female characters in the world of sequential art. *Eartha Kitt: Femme Fatale*, *Catwoman: The Game*, and *Arkham City* prove that Catwoman holds a wide range of racial and gender meanings in the twenty-first century, but the character's history, which begins with the famous cartoonist Milton Caniff, shows how the character also exists within a series of unpredictable (retro)transgressions.

In 1934, a few years before Jackie Ormes sought to insert the Black female image in comic strips and gags, Milton Caniff introduced one the most popular female characters of the twentieth century: the Cat. Caniff, the creator of the infamous and Orientalist-inscribed Dragon Lady caricature in the comic *Terry and the Pirates*, fashioned the Cat as a parallel personality to Dragon Lady, who was a European version of the Chinese, sexually volatile, and mistrustful femme fatale who used her sexuality to manipulate and entrap American heroes.[3] Like Dragon Lady, the Cat exhibited the cunning, conniving, and potent gesticulating of a slithering, man-eating animal. The similarity in appearance between the two characters is striking as well, as the Dragon Lady and the Cat both have fair skin, almond-shaped eyes, jet-black hair, high cheekbones, and a pouty mouth. DC Comics' writers Bob Kane and Bill Finger modified the character in the 1940 *Batman* and renamed her Catwoman. Unlike her female contemporaries in other comic books, most notably Wonder Woman, Liberty Belle, and Black

Canary, Catwoman's commitment to social justice, American exceptionalism, and wartime patriotism were ambiguous at best, and her sexuality—often used to manipulate, confuse, and shock—embodied the fear of and fascination with outwardly aggressive female sexuality.[4] According to *Batman* writers, the introduction of Catwoman, a working-class hairdresser-turned-socialite and jewel thief, meant to attract more female readers to the series and provide male readers with sexual gratification. In the minds of DC Comic moguls, women readers would admire the development of the character's beauty, strength, vulnerability, and intelligence.[5] DC believed that male readers would respond to Catwoman's exaggerated physique, as well as her less-than-subtle sexual innuendos. For example, in her first appearance in 1940s *Batman*, the caped crusader remarks to Catwoman, "Quiet or Papa will spank!" to which Catwoman responds: "I know when I'm licked!"[6]

An analysis of Catwoman offers fertile ground for interrogating the cultural politics of race, given the racialization, deracialization, and sexual representation of the character in comic books, graphic novels, television, video games, and film over the past several decades. Across these various popular mediums, the Catwoman character created and reconstituted narrative spaces for readers along the lines of race, gender, and sexuality. In *Batman*, Catwoman created a narrative space of heteronormativity that strategically undercut the perceived homoeroticism between the characters Batman and Robin in the comic book and 1960s television series.[7] The graphic novel *Catwoman*, in contrast, formed a gender and racial space to negotiate the two poles of transgressive and objectified sexuality, as well as a feminist sensibility and an autonomous sexuality. From her television and feature-film premier to the twenty-first century, Catwoman developed into a dubious mixture of 1960s civil rights protest, racial inclusion, and postracial cultural politics. The alchemy or fabrication of postracialism that creators of the character had her to embody narrates how race—specifically blackness—shapes production, perception, and interest among a wide variety of fans, as well as the cultural and political implications of this process.[8] To explore these conclusions and the narrative use of Catwoman vis-à-vis the cultural politics of race, I begin with a history of the character to situate her in space and time, and proceed to interpret the various meanings of Catwoman's characterology alongside several interlocking forms of difference. I argue that the various possibilities for understanding the effects that gender, race, and sexuality have on production and consumption intervene in studies on comic book and graphic novel fandom in which female characters' racial fluidity has yet to enter the scholarly discourse about comic books. In so doing, I establish that Catwoman's various meanings in engaging with blackness and additional aspects of difference constitute more than the sum of her nine comic book lives.

Am I to Be the Bride or the Burglar?
Catwoman as a Sexual Device in the Golden Age

While many audiences know Catwoman from the 1960s television series *Batman*, the character has been a part of the franchise since the comic book title's early inception in the pre–World War II years, a time nostalgically termed the "golden age of comics" by fans and scholars alike. However, Catwoman's comic book run in *Batman* came to a halt not long after her introduction in 1940. After World War II, DC Comics made the decision to retire the sexually overt character for a few years, after leading comic book distributors implemented the Comic Book Codes, a series of self-regulated rules to tone down sexuality and violence in comic book titles.[9] Catwoman reemerged in the early 1950s as a slightly less kinky but still hypersexual personality obsessed with Batman and matrimony. The timing of her reintroduction and character shift was a strategic maneuver on the part of DC and writer Bob Kane to appeal to a growing female readership.[10] Writers sought to deflect the criticism forged by psychiatrist Fredric Wertham's 1954 book *Seduction of the Innocent*, which suggested there was a latent homoerotic relationship between Batman and Robin, thereby making the series unsuitable reading for children.[11]

Indeed, Kane and DC vehemently denied an overt or subtextual narrative of same-sex desire between Batman and Robin, and soon introduced several female love interests into the lives of Bruce Wayne and Dick Grayson, Batman's and Robin's daytime personas. It should then come as no surprise that by the late 1950s, Catwoman's normative sexuality became compulsory, and seldom did she appear without relentless dialogue about domesticating Batman. In one panel of the *Batman* series, Catwoman leers over Batman and his superhero comrades, including the newly introduced crime fightress Batgirl, with the hopes of threatening Batman into matrimonial submission. As his comrades look on in fear, she seductively and assertively says to Batman, "My fate is in your hands, Batman! Am I to be the bride—or burglar? Before you answer, I must warn you that if you refuse my proposal of marriage—you doom not only yourself, but Robin and Batgirl as well . . . !"[12] (see plate 4).

Catwoman's obsession with marriage and securing Batman as her mate had as much to do with the character's written desires as it had to do with how writers used her as a tool to mediate Batman's relationship with other male and female characters in the series. From the beginning of the *Batman* series well until the early 1950s, Catwoman became a constant wedge and point of contention between Batman and Robin, who were the title's lead characters. In the 1940s *Batman* comics, a socialite named Julie Madison was the girlfriend of Bruce Wayne. Yet since she was the love interest of Bruce Wayne and not his alter ego, Batman, her appearances were limited to the briefer segments involving Wayne. Given that three quarters of the series dealt with the crime-fighting adventures of Batman and his boy wonder Robin, the addition of Catwoman, and later Batgirl, into the duo's secret lives as crime fighters created a triangle of sexual tension. In an early *Batman* installment, Batman allows Catwoman (then known as the Cat) to escape justice, thus perturbing the boy wonder:

> ROBIN: Watch Her! She's jumped overboard!
> BATMAN: Fancy that! (*As Robin makes ready to jump after the Cat, the Batman clumsily "bumps" into him!*)
> ROBIN: Hey!
> BATMAN: Oops. Sorry, Robin.
> ROBIN: Too late—she's gone! And say, I'll bet you bumped into me on purpose . . . so she might try a break!
> BATMAN: Why, Robin, my boy, what ever gave you such an idea![13]

Since the premise of the Batman/Catwoman narrative was to sustain sexual tension between the two and keep readers coming back by suspending the consummation of their relationship, DC writers could not risk the formation of an actual relationship between Catwoman and Batman, or between Batman and any other woman. Nineteen-eighties DC writer Frank Miller, who was the mastermind behind Batman's resurrection in the graphic novel *The Dark Knight Returns*, agreed by stating, "[Batman's] sexual urges are so drastically sublimated into crime-fighting that there's no room for any other emotional [or sexual] activity."[14]

As the late fifties grew near, Catwoman again disappeared from *Batman's* comic book world and did not reemerge until 1964. To sustain readership

2.1 Bob Finger, "The Cat," *Batman* #1, August–September 1940. © DC COMICS.

and appease the dual interests of male and female readers, DC writer Bob Kane developed a compromise to expand their marketing strategy. While in Gotham City, Batman and Catwoman met occasionally and remained friendly adversaries, but in the parallel universe of Earth Two, their alter egos Bruce Wayne and Selina Kyle married and had a daughter, the Huntress, who became a social-justice crusader. Kane's story line allowed for a bilateral reading in which singlehood and marriage could coexist within a metanarrative, resulting in a win-win for male and female readers. This approach also allowed simultaneous contestation of and conformity to gender and sexual codes, as both characters were sexually autonomous in one universe (Gotham City), and objects of domestication in another universe (Earth Two).

Catwoman's television appearance came about in the 1966 television series *Batman*, starring Adam West as Batman, Burt Ward as Robin, and Julie Newmar as Catwoman.[15] The framing of Catwoman's character on the television show *Batman* made significant references to feminist movements that reflected and distorted the changes of the times. Catwoman controlled an autonomous criminal empire and sometimes fought on the right side of the law, or with Batman, but, like the early comic book series, the television show relied on the sexual attraction between the two as a core narrative device. Conveniently, the unreliability of Catwoman's character and her propensity toward crime was the ongoing threat that would disallow the consummation of their relationship. Robin remained jealous of the tenuous relationship throughout the series, and writers seemed genuinely perplexed as to where Robin fit in as Batman and Catwoman pondered their hypothetical romantic future in the climax of nearly half of the first year's episodes. In a 1966 episode, the dialogue between Catwoman and Batman acknowledges Robin's unstable and ambiguous status in Batman's life, not to mention his centrality to Batman's—and Bruce Wayne's—phantasmagoric world:

CATWOMAN: I can give you more happiness than . . . than any one. . . .
   It can be you and me against the world.
BATMAN: What about Robin?
CATWOMAN: Well, I'd have him killed, of course—painlessly. (*Batman appears shocked.*) Well, he is a bit of a bore with his "holy this" and "holy that . . ."
BATMAN: (*Indignant.*) Oh! That does it, Catwoman! I thought you had a modicum of decency, but I see now that I erred in my judgment.[16]

The sexual development of the Catwoman character reflected the lifting of the sanctions imposed by the 1950s' Comic Book Codes, and of the increasing momentum of twentieth-century feminist movements. Catwoman on the *Batman* television sitcom considered Batman a sexual toy, but also an equal in the public sphere. In comparison, in a 1967 *Batman* comic panel, writers integrated the changing trajectory of gender relations by representing Catwoman as an ideologue who led a brainwashed, cloned mass of women freedom fighters in the name of the battle of the sexes (see plate 5).[17] In the comic book and television show, Catwoman expressed jealousy of Batman and Robin's collaborator, Batgirl, that was irrational and antithetical to mature feminist sensibilities. However, her consistent critique of Batgirl was also telling in the larger context of gender relations. In Catwoman's eyes, Batgirl was a sidekick reliant upon Batman and Robin for her identity and her actions. She was an extension of the caped crusaders, a female bat who mucked about blindly in the dark until Batman and Robin brought her into the crime fighting light. Catwoman, on the other hand, was a salacious, stealthy, and quick-moving feline who acted not on the prescriptions of others but as she pleased to act. In the urban landscape of Gotham City, more often than not, men were utterly incompetent when they came up against Catwoman, especially when faced with the Black Catwoman played by actor Eartha Kitt.

This Night's Work Will Catapult Me into the Headlines!
The Problem of "Race" and Catwoman in the Silver Age

The mid- to late 1960s, referred to as the "silver age of comics," became notable for its modern break with the confines of the Comic Book Codes, its expansion into television and animation, and its expansion of the superhero genre.[18] To heighten the visibility of the superhero, there in kind would have to be a heightening of the "superfoe" or villain. In 1967, Catwoman's persona—and Batman's television world—would change once again, as Black actor Eartha Kitt replaced Julie Newmar in the role of Catwoman on the television series, thereby leading the character to gather deeper meanings and expanded interpretations of race, gender, and sexuality.[19] Kitt's adaptation of the role was different from Newmar's, and so was the relationship between Catwoman and Batman. Kitt's voice inflection and enunciation of Catwoman's infamous cat phrases were impeccable, and the underlying sexual connotation of her portrayal was consistent with earlier versions of the character. However, the sexual inferences that constituted Newmar and West's relationship did not exist in the second season, when Catwoman's character took a sharp turn from feline fatale to plain fatal. The television show stood out for its unstereotypical and unique portrayal of a lead Black female character.[20] Notably, Kitt's performance stood in striking contrast to the roles available to Black women on television, insofar as she did not fit the proverbial mammy, Jezebel, tragic mulatta, and Sapphire stereotypes that were the norm on television and in the cinema at that time. Still, Catwoman's transformation to a power-hungry criminal, albeit an intelligent one, suggested that although the writers were open to a Black Catwoman, when it came to the sexual relationship between the new Catwoman and the existing (read "white") Batman, they replaced Catwoman's sexual innuendos with cunning and mischievous pursuits to avoid representing a holy Bat-abomination, that is, an interracial romance.

Kitt's colleagues embraced her inclusion in the television series, although the show's conflicting, colorblind rhetoric acknowledged and denied Kitt's blackness at the same time. In the documentary *The Many Faces of Catwoman* (2004), in reference to race and the casting of Kitt as Catwoman, Adam West declares, "Oh, and then we got a Black Catwoman! But her race did not matter. We did not think a thing about it. . . . When I first met her, I thought, here is this Black woman, and she's beautiful, too."[21] West's comment shows that, while one may purport not to see race ("We did not think a thing about it"), subconscious feelings about race are present ("When I first met her, I thought, *here is this Black woman*, and *she's beautiful, too*"). West's postracial rhetoric gives primacy to aesthetics over talent, and infers that blackness is generally antithetical to the illusory and nebulous marker of the dominant culture's conceptualization of beauty. These extratextual, ideological contradictions notwithstanding, Kitt's reinterpretation of Catwoman did challenge notions of space and blackness in the popular imagination, and the confines of the social relations of racial apartheid and segregation in the United States.

Kitt's first appearance in the 1967 *Batman* episode "Catwoman Dressed to Kill" did more than tout blackness, as the character would signify on Black attainment of space and the dominant culture's conceptualization of beauty, femininity, sexuality, and power, especially as it relates to blackness vis-à-vis whiteness. In this groundbreaking episode, Catwoman interrupts a fashion award ceremony for white socialites at the very moment Batgirl receives the "Batty Award" for the best-dressed crime fightress in Gotham City:

COMMISSIONER GORDON: (*Proudly.*) This award goes to prove that there is room for style, even in crime fighting.

CATWOMAN: (*Catwoman enters the room with white male sidekicks Manks and Angora.*) Ridiculous! I said ridiculous—foolish prattle. How can Batgirl be the best anything when Catwoman is around? (*Catwoman chuckles in a muted purr.*) No best-dressed list is complete without the addition of the queen of criminals, the princess of plunder—yours untruly. Right, Manks and Angora?

MANKS AND ANGORA: (*Together.*) Right!

CATWOMAN: In any comparison between Batgirl and myself, she runs a poor third.

COMMISSIONER GORDON: Just a minute, Catwoman, you cannot come in here and disturb a luncheon like this!

CATWOMAN: Ah, but I can, gentlemen. And I have. (*Catwoman gestures to a table of white female socialites.*) You ladies, with your fancy hairdos, what do you know about beauty? After you suffer the effects of my hair bomb, you will never be able to raise your heads in public again! Then we will see who is the fairest of them all. Hssss! (*Catwoman throws a sequined dust at the socialites, which explodes in their faces and turns their hairdos into finger-caught-in-the-light-socket-looking Afros.*)

SOCIALITES (*all*): Oh no![22]

There are several layers of meaning to cull from this scene in relationship to gender, race, and sexualities. Catwoman's insistence that she can enter into an all-white space, and has, asserts her right to belong and seize recognition. In view of West's earlier comment about Kitt, Catwoman's scorn of the white socialites and their vying to be seen as the "fairest of them all" in this 1967 episode is an ironic, signifying statement on whiteness, blackness, and beauty aesthetics at time when the slogan "Black is beautiful" was infused with political meaning. Hair is a significant, material sign of racialization, and Catwoman's transformation of the white socialites' hair into Afros (in contrast to Kitt's long, pin-curled locks) via a "hair bomb" blurs and overturns hierarchies of beauty, hair, and their dependent relationship to race. Catwoman's commentary before the explosion also invokes a direct confrontation with what bell hooks has coined the white-supremacist-capitalist patriarchy that is responsible for the white socialites' elevated racial, class, and gender status.[23] Further, while the 1940s *Batman* comic book used signs of heteronormativity to reify a heterosexual narrative structure with the inclusion of Catwoman, the televisual animation of Catwoman as played by Kitt made way for additional sexual frameworks and sexual-object relations.

A critical mass of viewers could and did view the roles of Catwoman's lackeys, Manks and Angora, as well as her comrades the Joker, the Riddler, and the Penguin, as powerful symbols of alternative white masculinity that did not rely upon hypermasculinity, heterosexuality, or brute brawn to define their manhood.[24] In this way, Kitt's appearance sets the stage for viewers to embrace a Catwoman whose blackness and allied relationship with unconventional white masculinities, without the insinuation of a sexual relationship, made her more socially significant in regard to the politics of race, gender, and sexualities. Her extradition from being the love interest of Batman was an unfortunate throwback to antebellum fears of miscegenation. Yet Kitt's role paradoxically opened the door for equal footing, in contrast to Newmar's and, later, actor Lee Meriwether's, interpretation of the character. Although Newmar and Meriwether both relied upon their wit to define the role, they relied more upon their sexuality.

It is more than ironic that an episode about a luncheon (i.e., "Catwoman Dressed to Kill"), which helped to usher in Kitt's career as a trailblazer in television, would symbolically foreshadow a White House luncheon Kitt would attend in real life, with president Lyndon Johnson in 1968. When asked about the Vietnam War by First Lady Johnson at the luncheon, Kitt expressed her ambivalence by stating, "You send the best of this country off to be shot and maimed. No wonder the kids rebel and [smoke] pot."[25] The First Lady took offense, and news of Kitt's forthright and antiwar commentary spread. Reactions to her comment included an aggressive movement to blacklist Kitt in the United States, but this opened the door to more opportunities for the actor and singer to perform at nightclubs in Europe and Asia. Furthermore, her queer-allied camp in *Batman* gave her traction in her overseas engagements and boosted her popularity abroad and in New York City.[26] If "Catwoman Dressed to Kill" foreshadowed Kitt's real-life rebellion, Kitt's Catwoman character also became a popular cultural icon months before the Stonewall riots for gay rights, and continued decades after Stonewall's intervention into the ideological state apparatuses retroprocessing of heteronormativity in the public sphere.[27]

Queer spectators and fans did tap into and rally around the transgressive performance of masculinities in *Batman* in the late 1960s (and in subsequent decades as the show appeared in syndication), but the characterization of sexuality in the television show was still problematic. As cultural critic Marti Jo Morris writes of the television and film series, while the expansion of masculinities and, by association, perceived sexualities of these characters may "produce a variety of readings both subversive and conforming, the subversive messages are more likely to solidify extreme opinion than to persuade people, gain power, and disrupt dominant ideologies."[28] I argue similarly that while the widely colorful costumes and eccentric stylization of Manks, Angora, the Joker, the Riddler, and the Penguin may have increased the prospects of subjectivity for queer-identified audiences, the majority of spectators would likely have seen these roles as queer minstrels or as evil, asexual villains. Kitt's Catwoman and her villainous colleagues represent the possibilities and contradictions that led to a diversification of the comic book and television viewing market, thereby expanding the fan base beyond any one particular race, gender, or monosexual distinction. At the same time, such camp performances, as Morris suggests, present little guarantee of subversion on a broad scale. Perhaps the most significant mediator of the unreliability of representation is representative action in the public sphere: the same role that made Eartha Kitt a camp icon also helped to influence her participation in activism on the behalf of lesbian, bisexual, and gay rights from the late 1960s until her death in 2008. Eartha Kitt as Catwoman writ large was more than a television character, and as an icon of sexuality and sexual freedom, the way she made use of the reaction to her Catwoman camp interpenetrated and interlinked the textuality of the visual with the political possibilities of the contextual real.

Dawn of a New Age: The Bronzing of Catwoman in Graphic Novels

Television's Catwoman laid significant groundwork for the racial and sexual transgressions of the character in the modern comic book era, but these could be retrograde or progressive depending upon the particular graphic novel or comic book issue. In the 1980s, *Batman* writer Frank Miller changed Catwoman's comic book history from that of a working-class hairdresser turned socialite and jewel thief in the 1940s and '50s and in the television series, to a former prostitute who specialized in sadomasochism. In this depiction, the character was again depicted with her original exaggerated anatomy, apparently for the gratification of young male readers. Catwoman's strong sexual innuendos in a 1986 issue of *Batman* were reminiscent of the era before the Comic Book Codes, as she seductively queries Batman, "Do I have to purr in your ear?" Batman responds with like repartee, "No, but maybe later you could scratch my back." Catwoman keeps up the sexual banter by replying, "What's the matter? No itches in the front?"[29]

Miller's sexualized *Catwoman* was congruent with a growing trend in 1980s' comics to present angry latex- and leather-clad ass-kicking women such as Barb Wire, Lady Rawhide, Witch Blade, Fatale, Black Widow, and She-Hulk. Cultural critic Jeffrey Brown writes, "To attract the attention of the predominantly male adolescent comics consumer, publishers flooded store shelves with new books [in the 1980s] featuring extremely leggy and buxom superheroines costumed in highly revealing, skintight outfits."[30] Catwoman's transformation paralleled the metamorphosis of the *Batman* comic book and, later, the animated series, into a graphic novel format in which Batman became more serious, mature, and disenchanted with the world—leaving the Boy Wonder behind to engage with the complexity of life and his disillusion with justice.[31] In Miller's version, Catwoman took vengeance on her pimp and advocated for women, especially sex workers. When Batman met Catwoman on the streets of Gotham City, it was generally to stop her from committing a crime or to save her from herself. This depiction departed from the former Catwoman's cross-gender appeal as an autonomous character with agency. The Catwoman of the past occupied the space of subject of desire. She controlled her own destiny; she did not wait for Batman to save her from demise.

Not until writer Mindy Newell and, later, writer Ed Brubaker took on the task of making Catwoman a graphic novel did Catwoman gain a genealogy and a serious feminist sensibility absent the exaggerated battle-of-the-sexes polemics of her 1960s comic book character. As writer Ed Brubaker writes,

> [The former] Catwoman was kind of disgusting the way she was
> always portrayed as this real sort of fawning, "Oh, I have to make
> out . . ." She couldn't have a guest appearance in any comic without
> kissing the main character in a really grotesque way. She could be
> really tough and smart and everything, and then she would do this
> fake shaking-her-tail kind of shit. I've never known a woman like
> that. . . . I like my version of her. . . . [I wanted to do something] a lot

different than what was going on in mainstream comics at the time, character-driven explorations, as opposed to straight plot-driven action. I remember I was talking to Judd Winick at a comic-book convention, the first time I met him. He said, "You know what I really like about *Catwoman*? It's the closest thing to an alternative comic that gets published by DC."[32]

In 1991, in her graphic novel *Her Sister's Keeper*, Mindy Newell, a psychiatric nurse turned writer, added a complexity to Catwoman beyond the eye-candy cat suit of yesteryear (see plate 6).[33] Catwoman became more than an avenger in this series; she became a vigilante by her own choice—one who championed the rights of the working classes of the east end of Gotham City. While she did remain an antihero, she was no longer a villainess—perhaps a temptress, but always her own woman. Newell's and Brubaker's Catwoman had a circle of friends and relatives that had less to do with the world of Batman and Bruce Wayne. The new Catwoman had a Spanish-speaking Latino mother who committed suicide, a white alcoholic father, a sister who had a mental breakdown, and a best friend, Holly, who is in a same-sex relationship and is a former child prostitute, runaway, and recovering drug attic. In short, holy prophesy! Newell and Brubaker made Wertham's worst nightmare come true. With the exception of ethnicity and the extended circle of family and friends, Newell's emotionally complex Selina Kyle/Catwoman became a loose model for Catwoman's appearance in the second installment of Tim Burton's successful Batman film enterprise, *Batman Returns* (1991). Unfortunately, the enhancement of race, gender, and sexuality did not transfer well to the representation or reception of the character in *Batman Returns* or *The Dark Knight Rises*, nor in the film feature *Catwoman* (2004). In all three films, blackness was absent or became a context and subtext that the creators of the character appeared unable to reconcile in the market.

Those Who Bother Cats Can Get Scratched! The Politics of Race, Production, and Consumption in *Batman Returns* and *Catwoman*

Casting directors faced a dilemma when it came to who would play Catwoman in *Batman Returns*.[34] Since the origin story in *Her Sister's Keeper*, Catwoman was assumedly a mixture of Latino and white, but the last visual representation of Catwoman on the small screen had been Black. Although rumors surfaced that producers had considered the R&B singer Jody Watley and actor/singer Vanessa L. Williams for the role, the film's decision makers did not select Watley or any other Black actor, and instead cast white actor Michelle Pfeiffer to play the dual personality of Selina Kyle and Catwoman. Given Kitt's brief but significant contribution to the *Catwoman* franchise, it seems the makers of the 1992 film faced the same dilemma as the 1960s television show, that is, questioning of viewers' potential reception of blackness, sexuality, and cross-racial desire in a romantic context. More than twenty-five years had passed since the television series had first aired, and the motion picture industry had produced many on-screen sexual portrayals of interracial liaisons. Still, makers of *Batman Returns* sought to fashion the film in accordance with the current Batman graphic novel series, *The Dark Knight Returns*, and apparently balked at presenting an interracial love theme. Creators of the 2012 *The Dark Knight Rises* followed suit by casting actor Anne Hathaway as Catwoman in what was a fairly lackluster and forgettable characterization.

In contrast to *The Dark Knight Rises*, Pfeiffer's 1992 interpretation of the character was successful on several accounts: the acting was sound, and Pfeiffer brought a sense of vulnerability to Selina Kyle and an unapologetic autonomy to Catwoman. As a reviewer in *Rolling Stone* wrote about Pfeiffer's portrayal, "Catwoman is no bimbo in black leather. Pfeiffer gives this feminist avenger a tough core of intelligence and wit."[35] In contrast, feminist critic Priscilla Walton writes in her analysis of *Batman Returns*, "Although Burton's film offers the potential of feminist agency in its depiction of Catwoman's outlaw performance, it also skins this cat by situating her firmly under the eye of male authority."[36] As discussions began about a Catwoman feature film in the wake of the deracialization of the character in Burton's *Batman Returns*, the film's producers and director would need to make a calculated decision pertaining to the race of the character.

In 2003, DC/Warner Brothers Pictures announced that actor Halle Berry would play the lead in their 2004 feature film *Catwoman*, directed by European director Jean-Cristophe "Pitof" Comar.[37] In the 2004 adaptation of *Catwoman*, Patience Phillips—a young Black artist who works in the advertising division of a cosmetics firm—replaces Selina Kyle. An Egyptian cat transforms Phillips into Catwoman after her own boss kills her for finding out the firm's secret: their best-selling face cream creates long-term paralysis and deterioration of the flesh. The love interest for Phillips in *Catwoman* is not Batman; rather, it is Tom Lone, played by the Latino and American Indian actor Benjamin Bratt. As the plot and the casting of this film demonstrate, the new Catwoman had no resemblance to the graphic novel character other than the name. Catwoman's self-assurance, strength, and cunning were completely nonexistent. Patience Phillips was embarrassingly self-effacing before she became Catwoman, and after her transition, she was less of a social justice crusader or jewel thief in the Robin Hood tradition, as the prior Catwoman had been, and more of a rebel without a cause. When Phillips/Catwoman steals jewelry from a downtown city museum, for example, she does this on a lark, returns it, and leaves a handwritten note that says, "Sorry." Even before DC writers infused Selina Kyle/Catwoman's character with a feminist worldview in the graphic novel, she never apologized for anything, and would certainly never say "I'm sorry" after a heist. *Catwoman* the movie departed from the gritty urban realism and the psychologically layered and character-driven writing of the contemporary graphic novel to become a romantic comedy tainted by artificial-looking computer-generated imagery (commonly referred to as CGI). Yet, *Catwoman* the movie suffered from more than the clichéd adage that the book is always better than the film.

Reviews of *Catwoman* were overwhelmingly negative, citing poor acting and poorly executed action scenes as the film's downfall, and fans of Catwoman were disappointed in the casting and the narrative. Reviewers accused the film of being nothing more than an opportunity to show off Berry's well-toned physique. "Catwoman's ensemble looks like she's been shopping at trick-toria's secret [with her] open-toed shoes, black slash pants and a leather bustier," said a sarcastic reviewer in the *Houston Chronicle*.[38] Aesthetically, Catwoman's movements in the film had more resemblance to a modern video game than the martial arts–inspired movements of Burton's film and those suggested by graphic novel illustrators. In the graphic novel series, Catwoman was not a superheroine with magic or exaggerated powers. Part of her appeal to the everyday reader was that she was an antihero whose fighting ability was derivative of martial arts and physical endurance training. Catwoman's ability to complete her missions using her well-honed physical agility in the graphic novel made her accessible and more realistic, which led to her long-term respect among readers. Over the years, Catwoman had been a working-class hairdresser, a socialite, a former prostitute, a jewel thief, and a US government spy. However, whatever her occupation, she had always been assertive, strong-minded, and, most important to modern readers, she had always been Selina Kyle. As one fan remarked in a newspaper exposé about readers' dismay concerning the film, "If you're going to put Halle Berry in a tight costume and give her cat powers, just call her tiger girl or something. . . . But if you call her Catwoman, give me the Catwoman I know."[39] While the character's identity had always been in a state of flux, and her origin had been reset more than once by Frank Miller, Mindy Newell, and, later, Ed Brubaker, Warner Brothers' filmic departure troubled the marketplace and Catwoman readers for reasons derived from a collision of liberal politicking, lack of business know-how, and culture.

Unlike Burton's *Batman Returns*, the artistic direction of Warner Brothers' *Catwoman* did not consider the desires of *Batman* fans. Rather, I argue that the film sought to redress the racially suspect casting of Pfeiffer in *Batman Returns* to broaden the viewership in three primary ways. First, producers likely hoped that the casting of Berry would remedy director Tim Burton's decision to shun Black actors for the role ten years earlier. Second, makers of the film counted on Berry's recent Oscar for *Monster's Ball* and role as the comic book character Storm in the films *X-Men I* and *X-Men II* to help secure the film's success. And third, the filmic team sought to appeal to fans of Berry, whom they thought might attract not only the general audience but also Black and "urban" audiences.

Berry shared the hope that Black moviegoers would support the film because of her role in it in several periodicals, including the popular Black periodical *Jet*.[40] Berry and Bratt appeared on the *Oprah Winfrey Show* in May 2004 to promote the July release of *Catwoman*, and mentioned that it was the first major action film in which a Black woman and a Latino man were the major stars. "More films with people of color in leading roles will be made," said Berry on the *Oprah Winfrey Show*, "if people go out and support this film."[41] Yet, in *Catwoman*, Lone and Phillips are racially ambiguous characters who show no ties to their ethnic ancestry; they bear no signs of ethnicity or culture to mark them in terms of race. A twenty-first-century Black Catwoman could not break new ground or carve out meaningful gender, racial, or sexual spaces while remaining squarely situated within a 1960s approach of inclusion by way of nonthreatening, colorblind representations. In this sense, Berry's racial difference in the film made little difference at all, and her role was less radical than that of her 1967 predecessor. The narrative in the graphic novel that accompanied the film's release is identical to that of the film; it is simply a print version of the digital work (see plate 7).[42]

The problem with Berry's and Bratt's romantic multicultural rhetoric on the *Oprah Winfrey Show* was that, in Patience Phillips's and Tom Lone's world, race does not exist. This postracial fantasy makes it problematic for the actors to assume that racial-ethnic audiences would engage with a film that was divorced from the same modes of difference the actors purported as being essential to expanding the roles of people of color in the film industry.[43] In response to Warner Brothers' and Pitof's departure from the *Catwoman* graphic novel, clusters of fans took the initiative to prove that computer animation and a large budget did not translate into an accurate or satisfactory representation in film by creating two film shorts, *Catwoman: Copy Cat* and *Catwoman: Nine Lives* in 2005. Both films were nonprofit ventures and underscore the significant meaning that Catwoman has to fans, as well as their need to challenge DC/Warner Brothers to address the needs and perceptions of readers. In the eyes of fans, bringing Catwoman to the screen was not a money-earning venture. The two fan films were aesthetically simple and had mediocre acting, but their plots interwove typical scenarios from the graphic novel, and, unsurprisingly, both films cast white actors to play the role of Selina Kyle/Catwoman.

Black Cat Got Your Tongue? Fans Read Gender, Race, and Sexuality into *Catwoman*

In my ongoing discussions with avid readers of the contemporary *Catwoman* series on DC Comics' Catwoman message board, I asked readers if they felt that the ethnicity of the character mattered, if men and women read the title for different reasons, if they thought Catwoman was a feminist, and what actor they felt best portrayed the character. These questions sought to ascertain how readers were decoding Catwoman's changing narrative in many of the forms of media in which she appears, and the significance of race, class, gender, and sexuality in the title's production. An advantage to using the DC message board was that I could correspond with a larger pool of fans than one-on-one interviews would allow; I could access international readers; and I could continue our conversations, thereby creating an ongoing dialogue. This approach was successful on many other accounts. The message board format allowed respondents the opportunity to take time with their answers, absent the pressure of an interviewer's anticipation of the answer that would fit the needs of an academician's research and hypotheses within the confines of a timed interview. Message board respondents are not casual readers; their participation in such a forum speaks to a desire to increase their engagement beyond reading the books and to access and connect with a global community of readers.

While not a cyber ethnographer, on the Catwoman message board I was part of a vernacular community of readers who make meaning in graphic novel consumption through the reading process and who participate in the various cultural circuits relevant to the art form.[44] In other words, on the DC message forum, I was what cultural critic George Lipsitz calls a maximally competent cultural reader and consumer, rather than an academic probing for answers that might lead to distortion or exploitation of the interviewees' voices.[45] Fans' voices reflect an undying commitment to Catwoman, and while their responses were sometimes contradictory, they were overwhelmingly thoughtful. I will cite readers' responses in succession here to underscore the legitimacy and intelligence of their voices and interpretations, and to avoid the problematic stance of the academician as *the* authority voice at the expense of the art form under examination, and at the expense of the consumers, who are the comakers of the art form.

In their responses, readers' interpretations of Catwoman's ethnicity show the extent to which race matters, but not in the ways that one might assume. This is apparent in fans' responses to my question concerning how the race of Catwoman might shape the meaning of the graphic novel's narrative and the reading pleasure of the fans. The fans' answers point to the necessity of not constraining the character within a stagnant identity;[46] yet, for the readers, the character's ethnicity, race, and character do require continuity:

RESPONSE ONE: To me I guess Catwoman is a thief and an American—and culturally haughty and catlike—no LA bimbo babe. I don't think Catwoman is defined by race BUT she has beginnings as a European woman. I am not a European nor am I American. I like Catwoman; the essence of her on TV has been great! Whether by Eartha or the others—she was a dominating femme fatale. I still pick her as European. And I would hate it if [she became a] supermodel [like] Vixen,[47] or all of a sudden was French European.

RESPONSE TWO: I don't think it really matters, as long as she is Selina Kyle, former prostitute turned costumed thief, turned vigilante, without powers of any sort. There was a Volume I with flashbacks in which her mother seemed to be Latin American and her father more white. Race would be an issue in her portrayal and how she is perceived—due to racial stereotyping. She is supposed to have emerged from the urban underclass in a big, American city, and that is not supposed to be consistent with being a WASP.

RESPONSE THREE: She is Caucasian, and Cuban, but Cuban is "American" and can imply mixed race. There are African blood Cubans, and Caucasian blood Cubans. I don't think that race is an issue with Selina . . . black hair, light skin and green eyes can mean different things, but I would assume some Irish in there and I believe her father was Irish. Some African Americans in this country I've known have had light skin, black hair and green eyes. I like her the way she is, but also liked the idea of some Egyptian blood—as it could tie back to the people who worshiped the children of [cats] in some of Ed Brubaker's [writing] last year with the title. That could make for some interesting reading. I would like to see more heroes of color though. . . . I would love to see a person(s) of color being trained by Selina—a young African American girl would be awesome. The character could be someone like [Catwoman]—a youth criminal of some kind, who had bad beginnings. After 60 years in comics, I think Catwoman could expand, and comics could certainly do with some more heroes of color. Oh, but I'm just a dorky white guy, so what do I know.[48]

For readers, Catwoman either was a mixture of Latino, Italian, and Irish, or possibly had Egyptian (African) ancestry. Several responses reflect a consciousness of the need for comic book characters of color, whether Latino or Black. In a follow-up query I posted to the DC message board concerning fans' preference for actor portrayals of Catwoman, an overwhelming majority of readers disclosed that they preferred the portrayals of Catwoman by Newmar, Pfeiffer, and Kitt—in that order.[49] One could conclude that their rankings reflect unspoken desires and racial attitudes. It is significant that some commentary did equate sexual prowess with ethnicity, thereby exposing malign ideologies of race that permeate and infect the reading process. Yet only a few readers (many of whom identified their own race) interpreted Catwoman as being ethnically white/European, and only one indirectly expressed prejudice toward the possibility of a Black Catwoman (as inferred in a comment, "That's the way we've grown used to them, so just don't change them"). Of course, there is always a disjuncture between one's true feelings and what one shares. This aside, my question concerning Catwoman's ethnicity ignited a critical discussion among readers about the boundaries and meanings of race in ways that represented Catwoman as a state of becoming rather than stagnant racialized criterion readers depended upon for identification or reading pleasure.

As for the effect that gender has on a reader's comprehension of *Catwoman*, forum participants revealed that men and women often read the title for different reasons, but their reasons were not bound to their gender identity. The extant literature on comic books and their fans focuses on comics directed at one gender, and provides an interpretation of readers that belong to one gender group. Although this approach allows for a close reading of the correlation between a gender-exclusive product and a gender-exclusive consumer, it may miss an opportunity to draw comparisons between men and women readers of the same cultural text targeted toward a mixed audience. While many studies conclude that women read to engage in a social experience and men read on an individualistic basis, readers of *Catwoman* muddle such distinctions.[50] For *Catwoman* readers, the reading process and the meanings they deduce from it are shared *and* individualistic, without either being derivative of the gender of the particular reader. Men cited the beauty of the character, and women the strength of the character as factors in their choice to read *Catwoman*, but these were not determinants in isolation:

RESPONSE ONE: As a female I think Selina/Catwoman is a great role model, and she's very realistically written with real human flaws (as with everyone else in it) so it's easy to relate to her and care about her. Along with all the personal character stuff it is also a really cool book with some of the best villains, situations and fights I've ever read in my limited comic book experience—it's like a great ongoing movie to me. It is smart, and I like that Selina is treated like a REAL woman and not a one-dimensional Playboy model-on-triple-silicone 'fanboy' fantasy.

RESPONSE TWO: If I may be so bold: From what I have seen from hanging out on this MB [message board] for the last four or so years, I really think we all read *Catwoman* for the same reason. Male and female—gay and straight. We like her because she is sexy, fearless, smart, tough, and does her own thing. Personally, I like Selina because she is unconventional, thumbs her nose at society and does not take herself too seriously, which is a refreshing change from all the duty-bound characters out there. Selina will fall on her derriere, get up, and start all over again. I really think that it is a misnomer to think that (straight) men only want to read about hot women with no brains. There are far too many strong, powerful, and highly intelligent women in comic books.

RESPONSE THREE: One of the things I've liked about the *Catwoman* series is her cast of supporting players. I love Holly and Karon, and I love Slam Bradley too. I think the supporting cast is one of the essential parts to my enjoyment of this book. It is nice to see Selina have someone to care about, other than herself. I love the hot/cold thing with Slam, and would rather see her partnering up with him over Batman. I love the older sister thing with Holly, too. Without these characters, I think Selina would lose a lot of her complexity and even vulnerability.

RESPONSE FOUR: She sexxxxxy. Mommy, I wanna taste!

RESPONSE FIVE: As a male reader, I would be dishonest if I said that looks and sex appeal didn't have some bearing into me buying *Catwoman*. That said, are there any truly unattractive "looks wise" female heroines? And can't that be said of male heroes as well? The reason I stick with *Catwoman*, and the character, is because I find her character interesting. She is noble in her willingness to fight for the underdog. Also, it is interesting to see a hero who isn't afraid to blur the line between right/wrong, but always seems to find a way to do the right thing. Like us, I think she is very human; she makes mistakes, but always struggles to correct her faults and clean-up after her own mistakes. Selina is self-confident, and a strong woman, but at the same time she is well grounded and humble (the combination of these qualities make her very attractive to me). I think for me that that quality (humility/accepting her own imperfection) is what separates her from *Wonder Woman* (DC #1 Heroine) who I have never really found a long-term appeal to read her solo-title.[51]

Readers' thoughtful and sometimes sexually colorful responses show that they are either self-aware or self-reflexive about their choice to read *Catwoman*. Men do respond to Catwoman's appearance, but they also respond to the same attributes that women readers respond to: her relationships with other characters, her strength, and her perseverance under extreme adversity. While beauty may draw male readers to the title as young men, the character's development over time (after the days of her exaggerated body parts in the pages of *Batman*) speaks to the concrete reasons that kept them reading not past but through her anatomy. Insofar as women readers are concerned, the aesthetic change to a more realistically drawn physique increased the character's popularity, indicating that women, too, need new antiheroes—ones that reflect realism that escapes many of the Amazon sheroes in male titles. Yet the gender and sexual dynamic of the reading of Catwoman raises another question, and that is, given the duality of the character as an antihero and underclass vigilante—and as independent and sexy—can such a mixture, in a reader's view, encompass a feminist sensibility at the same time? Is feminism relevant to the portrayal and consumption of female graphic novel characters, as many cultural critics assume about female-exclusive comic book titles? I asked readers if they read Catwoman as a feminist, and although fewer readers responded to this query, their responses did represent a range of understanding of this activist stance, which ran the gamut from stereotypes of feminism to complex ruminations:

> RESPONSE ONE: It depends on how you define "feminist." Defining it as a person who believes that men and women should be treated equally, then, I definitely believe that Selina is a feminist. She has risen above a difficult and suppressed life (this is a common element of all of her origins—the current one, as well as the Pre-Crisis abused wife origin and the *Batman Returns* secretary origin) and has made it her mission to help other lost souls, especially abused women. She does not need a man to control her life and is a very strong character in her own right.

> RESPONSE TWO: I think Selina is a feminist in the way that she wants women treated fairly, but with her past she does tend to be harder on pimps and other men that degrade and hurt women. Personally, I think she is mostly an East End-ist.

RESPONSE THREE: She's not an extreme feminist, but maybe a little bit. She won't let any man walk over her no matter how powerful they may be. Maybe that is why she is such an interesting character![52]

On the question of feminism, most agree that Catwoman embodies a feminist sensibility because of her work to address and avenge the gender inequities that led her into sex work as a young woman. The message board discussion further reflects that Catwoman fans construe feminism as the practice of equalizing ideological and material structures that limit women's access to power. Indeed, the question about whether readers considered Catwoman a feminist appeared to lead respondents to contemplate the meaning of the term and the importance of the practice. One of the responses seemed postfeminist, in that its interpretation of the activist term conjured up terms such as "East End-ist," which shows a concentration on region versus gender politics, or a hesitance to define traditional understandings of feminism as a necessary political approach in the twenty-first century. The last reader's insistence that Catwoman is feminist but not an extreme feminist suggests a stance that Catwoman's feminism speaks to modern times divorced from the misconceptions of earlier feminism as anti-male. Only one reader in a follow-up query made the false equation of feminism with lesbianism, indicating that many graphic novel consumers may see gender politics in ways that are savvy and rarely stereotypical.

An inclusion of fans' voices does not seek to serve as data to substantiate a preconceived relationship between production and consumerism as it relates to difference. Rather, these voices serve as examples of continuous dialogues in a reader-centered space that remarks upon the modes of difference that hold meaning to *Catwoman*'s intelligent and diverse constituency. In this sense, message board respondents show the relationship between the text and consumer as a continual unfolding of meanings that will change as readers mature into their readership. Several respondents made mention that, as they grew older and read other titles, and as the writers of the graphic novel changed, their interpretations and motivations to read the title changed as well. Their voices thus provide the material to strengthen an understanding of the gender, race, and sexual aspects of the graphic novel fandom experience as it collides with the individual encoding of *Catwoman*'s narratives by a given reader at a particular historical moment.

Some readers of yesteryear surely read *Batman* and *Catwoman* to consume soft-core porn, or to live vicariously through a character whose behavior they long to emulate. However, male and female readers on the message board claim to read the title because Catwoman represents a modern, fallible woman: women whom they know, or women possessing the identities and contradictions they already inhabit. The space of difference that the character holds for women readers is significant given the male domination of comic book and graphic novel production and consumption arena. Indeed, the last writer for *Catwoman*, Ed Brubaker, shared with me, "There were more women fans for that book than any other I've done."[53] According to a small pool of comic book store retailers interviewed for this study, *Catwoman*'s readership spans ages sixteen to fifty, includes an approximate 50/50 readership of men and women, and, as the message board responses reveal, readers cross national borders and sexualities embrace a spectrum of cultural politics.[54] *Catwoman*'s readership is gender inclusive; therefore, no fixed analysis of identity categories or reception of *Catwoman* the graphic novel and Catwoman the character is possible.

The Many Faces of Catwoman

A historical timeline of Catwoman, an analysis of her character in various forms of print and visual culture, and reader interpretations show that while gender, sexuality, and race mediate production, consumption, and reception, there are no guarantees concerning what the relationship between those variables constitutes. Today's Catwoman has left behind her witty cat phrases for social justice, philosophy, occasional relapses into a life of crime, and a riot grrrl attitude.[55] In a 2005 issue of *Catwoman*, for example, Catwoman quotes Nietzsche and contemplates the struggle of Gotham City's working class.[56] Her costume is now quintessential post-glossy-punk; she wears a realistically fitting leather cat suit and Doc Marten–style boots and a riot grrrl sneer. She is also more than a tool of compulsory heterosexuality. Catwoman has sexual liaisons with men, kisses villainous Poison Ivy, and flirts with the superheroine Hawkgirl, promising to show her things "Batman would neither approve of nor know about."[57] Her relationships with men are autonomous and contingent and her relationships with women do not exist within a narrative context for the sole pleasure of the male pornographic gaze. Twenty-first-century Catwoman can take or leave Batman, and in most cases, she leaves him behind to pursue social justice for Gotham City, while not missing the opportunity to partake in a heist or two.

In the 2009 issue of the comic book *Gotham City Sirens*, the once racially ambiguous or Latina Catwoman seems codified as white, and she joins her DC sisters Poison Ivy and Harley Quinn in criminal pursuits, returning to the old days.[58] Contemporary representations in the graphic novel notwithstanding, the character Catwoman could and did place blackness within a history of multiply inscribed difference, which writer Marc Shapiro's 2013 *Eartha Kitt: Femme Fatale* reaffirms. In the 1960s, a Black Catwoman made American history, while in the twenty-first century, a Black Catwoman was feared, sometimes embraced, or transformed into a riot grrrl and Afropunk surfer for a new wave of audiences. Catwoman thus remains a significant part of the historical lexicon and contemporary trajectory of comics and blackness. Unlike Catwoman, in the 1970s and onward, Black female characters in mainstream titles were seldom racially fluid. Instead, there was a tethering of popular characters such as Storm in *X-Men*, Vixen in *Justice League of America*, and Nubia in *Wonder Woman* to US fabrications and imaginings of Africa and its inhabitants.

AFRICAN GODDESSES, MIXED-RACE WONDERS, AND BAADASSSSS WOMEN

Black Women as "Signs" of Africa in US Comics

You can learn a lot about a culture from its stories. Nubia, for example, had her own story to finish.

—Doselle Young, *Wonder Woman*

I am Storm, leader of the X-Men. We come in peace.

—Storm, *X-Men*

Spirit of the lion I command you. Spirit of the fox I call you. Spirit of the antelope I need you. Come to me! Aid me! Need me! Let vengeance be mine!

—Vixen, *Vixen*

IN 2008, the media outlets and the blogosphere were abuzz at the prospect of an upcoming *Wonder Woman* feature film.[1] The attention garnered by the preproduction film had less to with the film itself (something that Wonder Woman fans had surely been waiting to see) than with which actor would play the lead role of Diana Prince/Wonder Woman. Black American singer, fashion designer, and actor Beyoncé

Knowles announced her interest in playing the lead in the film, raising the specter of Halle Berry's Catwoman from the DC crypt. As with the casting of *Catwoman*, fans protested, insisting that the casting of Beyoncé as Wonder Woman was inappropriate not because of her mediocre acting talent but because of her race. As one blogger wrote, "People *really* care about Wonder Woman. Men and women of all ages and levels of geekery were incredibly passionate about who was to play Wonder Woman; they all had very definite opinions, and there was little debate. Beyoncé shouldn't be Wonder Woman. End of story."[2]

Though not a self-avowed fangirl, Knowles told a *Los Angeles Times* reporter that she had met with DC Comics and Warner Brothers executives about her interest in playing the lead, and that she felt that, given her recent dramatic roles, it was time for her to do a light-hearted action adventure. The *Wonder Woman* project was reportedly attractive to Knowles because of the recent success of comic book–to-film adaptations. "After doing these roles that were so emotional," said Knowles in the *Times* interview, "I was thinking to myself, I need to be a superhero."[3] Knowles's thespian training and box office intentions aside, disgruntled Wonder Woman fans ignored two historical facts when proclaiming their dislike of the idea of a Black Wonder Woman.

First, one of the earliest African female comic book heroines appeared in the comic book *Wonder Woman* and was billed as the "Black Wonder Woman." Second, the actor Lynda Carter, who played Wonder Woman in the 1970s television show of that title, is one half Mexican American (Carter self-identifies as "Latina"). These two bits of DC history prove that, although Wonder Woman is read as white by some fans, her race has never been racially fixed as white. Still, on the *Wendy Williams Show*, the former radio show host, who is African American, told Lynda Carter during an interview about the upcoming film that Wonder Woman should not be Black because fans know Wonder Woman as white. "That is how they ruined the *Honeymooners* remake," joked Williams, while gushing over Carter and a table of Wonder Woman memorabilia. A Black male blogger, apparently agreeing with Williams and seeking to defuse accusations of racism among Wonder Woman fans, wrote on the offense as well: "I've said it before. No Beyoncé (I am black, I will mention, and I still don't want her)."[4] The controversy and commentary about Knowles playing the role of Wonder Woman throws a wrench into the idea of colorblindness across racial and ethnic identities and communities, and shows the extent to which the Black female body and race remains confined in the US popular imagination. While fans may seem slow to see and accept Black women in the roles of superheroines on the silver screen, for the past several decades, comic book writers have used illustrations of and ideologies about the Black female body to signify the fetish, fear, and fabrication of Africa.

To explore the mass-mediated relationship between referents of Africa and the fetish for female characters of African descent in comics, I examine three reoccurring African superheroines in titles with wide readerships: Nubia in DC Comics' *Wonder Woman*, Storm in Marvel Comics' *X-Men* and *Storm*, and Vixen in DC Comics' *Vixen*, *Justice League of America* (*JLA*), and *Suicide Squad*. All three of these characters operate within fictional American and African landscapes in their respective titles, and two of the three are African transplants who use superpowers to deter the corruptive forces that threaten the nation state of America and their African homelands. Although different writers and artists created the titles, a common denominator is that Africa exists as a contradictory sign of origins. The etymology of Nubia's name, for example, would locate her within an area of southern Egypt that extends to the Sudan; yet writers define Nubia as a descendant of the Greek mythos of the women warriors known as the Amazons, located in Pontus (today an area within Turkey). Storm's comic book heritage is East African, Marvel writers tell us; however, in the pages of *X-Men*, writers also claim that she is a descendant of a line of white-haired, blue-eyed African priestesses. Yet again, a coherent geography escapes comic book writers; Storm's ethnic composition would more accurately situate her within the North African tribes of Morocco.[5] Vixen's African heritage has no ties to a factual Africa. She is a descendant of an African leader and warrior named Tantu, and the magic necklace that she wears, known as "the totem," allows her to conjure the powers and abilities of the entire animal kingdom. Writers therefore signify Vixen's Africaness by her phantasmagorical legacy and a predictable relationship to nature; she is African simply because her voodoo ways and ability to tame the wild marks her as African.

These lapses in geographic continuity may appear insignificant or simply congruent with the work of popular fiction, which engages in the imaginary, embellishes, and fabricates reality. However, the point I wish to make with these examples is that the ethnic and geographic origins of the characters act as launching pads for a continual process of ethnic extraction from Africa to uphold Occidental or Western conceptions of Africa.

Within this framework of Occidental ideology masquerading as African cosmology, Nubia, Storm, and Vixen are *comic book blood diamonds*. That is to say, these characters represent embellished African gems extracted from imagined cultural contexts and artfully reshaped for commodification in the global marketplace, allowing readers the opportunity to gaze and graze upon Africa. While clearly situated to "eat the other"—to borrow metaphoric phrasing from bell hooks—African female comic book and graphic novel characters represent the contradictions inherent in many forms of popular culture.[6] At different narrative and historical moments, Nubia, Storm, and Vixen work as ideological tools of American nationalism and colonialism. Yet, they paradoxically function as initiators of anti-colonialist political thought and action.

The questions addressed here include the following: What expansive possibilities in relationship to gender, race, and nation are present as well as undermined in mainstream comic book titles and graphic novels that feature women of African descent in the 1970s, 1980s, and later—titles that predominantly white men draw, author, and ink? Additionally, how do the writers of these texts imagine bicultural identities, that is, how do they pen the characters' negotiation of two cultures and two continents in troublesome and in productive ways? In what ways is the deployment of the sign of Africa legible through transcultural circuits of meaning in the titles that confirm a complex African identity and ancestry even as they exploit, disfigure, and misconfigure it for their interracial audiences? Finally, how do the proposed alternative narratives by Black male writers figure into the equation of Black female representation in comics, especially insofar as the maintenance of transnational Black cultural politics and intergender relationships are concerned? These broad inquiries lead to unpacking the cultural work and cultural morass of comic writers' ideological engagement with Africa and the Black female body.

Nubia: A Mixed-*Raced* Wonder Meets Pop Feminism

Of the female comic book heroines, Wonder Woman is the most iconographic. From the pages of writer and creator William Moulton Marsten's *Wonder Woman* comic book to the popular 1970s television series of the same title starring actor Lynda Carter, the idea and image of Wonder Woman remain integral components of the historical lexicon of women in comics.[7] As a term, "Wonder Woman" signifies women's strength and ability to conquer with ease multiple tasks at suprahuman levels. It is likely not surprising, then, that the first issue of *Ms. Magazine* in 1972 had a picture of Wonder Woman on its cover, as did the magazine's thirty-five-year-anniversary cover in 2007. The magazine's January 2009 special inaugural issue returned to the comic book theme, this time by presenting a Photoshopped image of president Barack Obama as Superman with the following caption: "This is what a feminist looks like."[8] *Ms. Magazine*'s inaugural issue caused a controversy for its apparent and consistent lack of support of senator Hillary Rodham Clinton as a 2008 presidential candidate, and in the minds of some feminist critics, the magazine suggested that feminism might no longer need women. There was no mention as to whether or not the magazine's flirtation with superherodom should make room for Black women, but a *Wonder Woman* comic book in 1973 dealt with this question via the character Nubia.

Nubia made appearances in ten *Wonder Woman* issues, but she has had notable spin-offs in other titles, including DC Comic's *Super Girl, Super Friends*, and *Birds of Prey*. Although the Harvard PhD and psychologist William Moulton Marston created Wonder Woman as a social justice crusader born into the Amazon female utopia of Paradise Island, writers Robert Kanigher and Cary Bates took the project over in 1973. They rewrote the origin of the Amazon princess to accommodate the introduction of Nubia, DC's first Black female superhero. The new Wonder Woman was one of two "wonder women"; one was marked racially as white, and the other (Nubia) was marked racially as Black.[9] In the pages of the comic book, mysterious gods conjure the two superheroines whom the Amazons' female leader, Queen Hippolyta, later brings to life through the magical caress of her hands. These virgin births explained the racial differences of the wonder women through elementary formulations based upon a precarious form of fantasy myth making: once upon time, Kanigher tells his readers, there were two masses of clay for which the Amazon queen of Paradise Island was responsible. One mass of clay was light, and thus the gods brought the child to life as white to bless Hippolyta. One mass of clay was dark, and thus the gods brought the child to life as Black to bring anguish to Hippolyta. The villainous Mars (a corrupt white male warrior) tears the "Black" infant from the arms of her white mother and trains Nubia to resent the white Wonder Woman and to battle her in a series of *Wonder Woman* issues titled "The War of the Wonder Women!" Certainly it is debatable whether *Ms. Magazine* meant to propose with their choice of Barack

Obama as feminism's Superman on their 2009 cover that feminism no longer needed women. Yet, did 1973's *Wonder Woman* suggest through Nubia that feminism was, at the time, plagued by or dependent upon the place of Black women in feminist politics and in nation making?

Nubia's introduction into the comic book world has ties to the ideological presuppositions of gender, race, and sexuality in popular literary genres. As in the nineteenth century's tragic mulatta genre, Nubia's parentage makes fictional claims to whiteness as a process of titillating exoticism while circumventing the messy history of miscegenation and amalgamation. Where else did Kanigher and Bates *mine* from to create the character Nubia, and what was their motivation to present readers with such an idea about sex, race, and procreation? Kanigher claims that the basis for Nubia's story was an African myth about the origins of the races, but he does not name the tribe in question. This was only the beginning of Kanigher's imaginary yet symbolically significant Africa.[10] A similar version of Kanigher's comic book creationism does appear in Yoruba, Egyptian, Polynesian, Greek, and Muslim religious lore, as well as in the Hebrew Bible's and the Old Testament's book of Genesis.[11] Given the mythology of Wonder Woman, a connection to Greek mythology's Prometheus molding man from clay seems most applicable to Kanigher's narrative, but it appears that the writer combined parts of Yoruba, Greek, and Polynesian creation stories to explain the creation of the races. In so doing, *Wonder Woman*'s postreligious narrative tells us that multiracial and Black Americans are the products of mystery, mysticism, and the length of time clay cooks in a kiln rather than the cohabitation of real, Black and white bodies. In *Wonder Woman*, Nubia says of her own curious parentage (or lack thereof) that she has felt "lonely" since the day she was born. "So long ago I can remember no mother, no father," Nubia cries, falling to her knees and burying her face in her hands.[12]

It is ideas of African cosmology that mediate this common American literary trope in *Wonder Woman*, making it more than an iteration of tragic mulatta literature. Kanigher's plots in the "The War of the Wonder Women!" series interweave purposeful references to Africa as the symbolical sign upon which Nubia was forced to negotiate an imagined African landscape, her utopist Amazon birthright, and an American society fraught with the social and political problems of the early 1970s, for example, women's and racial-ethnic rights. Congruent with Sojourner Truth's infamous rhetorical statements about Black women's place in the struggle for women's rights at the Seneca Falls Convention of 1848 (i.e., "Ain't I a Woman?"), in the pages of *Wonder Woman*, the narrative treatment of Nubia grapples with a similar question regarding Black womanhood.[13] In the first issue in which Nubia appears, the comic book's narrator introduces her as "an astounding intruder." Nubia enters the scene wearing clunky metal armor and carrying a long, sharp sword. She challenges Wonder Woman's position as the savior of the Amazons and of the free world by insisting, "I am Wonder Woman!"[14] Despite Nubia's views of her leadership qualities, fantasies of African primitivism, which is signaled by her style of dress and warrior mentality, serve as the phantasmagorical myth that nullifies her capacity to serve as a legitimate Wonder Woman of the Amazons and of the nation state.

Diana Prince and Nubia are sisters, brought to life by the same white mother and made from the same brand of "clay," but it is Nubia's imagined Africaness and symbolic blackness that apparently makes her susceptible to violent behavior and, perhaps most erroneous, masculinist and supremacist ideology. The colorful cover art of this first issue provides several semiotic references to underscore this reading. On the cover, the colorist depicts Wonder Woman in her typical patriotic costume of red, white, and blue, conjuring up the image of the American flag. In contrast, Nubia wears a tiger-print body suit adorned with a banana-leaf skirt, thus conjuring up a mix of Josephine Baker nostalgia and African primitivism. A black-and-white sketch of the white male warrior Mars is a watermark in the background, indicating that the women are subconsciously vying for the power associated with the dominant male power structure.[15]

Robert Kanigher's "The War of the Wonder Women!" dealt with this power struggle, and his introduction of Nubia indirectly correlates with the cultural and social environment of the early 1970s. At the time of the printing of the issue, the Civil Rights Act of 1964, the Voting Rights Act of 1965, and the Immigration and Nationality Act of 1965 were law. In addition, Congress had approved the Equal Rights Amendment for state ratification in 1972, and in 1973, *Roe v. Wade* had made legal abortions possible and Title 9 of the Education Amendments had banned sex discrimination in schools. These legal changes facilitated changes in social relations, especially insofar as interracial and intergender relations were concerned—a matter that would subsequently intensify in the now proverbial culture wars. However, Kanigher and Bates's writing and the comic books' illustrations tell us that it is mostly the gender wars—or, more precisely, an amorphous patriarchy, which takes form in the character Mars—that divides Nubia and Wonder Woman, not inequality based on race. Though both wonder women are generically "feminist," neither character represents the nuance or litany of concerns of the modern feminist movement, such as equal pay for equal work, sexual freedom, and gender equality, nor the core aspects of Black feminist thought, which would include racial, gender, sexual, and class equality. For example, when Wonder Woman says to Nubia in a 1973 issue, "Women should stick together and battle against our common oppressor. *Man* is making a battle ground of the world," Nubia responds with, "Not us, Amazon, it is our fate to fight for supremacy!"[16]

Nubia repeatedly questions her marginalization and the lack of acknowledgment of her potential as a leader of the Amazons, but because her questioning remains within the realm of irrational rhetoric, it is easy to dismiss her claims as grandiose and delusional. This narrative framing overshadows the race and gender inequality that Nubia's actions and words might otherwise expose as a part of womanist ideology. Kanigher's pseudofeminist narrative and Nubia's African nationalist diatribes do double ideological work by situating the absorption of patriarchal norms, supremacy, and violence on the Black female body and, therefore, upon Africa itself. Indeed, in the "The War of the Wonder Women!" Wonder Woman signifies rationality and peace, which is invariably, even if covertly, tied to her whiteness, and she lays the blame on mankind for the world's problems. Nubia, in contrast, is a Black female savage with inane or naïve cultural politics—that is, until she decides to join Wonder Woman in the "gender war." This gender war is most apparent in the last installment of the series, where Nubia curiously appears in a regional setting marked visually as Africa. She has transformed from a vengeful supremacist to a counternationalist superheroine who, with the help of Wonder Woman, fights the tyrannical African patriarchs Goolah and Kenyah for her freedom and for her title of African woman warrior and leader. Nubia stands tall in front of a crowd of scantily dressed African peasants, and Wonder Woman miraculously appears to advise Nubia to "let Athena [read: white womanhood] guide her." In kind, Nubia exclaims, "No man will ever own Nubia." She asserts that she fights on "equal ground" for her self-autonomy and proceeds to triumph over her African male foes.[17]

Nubia's triumph over African patriarchy ironically ushered in her comic book demise. No longer concerned with gender inequity in an intraracial context, and living in apparent bliss in her role as the Moynihan-

3.1 Cary Bates, "War of the Wonder Women!" *Wonder Woman* 32, #206, June–July 1973, 15.

esque African matriarch writ large, Nubia did not return until the early twenty-first century, when she appeared in two *Wonder Woman* issues. This time introduced as Nu'bia and depicted with dreadlocks and in a scantily clad sheath dress adorned with the face of a lion, she appears out of nowhere to confront Wonder Woman with the following cryptic sentences: "Many leagues from the kingdom of light have I traveled. Through the province of Nox and the territory of shades have I hunted the demon-king Ahriman. Finally, to track him here, to Patriarch's World . . . to my ancient FARAWAY HOME. How passing strange it is then, Princess, that I should find you here, as well."[18] Nu'bia's dialogue introduces a familiar story line for the Black Wonder Woman, one that indicates a search for—as one might guess—an African patriarch. Indeed, with Nu'bia confined to an imagined African island, obsessed with her intracultural liaisons, Wonder Woman remains the leader of the Amazons and is unencumbered in proceeding with her usual adventures: battling criminals and protecting the United States of America. DC's most recent iteration of Nubia in 2009 pairs her with a Black Superman in a parallel multiverse; the two work with Captain Marvel and other superheroes to save the world from an alteration of reality spearheaded by the villain Darkseid. In this version, writer Grant Morrison softens Nubia's rhetoric and her position on war and violence: "The Wonder Women of Amazonia bring only anti-war technology into the world," says Nubia to her Super(Black)man before a battle to save the universe (see plate 8).[19]

In the 1970s, the battle of the wonder women becomes not only a sign for and of American colonialism refigured as the territory of a fictionalized Africa, but also a sign for and of the 1970s feminist struggle itself. Wonder Woman and Nubia's strained relationship raises the following question: How do white women and Black women situate themselves in relationship to each other and in relationship to the forces of domination and subjugation? In the pages of *Wonder Woman*, the answer to this question is that the Black subject is ill-equipped to handle conflict and strife, and therefore a white intermediary figure—whether it is Wonder Woman or Mars—is necessary. A prime example of this occurs in a 1973 issue in which Wonder Woman saves Diana Prince's dashiki- and Afro-wearing Black female roommate (who is, of course, really Nubia in disguise) from a multicultural protest rally where protestors were trampling bystanders. "Suffering Sappho!—a full scale riot," says Wonder Woman. "This calls for emergency intervention. With male hot-heads on the rampage, my magic lasso is called for." After Wonder Woman brings the roommate to safety, she heartily thanks Wonder Woman and exclaims, "That pole would've mashed me into soul food if it weren't for you!"[20] Kanigher and Bates's use of corny Black vernacular aside, this scenario again infers that a white intermediary figure must speak for, save, and protect the incompetent African. While Kanigher's intentions to introduce a Black Wonder Woman into the DC universe were good, Nubia's and Wonder Woman's dialogue is boiled down to sound bites of women's rights and racial-ethnic rights. The DC writer failed by suggesting that the answer to the world's problems and peace lay solely within a limited interpretation of feminist consciousness and multiculturalism. Whereas Kanigher's battle of the wonder women was a mixture of pop-feminist psychology and postreligious, racial-ized biology, Marvel Comics' ethnically diverse and multinational *X-Men* penned alternative narratives in which counternationalist and bicultural consciousness began to take hold in the form of a character named Storm.

Storm: The African Goddess and the (Post)Colonial Bait and Switch

Actor Halle Berry made no secret of her dismay over the limited screen time given to her character, Storm, in the first two *X-Men* films. Viewers might have blinked and missed her appearances in the first few install-ments of the filmic franchise, which was an adoption of the popular comic book of the same title. Fans found Storm's secondary place in the films puzzling, since in the comic book and animated series *The Adventures of the X-Men*, she is one of the leaders of the collective. When a third *X-Men* film was on the table, *X-Men United: The Last Stand* (2006), Berry decided to take her own stand by insinuating in interviews and with various news sources that she may not appear in the film unless there was an upgrade of the Storm character. While such gestures might read like diva behavior, Berry rationalized her stance in the name of equity in representation. It made little sense, given the comic book's depiction of Storm and Berry's immense (although not always successful) filmic repertoire of the previous two decades, for the Storm character to remain an incidental element. In an interview about her character's evolvement since the first film and her decision to decline a short-shift role again, Berry, explained: "I thought that I somehow had to scare the shit out of [studio heads] and get them to give Storm a point of view. . . . Not really more screen time, because I know it's an ensemble, but if Storm spoke for five minutes, then I wanted it to be five

3.2 Cary Bates, "War of the Wonder Women!" *Wonder Woman* 32, #206, June–July 1973, 4.

minutes that meant something; five minutes of character development; five minutes of a point of view and 5 minutes of some back story history, not just 'go get the plane' or 'come on kids, let's go.' I really wanted her lines to mean something."[21]

Berry's argument for equality in representation took heed. The third film, in line with the comic book, charted the rise of Storm and situated the character as central to and as an indispensable part of the work and existence of the X-Men. Cinema's failure to move apace with the changing times, or, more pointedly, its slow progress toward meaningful representation beyond the symbolic, showed a glass ceiling that even a deserving, seasoned actor struggled to break through. Storm's paramount position in the *X-Men* comic book decades before her cinematic introduction shows her initial brief appearances in the first two films as erroneous at best, and tragically ironic at worst. *X-Men* the comic book, was leaps and bounds ahead of the cinema in the depiction of Black female superheroines.

In comparison to Storm's watered-down role in the first two *X-Men* films, as a part of the *X-Men* comic books, Ororo Munroe, also known as Storm, functions as a significant part of the minority collective of human mutants known as the X-Men. Born with telekinetic abilities, enormous strength, and nonnormative anatomies, the X-Men were the brainchild of Stan Lee and Jack Kirby in 1963. In their half sci-fi, half action comic adventure, Lee and Kirby present a paradigm of unequal power relations spurred by anxieties of difference in *X-Men*: the majority of the population fears mutants because of their anatomies and their omnipotent, magical powers; they therefore wish to exterminate, assimilate, or control all mutants, including the X-Men. It is the work of the X-Men to counter this assault to ensure mutant survival. Their superhero missions represent counterhegemony at work as they commit to the battle for a more just environment in which mutants and nonmutants alike can live without assimilation or violent confrontation.[22]

Scholars and fans alike have interpreted the *X-Men* series as an allegory of the plight of Black Americans, Jews, sexual minorities, and other historically marginalized groups in the United States and abroad. One of the series creators, Stan Lee, has admitted that he conceived of the different yet at first racially homogenous characters as a reflection of the Holocaust and race relations in the United States. The Marvel writers incorporated ideas from critical US thinkers of the time to pose philosophical dilemmas to their readers. Writer Stan Lee, for example, fashioned the two opposing mutants in the *X-Men* as the ideological mouthpieces of Martin Luther King (professor Charles Xavier, a.k.a. Professor X) and Malcolm X (Magneto). This avowed intellectual and racial consciousness among X-Men writers did not stop Lee and Kirby's series from creating Occidental images of Africa. In one of *X-Men*'s earliest stories, the then racially homogenous X-Men battle the dark forces of evil (i.e., brown bodies) in a Tarzan-like atmosphere.

In 1976, writer Len Wein introduced the Kenyan-born mutant Storm, who has the ability to create dramatic shifts in the weather. Storm's origin story tells us that after her Kenyan mother and African American father died, she became a street urchin forced to make her living as a petty thief during the Suez Crisis in Egypt.[23] As a young adult, Storm joins the X-Men, who, unlike the early 1960s lineup, now stand as an international and ethnically diverse social justice collective. While most journalistic literature and fan sites recognize Storm as a central character in *X-Men*, some critics have not been so kind. Cultural critic Anna Beatrice Scott, commenting on the first issue of *Giant X-Men* and the first two critically celebrated films about the X-Men, dismisses Storm as nothing more than a sidekick and "magical negress."[24] The beginning of the series and the first two films warrant such criticism; however, after reviewing a sampling of *X-Men* titles from 1976 to 2008, assessing the animated series, and taking into consideration the transformative aspects of the third *X-Men* film, I find that Storm's metamorphosis over the years represents a visionary social subject that propels social change. Although Storm was originally under the tutelage of Professor X, the intellectual guide of the X-Men, neither white male nor white female authority speaks for her; she is a leader of those deemed different by the dominant ruling force.

For the first four years of Storm's run in *X-Men*, she served as an example of the bicultural consciousness that emerges because of being a displaced African in America. In a 1982 issue, Storm tells one of her fellow mutant comrades, Scott, that although her spirit was wasted as a result of her displacement and longing for "Africa," her destiny was to "find and mend the missing, ravaged pieces" of herself.[25] With an introspective sentiment similar to the double consciousness expressed in W. E. B. Du Bois's the *Soul of Black Folks* about how to negotiate a national and Black identity in view of the dominant culture's perception of blackness, Storm continues to query to the reader in a dialogic fashion, "How can a body live without its soul?"[26] In another early installment of the series, when burdened by an unwanted pregnancy, Storm self-aborts and cautions the reader not to judge her decision, noting that the loss of her embryo was "a critical personal balance restored."[27] In a 1983 issue, after winning a significant battle, Storm's status changes from being a member of the social justice collective to being a leader of the X-Men. As Storm announces to her fellow mutants after the death of their battle leader Cyclops, "By right of combat, I, Storm, am now your leader. My word is law."[28]

Unlike *Wonder Woman*'s Nubia, *X-Men* writers did more than pay lip service to feminism; Storm embodied it in her struggle as an African woman, as a team member, and as an eventual leader of the X-Men. Yet, it is the young Storm in Africa that concerns the rearticulation of her origin in the graphic novel *Storm*, written by Black American romance writer Eric Jerome Dickey.[29] I shift to a discussion of Dickey's graphic novel because, although Marvel Comics solicited its creation, Dickey adds a significant understanding of how and why a Black male writer might reimagine African women in comic books. Dickey's graphic novel further depicts how such imaginings are inextricably bound to the history of Africans in America, and how this history shapes the ever evolving complex relationship between Black men and women in the public sphere (see plate 9).

If *X-Men* serves as an allegory of race relations in the United States, Dickey's *Storm*, published in 2007, serves as a direct representation of European colonialism in Africa. Dickey signed on to write *Storm* to establish the background story for Storm's upcoming marriage to the African superhero the Black Panther, also known in the Marvel universe as T'Challa. Dickey transforms the signifier of the African outsider in a foreign land as seen in *X-Men* into the African insider/outsider who battles with white foreigners and, at times, with other Africans. This is perhaps most apparent in the reaction of others to Storm's seemingly unusual appearance. In Africa, Africans tease Storm that she "pretends to be of mother Africa, but is really American," and white Europeans refer to her as "the blue-eyed witch." Storm's reaction to the taunting reflects an internalization of the fears and anxieties of those around her, as seen in her decision to conceal her long, white hair under an Afro wig, to suppress her telekinetic powers in public, and to downplay her strength so that others will not find her presence and her multiple attributes a threat (see plate 10).

While this depiction of Storm (as seen with Nubia) might seem to walk a thin line between the melodramatic binaries invoked by the tragic mulatta genre, Dickey's portrayal of Storm more accurately represents the precarious position of Black Americans within an imagined Africa. Storm's patrilineal heritage signifies America (recall that her father is American), and the character therefore signifies whiteness, betrayal, and colonialism to other Africans. Conversely, for white colonialists in Africa, Storm's matrilineal heritage (recall that her mother is African and that Storm was born in Africa), appearance, and powers signify an African-ess not easily placed within the phenotypical traits associated with the continent. Storm's long, white hair, blue eyes, skin color, and mutant ability make it difficult for white colonialists to codify her within their own distorted racial logics of Africa and its inhabitants. Thus, part of the European soldiers' colonial endeavor in Africa begins with an attempt to capture and control Storm. Ironically, her fellow African comrades collude in her capture.

Unlike the order of the day in mainstream comic book titles, in Dickey's Africa, white Europeans are not victims of savage others, nor are they savage tamers; they are a menacing threat to the freedom of African peoples. This is apparent during a telling conversation between white soldiers that takes place as they search for Storm in the African bush. The conversation centers on how colonial endeavors in Africa have affected the slave trade, and the soldiers acknowledge Europeans' role in isolating and disenfranchising Africans throughout the Diaspora:

> SOLDIER ONE: Never understood all of their civil wars. That thing in Rwanda ... Hutus ... Tutsi ... that Ethiopian thing ... Sudan. And in America. America probably has the dumbest of it all. Darker skinned don't like light skinned ... never will understand that one.
> SOLDIER TWO: Read *Willie Lynch—The Making of a Slave*—and you will understand their mentality. Why they were bred to betray each other.
> SOLDIER ONE: Willie Lynch—that American doctrine, right [sic]?
> SOLDIER TWO: Your point?
> SOLDIER ONE: We're in Africa.[30]

They are indeed in Africa, but, as the dialogue indicates, the specter of slavery and its transhemispheric effects informs the social relations depicted by the graphic novel. Willie Lynch was a product of rumor and lore; many have described the mythic character as a slave owner who delivered an infamous speech in Virginia in 1712 about how to incite distrust among African slaves in America: divide them by color.[31] Allegedly, Lynch was British, just like the soldiers in Dickey's graphic novel. One might consider the story of Willie Lynch as an embellishment of real life, ethnic subterfuge, or as fictional as Dickey's graphic novel, but the color apartheid that emerged among people of African descent in various regions in Africa and throughout the United States is real. This redeployment of racial, national, and geographical signifiers makes Dickey's Africa a complicated web of strained interactions and contested meanings that Storm seeks to disentangle as she develops her mutant powers, comes into womanhood, and forgoes the temptation to adjust her actions and appearance for the comfort of others. "In many ways," writes Rebecca Housel in her analysis of female characters in X-Men, "Storm is the perfect superhero and leader. She has moral complexity and masters ethical duality. She is not bound to one conception of ethics over another. She understands that different situations require different ways of thinking. She has mental and physical toughness and a focused rational side. [Finally], she realizes that justice and duty require carefully tailored action and emotion."[32]

Unfortunately, there is scant development of these attributes in Eric Jerome Dickey's graphic novel. Dickey is keen on grappling with intracultural and intercultural prejudices but presents a troubling depiction of gender relations. He at times makes clumsy shifts from politics to romance, which results in Storm being portrayed as needy and helpless, thus necessitating that the Black Panther come to her rescue. More than backwards gender politics or romance genre writing, this approach to Storm is likely a purposeful rewriting. In X-Men's version of the first meeting between Storm and the Black Panther, written by the white writers Chris Claremont and John Byrne, Storm saves the Black Panther during a battle when they are both adolescents. This is the opposite of the scenario in Dickey's graphic novel Storm, in which the young Black Panther saves the adolescent Storm from sexually aggressive European soldiers. Dickey's narrative departure may have been a bit of historical mending, reminding readers of the sexual exploitation of African women by white men, or a deliberate effort to restore the representation of Black manhood. Unfortunately, Dickey's compelling narrative of white colonialism in Africa and intertribal conflict belies Storm's power, and it is largely only in the pages of X-Men that she exists as a strong, autonomous, and assertive leader.

Vixen: One Baadasssss Woman on a Suicide Mission

Vixen, like Marvel's Storm, is part of a popular superhero collective, in this case the Justice League of America, created in 1960 by DC Comics' writer Gardner Fox. DC Comics had plans for Vixen to appear as a feature character in her own graphic novel in 1978.[33] However, DC lost faith that there was a concrete audience for a series with a Black female lead, and cancelled it after the first issue. The decision to launch *Vixen* in the first place might seem curious without the reminder that *Vixen* came at the heels of the lucrative 1970s blaxploitation film era. The original Vixen bears a significant visual likeness to Jim Lawrence's Black American heroine comic strip *Friday Foster*, done for the *Chicago Tribune* between 1970 and 1974, which was later made into a comic book by Dell Comics in 1972, and a film starring Pam Grier made in 1975.[34] As with notable blaxploitation actors, such as Grier and Tamara Dobson, there was something intriguing and seductive about Vixen's baadasssss ways, or, as Vixen proclaims to those who get in her way, her "five knuckles of talent." The cover of the inaugural *Vixen* issue asserts the connection between blaxploitation cinema and *Vixen*'s first issue, as it is a replica of the posters used to promote Grier in the films *Foxy Brown* and *Coffy*.

Vixen's image, like Grier's in the movie posters, appears in a round circle composed of multiple frames in which a curvaceous figure fights crime, leaps into the air wearing a fox costume, glares at an assumed spectator in a revealing nightgown, seductively embraces a male suitor, and poses as a fashion model. This cyclical iconography marks the various spheres Vixen negotiates as a crime fighter, lover, and fashionista. Yet, labeling *Vixen* a blaxploitation heroine incarnate limits the discourse to a particular set of enclosed meanings usually associated with the blaxploitation genre. Vixen's character and crusades are in many ways representative of the tenuous relationship between the United States and Africa, and the role the United States played (or failed to play) in African and in Black American economic, social, and political policy.

As one might expect, Vixen's story begins in Africa. She is an orphan whose life's mission is to secure a sense of belonging in the United States and to reconcile her attachment and responsibility to an idealized, imagined, and, at times, vilified African nation. Born in the fictional African village of M'Changa, Vixen leaves Africa after the death of her parents. When not involved in crime fighting, she takes on the persona of Mari McCabe—

3.3 Geary & Carla Conway, "The Vixen: Is a Lady Fox." Vixen #1, August–September 1978.

a New York high-fashion model. In the pages of the graphic novel *Vixen*, McCabe declares that she feels "new, vital, and precious" as Vixen and that she would not "trade such a feeling for all of the furs and cosmetics in the world." Writers signify the character's existence as both a part of and apart from the United States by penning reoccurring calls back to her village in Africa, where the expectation is that she will bring peace to warring African factions. Vixen's primary goal when not fighting for social justice on the North American continent, then, is to attend to strife on the African continent. While in Africa, Vixen also seeks to avenge her father's murder by killing the African dictator General Manitoba, who is responsible for her father's death. Vixen's crusades in Africa are more than personal, and her social justice work is more than the pull of ethnic duty. General Manitoba threatens to rule all of Africa by force, and once he has succeeded, he promises to colonize the United States of America as well; therefore, Vixen must stop him, and of course, she obliges.

Vixen the graphic novel is akin to a host of comic book narratives with Black characters (such as *Wonder Woman*'s vengeful Nubia) where the larger systems of American colonialism and white imperialism remain unquestioned, and African or Black microcriminality take center stage. At one point in the graphic novel, Vixen draws an analogy between the African dictator Manitoba's desire for a new world order and Adolph Hitler's Nazi rhetoric. Here, DC writers present Black and white social relations reimagined as African tribalism and its imagined threat to the United States. *Vixen*'s narrative and the actions of her character affirm the ideological presuppositions of American exceptionalism. Vixen is also an intermediary figure between the United States and Africa, and between African dictators and the African masses. Her story line replicates the "black problem" framework of much of the sociological literature of the time that found its way into mainstream comic book titles featuring Black characters. As cultural critic Rod Lendrum argues in his analysis of Black male superheroes in the 1970s, in many comic books, "Black problems were created by Blacks and were to be solved by Blacks; white male writers, to a large extent, had accepted Moynihan propaganda."[35] Through this sociological and ideological prism, conceptions and perceptions of African tribalism became a tool for evading discussion of colonialism in North America and in Africa.

When Vixen made the downward leap from her own self-title to DC's *Action Comics*, *Animal Man*, and *Justice League of America (JLA)*, she worked with an unarmed and unsanctioned police force that sought to protect the

United States from foreign outsiders and wayward outlaws. Though clearly a part of the US national machine as a consistent and often primary character in the *JLA*, Vixen transcended the typical trend to make Black characters marginal or sidekicks in comics; she was often the most powerful of female characters. Unlike the X-Men, the JLA team is comprised of well-known and already existing superheroes, including Superman, Batman, Wonder Woman, and Aquaman, all of whom lived in the fictional town of Happy Harbor in real-life Rhode Island. When the JLA moved to Detroit in the early 1980s, Vixen joined the superhero lineup and held her own among the other characters. Having previously worked with Superman in DC's *Action Comics* to address big city sins, Vixen found the postindustrial site of Detroit an ideal place to fight urban crime and to reunite with Superman, with whom the character had an ongoing flirtation.

In a 1984 issue of *JLA*, Vixen had top billing on the cover, alongside Superman, and the narrative flirts with the idea of Vixen and Superman being romantic partners. The writers introduce Vixen as a mysterious and exotic sex symbol:

> NARRATOR: Below her, the city glitters like a bed of pearls. She doesn't move, scarcely breathes . . . a statue sculpted in flesh and blood. At last he comes—the one she's waited for. And she goes to him!
> VIXEN: About time you showed up Superman! Let's talk!
> SUPERMAN: W-What? Vixen! Where did you come from?
> VIXEN: I didn't wait on top of the galaxy broadcasting building for two hours just for the view!
> SUPERMAN: Isn't that flattering! All right, Vixen, you've got me curious. Let's go somewhere where we won't be interrupted.[36]

Vixen and Superman's flirtation, a common trope in *JLA*, quickly and safely turns from romance to crime fighting. This narrative shift underscores that while the writers may have hinted at an interracial sexual liaison to arouse male readers, in patriotic comics the focus was ultimately on the task of securing the safety of the nation.

When the president of the United States demands that the JLA disband because he disapproves of their brand of vigilante justice, Vixen retires from crime fighting—but not for long. After a failed trip to Africa, during which she had hoped to "make a difference in her homeland," Vixen joins the Suicide Squad—a for hire group of superheroes. In a 1988 issue of *Suicide Squad* Vixen tells the reader, "I stopped being Vixen then; quit the whole superhero game. Went to Africa seeking my spiritual home-land. I found Ethiopia instead. There's so much misery there. There's only so much you can do. I got burned out, got broke, so I came back to make some money. Full circle."[37] There was scant basis for the feeling of hope-lessness that Vixen expressed in *Suicide Squad*. At that time, Ethiopia was nearing the end of a violent civil war between the Ethiopian government and Eritrean nationalists.[38] Vixen's statement thus has no grounding in historical fact, and she never returns to the topic of Ethiopia, nor does she ever explain what made the situation appear helpless. Instead, the book provides a visual cue as to what was most hopeless about Africa: child star-vation. In the same issue, Vixen looks at two African boys with pity after she declares her decision to join Suicide Squad. The children wear white loincloths and have swollen bellies. Vixen's sad look at the two young boys encourages a visual "sigh" from the spectator.

Vixen's ill-perceived statement about the impossibility of change in Africa and its misery fits squarely within the sign of Africa as a starved and ravaged continent worthy of pity and beyond repair in the US popu-lar imagination. Further, this portrayal mirrored the earlier Reagan-Bush administration position on apartheid in South Africa in the early 1980s—known as "constructive engagement"—which limited, but did not end, US business dealings with the region. Instead, constructive engagement made rhetorical proclamations about supporting the end of apartheid.[39] Though Vixen's rhetoric is congruent with the ideology of constructive engage-ment, and her visual empathy is a replica of tear-jerking, late-night Afri-can hunger-relief advertisements, DC writers seemed less interested in the real Africa than in how an imagined Africa might fit within the fantasy myth making of the DC universe. In the wake of her African spiritual jour-ney, Vixen ceased working with the Suicide Squad, and in the 1990s, she returned to the JLA and to her duties as a defender of US national security. On the vibrant cover of a 1994 issue of *JLA Taskforce*, Vixen and her super-friends were "trapped in a savage world" that required taming.[40] The phras-ing echoes the language of imperialism: moralistic crusaders, presented as a well-intentioned superhero collective that sought justice for the United States, had a divine right to conquer, civilize, and tame the wild. Well into the twenty-first century, the JLA's efforts and intents remained consis-tent, and Vixen continued as a central character in the superhero line-up, appearing not only in the comic book but also in the *JLA Unlimited* series, which aired on the Cartoon Network from 2004 to 2006. In 2015, DC made the announcement that Vixen would appear in her own animated digital series on the CW Seed website.[41]

In the 2009 resurrection of Vixen in her own self-titled graphic novel miniseries, *Vixen: Return of the Lion*, the characterization is still a complex and dubious mixture of sex symbol, animal, and baadasssss freedom fighter.[42] The female writer Willow Wilson, who has a degree in history and Arabic language and literature from Boston College, wrote DC's latest incarnation of Vixen. More than thirty years had passed since DC attempted to promote Vixen in her own series, but unlike in the 1978 version, by the early twenty-first century, the character had a long history of appearances in many comic book titles. In several of them, such as *JLA* and *Suicide Squad*, she was the star of the series, and their popularity surely convinced DC that Vixen was once again ready for her own title. As with the character Nubia, the passing of time brought about a visual change. 2009's *Vixen: Return of the Lion* presents Vixen with a modern pixie haircut and soft, modern features, but her new self-titled comic book returns to the 1978 trope of revenge and a warring African nation in need of intervention. The cover of *Vixen: Return of the Lion* places Vixen in a jungle-type atmosphere, apparently in Africa, leaning against a lion, her body sprawled and a "come hither" glare in her hazel almond-shaped eyes (see plate 11). The narrative begins with the iconic Superman sharing with Vixen that the gang who killed her mother is still on the loose in Zambesi, a name similar to that of the Southern African country of Zambia (Zambesi, more commonly spelled Zambezi, is a river in Africa). Vixen returns to Africa, this time to the Dagombi Plains, to bring her mother's murderers to justice. When Vixen arrives, African villagers greet her in a sandy area surrounded by mud huts and speak to her using the following phrases: "Wo fri he?" "Te Ferew Sen?" "Ko Ko!"[43]

Vixen's female friend, Abiesa, code switches to English, warns Vixen that her crusade of vengeance is dangerous, and suggests that matrimony might take her mind off of her frivolous pursuit of social justice. "If you do not find a husband to civilize you," says Abiesa, "you may begin to bleat [like a goat]." Vixen ignores Abiesa's warning and, unsurprisingly, soon faces a group of African patriarchs whose leader, Kwesi, chastises Vixen. Kwesi glares at Vixen in disapproval as he queries with condemnation: "So this is the uncircumcised slut?" In a subsequent issue, Vixen contemplates, with one of her African comrades, the consequences of US soldiers in

3.4 John Ostrander, "Blood and Snow," *Suicide Squad* #11, March 1988.

Africa vis-à-vis a Zambesi independent nation run by African insurgents. "This is about keeping Zambesi from being destroyed by warlords," argues Vixen, to which her unnamed African comrade replies, "What would you have instead? Foreign troops on the ground, our resources snatched away from us? Another African tragedy? Kwesi is a thug. But at least he is a Zambesi thug."[44] Their pondering about Africa's future ceases when Vixen learns that the warlord Kwesi has plans to mind-control and destroy Superman; thus, her calls to save a war-torn Africa are interrupted by the more important duty to save Superman and, therefore, to metaphorically save America.

Willow Wilson did integrate aspects of feminism and the gender concerns of some African women into the graphic novel, likely because of her education and experiences as a progressive Islamic writer living in Cairo. Still, thirty-six years after the introduction of the graphic novel *Vixen*, in her return in *Vixen: Return of the Lion*, the character remains entangled in colonial discourses of US national allegiance and the idea of a primitive, patriarchal Africa. References to circumcision and intravillage conflict serve as decontexualized facts to affirm African pathology and primitivism, thereby showing that Africa remains a convenient sign of difference that appears to infatuate comic book writers, resulting in inventive and erroneous ends. Some titles that feature Storm and Vixen question US foreign policy on Africa, but more often than not this questioning is forgotten in favor of writers' repetitive representations of African essentialism and savagery. The words of Wonder Woman in a 2000 issue further exemplify writers' stagnant Africa and the ideological presupposition that the United States is morally superior. In this issue, titled "Three Hearts," Wonder Woman scolds Nu'bia as if she were a child after Nu'bia apparently scares some civilians while she is fighting criminals. "Nu'bia!" says Wonder Woman condescendingly. "You can't . . . petrify people. This isn't the underworld. There are rules here. Laws of conduct."[45]

The comic writers' idea Africa and its inhabitants, and their fabrication, extraction, and exaggeration of Africa, does more than serve as building blocks for a troublesome depiction of African nations and the African female subject. What appears as an irrational fetishization of Africa may allow for a curious avoidance of penning narratives about Black American female superheroes. The question then becomes, what is the rationale, whether conscious or unconscious, for this inclusion of African women and apparent exclusion of Black American women? Cultural critic Ann

Ducille writes that in the intellectual scholarship of postcolonial studies, the preponderance of works that focus on colonialism outside of the United States locates oppression conveniently "elsewhere," and thereby "not here in the United States," which increases its appeal and commodification in the mainstream academy.[46] In other words, American Blacks are too familiar a trope, whereas Africans offer newer, fresher, exotic ground. In these comic books, Africa and African women may serve a similar ideological purpose by displacing and locating imaginings of Africa not as a way of understanding and explaining Africa but as way to discuss race issues absent of US responsibility. African characters create a safe distance of representational responsibility, but their circulation in the United States provide just enough representation to make claims to ethnic inclusion without the burden of US guilt. A Black American superheroine, for example, might be less concerned with fighting African patriarchs and risking her life for patriotic missions in the name of US nationalism, and more concerned with addressing and avenging one of the primary concerns of people of African descent living in America: the legacy and continuance of US racism. This is, in fact, the goal of Rocket, one of the few and most notable African American female characters in the Black-owned Milestone Comics title *Icon*.[47]

African Female Comic Book Characters as Black Cultural Traffic

In their anthology on Black performance and popular culture, *Black Cultural Traffic*, cultural critics Harry Elam and Kennell Jackson offer a wide range of historical and contemporary examples of the transnational circulation and commodification of blackness. "Black cultural traffic" refers to the transport and representation of Black bodies through mass-circulated artifacts. The editors gather critical essays that speak to the limitations and possibilities in circulation, as articulated in the foreword by cultural critic Tricia Rose. Metaphorical and representative cultural exchanges of blackness, Rose writes, are "tethered to the traffic in black bodies on which these cultural exchanges are based. They share several disheartening characteristics: similar trade routes, unequal forms of exchange, and often, a soulless focus on capital gain. These respective black traffics also share powerful traditions of possibility, such as strategies of refusal, revision, generative exchanges across . . . boundaries, style and innovation as life-saving devices and unexpected alternative routes."[48]

DC Comics' and Marvel Comics' Africa, as well as their miraculous African orphans Nubia, Storm, and Vixen, provide relevant case studies for understanding the deployment of the sign of Africa as a process in Black cultural traffic. Africa and women's bodies sell in comic books, especially when presented in the narrative trope of Africa as exotic yet dangerous, and African women as sexual enticements for male characters who are also centrally focused on protecting the nation. Although their subject content tightly focuses around these themes, their use nevertheless sheds light upon the larger field and purpose of comic books and comic book studies.

Comic books, like other forms of popular literature, are social objects; that is to say, comics function as forms of material culture where writers and readers metaphorically work through social relations.[49] Nubia, Storm, and Vixen, while wide-ranging in their representation and political uses, were vessels through which writers imagined a relationship between Africa and the United States. As Rose articulates in her discussion of transnational Black popular culture, these superheroines possess problematic ideologies as well as progressive politics that have the capacity to do relevant, though at times contradictory, cultural work. DC's Nubia is as much a mixed-race wonder and puppet of pop feminism as she is a challenge to the withholding of fully actualized citizenship from Black women. Marvel's Storm, whether the savoir of the Black Panther or herself the saved, is an African goddess on which the future of a tolerant anti-imperialist nation, and mutant revolution, relies. DC's Vixen is the fierce fighting baadasssss of American nationalism, who, although buxomly brazen with her "five knuckles of talent," struggles to think through and fight for justice on two continents.

African female characters are thus contradictory referents for Africa in mainstream comics, yet they also remain integral to the political theorizing and fight for social justice upon which writers hinge and interweave their plots, even if not always in perfect or satisfactory ways. The power of these African female characters, then, may lie in their caring about social justice and in their actions, even if not always in the image and the totality of the message. As evidenced in the following chapter, if print culture may exist as a site for thinking through the circulation of ideas of Africa in the US popular imagination via female characters of African descent, then their articulation in the moving image of anime across the Pacific Rim shows how such discourses are not bound by North American production.

ANIME DREAMS FOR AFRICAN GIRLS

Nadia: The Secret of Blue Water

It is 1889, when countless ships are being subsumed beneath the waves of the Atlantic Ocean. World powers grab at each other for new colonies in Africa and Asia. The threats become terrible warfare. As the twentieth century draws closer, civilization grows richer. But the people tremble in fear, and the clouds of the world war darken the horizon. *And so our story begins.*

—Beginning voice-over, *Nadia: The Secret of Blue Water*

NADIA: *The Secret of Blue Water* (*Fushigi no umi no Nadia*) is the first Japanese-produced anime series to feature a young girl of African descent.[1] Film and anime producer Hideaki Anno, born in Ube, Yamaguchi Prefecture, Japan, in 1960, cowrote and directed the show; a total of thirty-nine episodes aired on television between 1990 and 1991 in Japan, the United States (on the Anime Network), and Europe. The show's director fashioned the series as a postmodern reinterpretation of French writer Jules Verne's 1870 half science fiction, half travelogue adventure story *Twenty Thousand Leagues Under the Sea*.[2] Anno's treatment incorporates many aspects of Verne's core narrative: *The Secret of Blue Water*, like *Twenty Thousand Leagues*, takes place in the mid- to late nineteenth century, depicts the uncertainty of sea travel, exhibits ambivalence about technological production, and chronicles the adventures of protagonists captured by US submarine navigators. Anno also works from the travelogue literature genre, insofar as *The Secret of Blue Water* serves as a visual and narrative record of events as well as the interior and expressed thoughts of travelers as they negotiate dangerous journeys. Yet Anno departs from *Twenty Thousand Leagues'* narrative structure in a critical way, as his story is profoundly political in its attention to how race relations and African ancestral displacement affects the lead protagonist, Nadia. In so doing, Anno tropes travelogue literature into a utopian televisual experience that translates into a phantasmagoric transatlantic ride— a Japanese dream for an African girl.

The Secret of Blue Water centers on the character Nadia, a fourteen-year-old Kenyan-born girl (later revealed as a fictional Atlantean princess), who performs trapeze and lion taming routines as a featured attraction at the Paris Universal Exposition of 1889. After being pursued for a magic necklace Nadia owns and wears—which she refers to as the "blue water"—she joins a ship crew of explorers as they sail in search of a threatening force (sea monsters) and face a supremacist foe (Gargoyle) who wishes to control the planet. Anno's narrative constitutes a useful critique of race prejudice and international imperialism through the television show's postmodern narrative of the nineteenth century and the use of dialogue that voices rhetorical strategies of gender and racial liberation and agency for the main character, Nadia. Yet the show is also colonialist in its visual and at times narrative execution, making Nadia's transpacific and mysterious African identity as much of a matter of sexualized spectacle as it is a matter of subjectivity and representation in the larger field of sequential art.

While the representation of a young Kenyan girl marked a racial shift in anime production and in consumption, Nadia's insertion within the spatial logics of the European, American, and Japanese empires situates her as a changing same that is in alignment with many other Black female characters of African descent in sequential art. Nadia might be thought of, then, as an adolescent version of *X-Men*'s Storm, *Wonder Woman*'s Nubia, and *Justice League of America*'s Vixen, all characters whose displaced status outside of their mythical African homelands posits them as both conduits and consequences of the transnational circulation of Black cultural traffic. That is to say, while Nadia's Black presence in anime broke significant representational ground in the 1990s, especially given the form's tendency to depict Anglo or ambiguously Asian characters, when situated within the larger field of sequential art (i.e., comics, graphic novels, and anime), Nadia's characterology is a part of a familiar pattern. In particular, Nadia is strikingly similar to Vixen, as both have the ability to communicate with animals (particularly lions), wear magic necklaces, and oscillate between yearning to return to Africa and feeling weighed down by what repatriating to Africa might mean. The perceived and real orphanhood and ancestral displacement of all four characters (Nubia, Storm, Vixen, and Nadia) allow for the forming of a psychologically layered and transcultural identity where characters contemplate and negotiate multinational identities. Yet, in so doing, Africa serves as little more than a mystical and marginal global signifier.

Unlike the other three sequential art characters who are codified as African in the United States, Nadia is an African subject living in Paris, and a product of international Japanese commodity circulation. Her cultural roots and lack of "rootedness" remark upon US race relations rather than (as with Nubia, Storm, and Vixen) an imagined relationship between the United States and Africa. This narrative shift from the more common treatment of African subjects in sequential art exemplifies an understanding of the relationship between African peoples as being contiguous to the concerns of US Blacks. The identity category of Black and the racial discourse in France, as cultural critic Trica Keaton writes, differ from the identity category of Black and the racial discourse in the United States; a Black Parisian's experience and history are not identical to those of a Black American.[3] At the same time, the producers of the show adeptly situate blackness as a diasporic identity throughout Asia, Africa, Europe, *and* the United States, thereby emphasizing the postimperial concerns of the wider Black Atlantic. The negotiation of race relations in African America in the television series thus exists as a site of interrogation and cultural legitimacy rather than a derisive circumvention of the place of Black Americans within a larger discourse of the African diaspora. As a character who is the product of global flows throughout international markets and one who is closely aligned and armed with postcolonial politics, Nadia is a character who occupies what Jodi Kim refers to as a "postimperial exile or refugee status, who simultaneously is a product of, bears witness to, and critiques imperialist and gendered racial violence."[4]

An aesthetic, textual, and theoretical interrogation of the series shows a televisual coding of sea travel as a maritime carrier of what I define as *empire in movement*, that is, how empire travels to affirm and disrupt imperial or colonialist domination. The work here is to consider the consequences and possibilities of bearing the burden of colonialist fantasy and postcolonial liberation on the body of an imagined African girl to address the following concerns: How do the grammars of anime re-envision nineteenth-century social relations by depicting and critiquing erroneous ideas of technology, gender, race, and sexuality propagated by the Paris Universal Exposition of 1889? In what ways is Nadia's codification as African and ambiguously Asian a way of reconstituting a productive identity suture into that of an Afro-Asian and transpacific subject? What does the sexualization of Nadia in pinups and as performed by adult women in cosplay reveal about the dialectics and displacement of chastity and sexuality onto an imagined adolescent body? An engagement with key episodes that address these questions and a cartography of the conventions, business, and visual work of anime reveals Hideaki Anno's Japanese dream for an African girl as an example of the way the ideological forces of empire travel through the modes of production, thereby permeating the spatial logics of Japanese, European, and US consumer culture.

"Infiltration of the Secret Base": The Business, Narrative, and Visual Grammars of Anime

Anime has emerged as one of the most lucrative engines of sequential art production. It owes its popularity in the United States to changes in animation production, globalization, and the commodification of Japanese culture.[5] One half of the US Cartoon Network programming is either Japanese anime or consists of American versions of anime. As of 2007, eighty new anime shows emerged each week on Japanese television.[6] Television on demand, the online streaming of content by subscription, YouTube, fan sites, mobile video applications, and DVD sales and rentals have expanded access to and dissemination of the anime form in the twenty-first century, but the beginning of its popularity in the United States reaches back to the mid-twentieth century. Scholars attribute anime's earliest form to the Japanese television show *Astro Boy* (*Tetsuwan Atomu*), the first show of its kind to air in serial form. From 1963 to 1966, *Astro Boy* ushered in what cultural critic Marc Steinberg refers to as the "media mix" of the anime system, and Thomas Lamarre as the "transmedial network" of anime, that is, the simultaneous marketing of an anime character's image and its dissemination through interconnected media.[7]

In the United States, most Americans' first contact with anime came about through the television premier of *Speed Racer* (*Mahha GōGōGō*). Adapted from a 1958 Japanese manga and anime series, *Speed Racer* aired on American television from 1966 to 1968. The show presented race car driver Speed Racer, his circle of friends, his girlfriend Trixie, and his ongoing competition with his older brother, the ominous race car driver Racer X. In addition to thrill-riding racing scenes, Speed Racer would on occasion confront the acts of treacherous villains. In the show's US adaptation, the names, musical score, and origin stories of the characters were re-created to attract American audiences, but Peter Fernandez, who was the show's director, producer, writer, and voice of many of the characters (including Speed Racer), self-consciously sought to maintain the experimental and complex structure of the anime form in the US version. *Speed Racer* is arguably the US starting point of Steinberg's anime system theory, as its cross-fertilization into action figures, films, and video games made way for its entrenchment within US popular culture, continuing on in the twenty-first century through motion pictures and syndication.[8] Anime as a big business, then, began to flourish decades before *The Secret of Blue Water*'s introduction to international audiences, but the workings of that business shaped the execution and the reception of the show.

Writer and journalist Roland Kelts argues that the cornerstone of the anime business lay not only in returns on production brought about by global consumption alone but also in the business behind the business, that is, in training animators in private institutions to keep up with demand. As anime became increasingly popular as a global cultural form by the late 1980s, animation emerged as a legitimate occupation in Japan and thereby increased the demand for formal training in the field. Private art institutes and degree programs in anime capitalized on this demand among prospective artists and animators, who aspired to take part in the lucrative global commodification of the anime form.[9] The name of Digital Hollywood University (DHU) in Akihabara, Japan, reveals how the business of anime was able to expand exponentially by the twenty-first century and adopt a Hollywood-sized production scale.[10]

Digital Hollywood University, a private four-year university founded in 2005, offers a bachelor's of digital content. At the university's website, their mission is conveyed as energizing the world with Japanese digital content; they are dedicated to helping their graduates create "cool Japan" in Akihabara, which is defined as "Japan's pop culture hub."[11] The increasing corporatization and professionalization of anime, as seen with global marketing and training machines such as DHU, has led to an increase in the quantity of production, and, as some purists and critics contend, a decrease in the quality of the form. Kelt reasons that one of the easiest ways to make money in the field of anime is to train aspiring animators, but a result of this mass training, beyond the greed and a flooded and exploited labor pool, he argues, is an aesthetic shift in contemporary anime that is increasingly less experimental and more commercial or Hollywood.[12] At an Anime Expo in the late 1960s, Hideaki Anno described the modern landscape of the anime business and its possible consequences for the future of the form: "The creators have to change their frame of mind for the field to advance. And it doesn't look too hopeful in today's Japan. It's in a critical condition right now. I don't think there's any bright future. . . . The people who make it, and the people who want it, they're always wanting the same things. They've been making only similar things for the past ten years, with no sense of urgency. To get it going once more, you need to force people to go outside, to go out again."[13] "Going outside" for Anno meant going outside of the formulaic conventions to create the genre anew. Large-scale production, he suggested, had shifted creators' focus away from the art and toward consumer demand.

The mode and transformation of the production of anime is significant to the contemplation of the cultural work of anime in general, and of Anno's *The Secret of Blue Water* in particular. Anime's expansion reveals the effects of neoliberalism on the market: forms of cultural production become privatized commodities through the work of institutions of higher learning and through global circulation. As an economic force, neoliberalism is the process of market expansion in the global economy with limited state intervention or regulation; it entails the free movement of capital and goods, and requires the privatization of national or government-sponsored industries.[14] It is within this larger anime arena that art, economics, and culture collide. Indeed, the economic havoc caused by neoliberalism has had a direct effect on the field and on some of the aesthetic choices of the visionaries who introduced Nadia to television audiences across the globe.

Director Hayao Miyazaki brought the original concept of Nadia to Japan's public television network *Nippon Hōsō Kyōkai* (NHK), and the network passed the project on to Hideaki Anno, a former Osaka University of Arts student, for further development. From then on, Anno became the chief agent of the show's production, as he reworked the show's concept, directed and shepherded the series, and collaborated on the writing of the script.[15] Anno won the Animage Anime Grand Prix Award for *The Secret of Blue Water* in 1991, but the show's accolades and popularity resulted in a mix of professional riches and personal ambivalence.[16] Many elements of the show reflect Anno's training in independent filmmaking and his postmodern narrative and visual style that aimed to, in his words, "fix Japanese animation," but Anno expressed in interviews his dismay over not having complete control over a show that was seen as representative of his best work to date. In comparison to his experience with *The Secret of Blue Water*, in an interview about his artistic process and his success in the field, Anno asserts that Gainax, the anime studio corporation that he cofounded in 1984, gave him carte blanche for his second award-winning anime series, *Evangelion,* which fans and the industry now consider his magnum opus.[17]

Though some critics and some animators, such as Anno, argue that anime aesthetics are in an era of declension brought on by the increase in mass-market production since the early 1990s, anime's perceived though not always substantial difference from US animation continues to situate it as distinct from the likes of animation conglomerates Disney and Pixar. Narratives of anime shift, but there are key elements of its structure that situate it as a subgenre within the larger field of sequential art, or what I refer to as the *narratological* and *visual grammars* of the anime form.[18] These elements include the sublime terrain of postmodern narratives. That is to say, the story lines in anime foster an intellectual space that seeks to move spectators into alternative ways of seeing by decentering and deconstructing grand historical, social, and political narratives. The form's postmodern impulse further constitutes the deceiving aspects of authorial presence and an experimental avant-gardism that encourages aesthetic reflection. Anime illustrations consist of fantasy-themed adolescent characters who often perform adult roles or operate within adult situations. Their disproportionately drawn large eyes and heads, minimal noses, and small mouths allow the eyes of the characters to serve as the central expressive focus, while their elongated bodies ebb and flow between rapid movement and momentary stasis. Lush watercolored landscapes and panoramic views in duplicate serve as the setting for anime, where the frequent insertion of live-action sequences, multiply drawn perspectives and angles, and cross-cutting sequences magnify the quick, truncated action scenes.[19]

Anno describes his own aesthetic as an attempt to use visual and narrative improvisation and to replicate the experience of a "live concert": "A cartoon is composed of simple signs and therefore from the outset, it is a fake world, right? Nothing but an optical illusion. Nobody would imagine that it's a documentary. Trying to integrate a documentary aspect into the film, that's my personal feeling of being 'live.' I think the deconstruction of these signs is rare in cartoons that are shown on TV. I tried to go to the rescue of Japanese animation."[20] In all forms of sequential art, a character's eyes are typically drawn to express emotion and mood, but Anno and his visual collaborators also use the framing and animation of characters' faces to imply an idea or an assemblage of ideological positions. Anno's calculated decision to use adolescents as key protagonists, he says in a 1996 interview, stems from their ability to relate to younger adults, who may make direct correlations between characters' fictional worlds and aspects of their own material lives. Adolescent characters may further provoke nostalgia in adults, which broadens the audience base. Anno creates adolescent characters, especially characters who are the age of fourteen, because, as he says, they are "no longer a child but not yet an adult. Considering 'age fourteen' as that in which an independence of mind starts manifesting, I found it proper to include this in my work."[21] The emotional aspects of Anno's narratives are not detours from the action sequences or the political content; rather, self-introspection, intimate relationships, and yearnings of the heart are woven into the story lines to convey the ways modern society, technology, and materialism cause emotional alienation. As a product of anime, *The Secret of Blue Water* bears all of these narrative and visual elements, and exerts a postmodern influence in its trenchant critique of race, authority, national belonging, and empire.

"The Girl at the Eiffel Tower": Markets of Racialization and National Belonging

The first episode of the *Secret of Blue Water* series, "The Girl at the Eiffel Tower," exemplifies anime as a form of narrative historicization, racial resocialization, and sexual fantasy. The show introduces the audience to a white Parisian inventor named Jean who is one of the main protagonists and who also serves as Nadia's romantic interest. Jean has strawberry blonde hair, large blue eyes magnified by wire-rimmed glasses, and a modestly drawn masculine physique. Like Nadia, Jean is a fourteen-year-old orphan; he attends the Paris Universal Exposition to enter an airplane that he has built with his uncle into the young inventors contest. His attention to scientific invention is averted, however, when he sees Nadia—a brown-skinned girl dressed in upper-class Parisian attire, whisking by on a bicycle. Nadia's dark brown skin, jet-black hair with blue-violet highlights, and distinct anime features provide a contrast to the other white-skinned characters, thereby intensifying her difference and use as a postmodern subject. In other words, to draw Nadia as an embodiment of anime conventions and to attribute more generalized features to the peripheral characters allows animators to imply the progressive codes of anime with Nadia, thereby also intensifying the character's use as social critique. In contrast, animators portray the young Jean as an anime/animation hybrid visual mix, which situates him as an intermediary character sympathetic to and an ally of Nadia's postcolonial circumstances, but still decidedly European and therefore an example of the more benign aspects of cultural misunderstanding.

When Jean first sees Nadia riding across a bridge on her bike, he is transfixed—erect even—and the frame freezes to highlight his expression of sexual excitement (see plates 12 and 13). Then the animation switches from stasis to rapid movement as Jean lets out an intense and prolonged gasp and begins to pursue Nadia on foot as she rides toward the Eiffel Tower. The scene then switches to Nadia standing at the top of the tower and crosscuts to Jean, who trails behind on foot. Nadia gazes out at the picturesque countryside that expands within the view of the frame and says aloud, "France, Spain, Italy, Egypt, Africa." She then turns to her pint-sized pet lion named King to ask, "King, do you think I was born in Africa like you were? Or is it someplace we have not thought of yet?" As a hot air balloon flies by, Nadia smiles in amazement and says, "How wonderful. Maybe we could find [my home] if we could fly." Jean, standing in the corridor behind them interrupts with, "Oh, but you can fly!" Nadia and King both turn and frown at the intrusion, and Nadia and Jean's ensuing exchange frames the logics of race, empire, and national belonging that is a core theme of the series:

JEAN: Where are you from? Is it India?
NADIA: I'm sorry, but I won't give out such personal information to a
    complete stranger.
JEAN: Oh good, you understand what I am saying. I wasn't even sure if
    we spoke the same language.
NADIA: Hmf.
JEAN: I'm sorry, but I didn't mean to offend you.
NADIA: Really? So I don't suppose you find my dark skin funny?
JEAN: Oh, no!
NADIA: Then what do you want from me?
JEAN: I thought we could both become friends since we are in Paris
    together—don't you think?
NADIA: No.

Nadia and Jean's first conversation defines the cultural barrier that haunts the two throughout their relationship. Though Jean hears Nadia speaking English as she wonders how to return to her homeland, and she answers his question in English, Nadia's visual blackness supersedes what he hears. French and Japanese versions of Nadia present the same language framing. In each version, Nadia always speaks the same language as Jean, and she shares enough in common with the other characters culturally to allow her to operate within white European society. Yet as a vegetarian, an advocate of nonviolence, and, as she repeatedly reminds the characters, an assumed African, her worldview remains distinct from that of those around her, and her physical difference is obvious to all. Indeed, Jean's "Where are you from?" signifies that her appearance—primarily her dark skin color—provides visual evidence for him that she is not a native of France.[22] Seemingly innocuous questions such as "Where are you from?" and "Do you speak English?" infer nonverbal assumptions about race, difference, and national belonging. Though his query is misguided, Jean's intentions are not nefarious. His attraction to Nadia and his zeal to protect her from harm throughout the series, and, later, their romantic relationship and marriage, offer the promise of interracial exchange rather than the problem of xenophobia.

Later in the series, we learn that Nadia is not a South Asian from India. Though exposed as a princess of the fictional Atlantis, her identity straddles ethnic markers, which leads spectators to place her as a South Asian Kenyan or a Black North African. The historical moment depicted in the show, that is, 1889, predates South Asian migration to Kenya by nearly a decade (1896), but Anno's postmodern conventions are not beholden to history, and his narrative loosely reinterprets and represents history to reweave racial solidarities and antagonisms. For Black characters in sequential art, Kenya as a site of origin is a popular racial and international trope, perhaps because it allows illustrators and animators to depict tribal characteristics that are starkly African and therefore different from Anglo characters, yet with intermittent "refined" Anglo features, such as lighter-hued eyes and loosely curled or straight hair, that are associated with and seen in North and East Africa. We see this aesthetic mix in the Kenyan character Storm, as well as in Nadia, whose dark skin, coarse straight hair, and blue to hazel eyes situate her as exotically African and as a visual racialized enigma to Europeans.

Fans report that Anno and his collaborators wanted to illustrate Nadia with coarse, curly hair, but conceded that if she was too conspicuously

Black, Japanese and international audiences might not relate to the character. Rumors exist that an early sketch released before the show's production in which Nadia's hair seems to unquestionably codify her as a Black African contrasts to the final version of the character in the series, which depicts Nadia as a mix of dark, ethnic, but not "too ethnic" features.[23] The point here is not to disprove Nadia's Asianess to essentialize her within a Black historical imaginary. Rather, my analysis seeks to think through the convergence of Black and Asian history throughout the African diaspora; it is interpretive of the director and writer's interweaving of African and Black American experiences onto Nadia, and attendant to the way fans read race onto the character. The business of anime influenced artistic choices that were laden with cultural and political meanings, and that served the interests of the anime industrial complex and, as it would turn out, a broader base of fans. In other words, visually marking Nadia in a more ambiguous fashion, that is, as African, Asian, and ambiguous Other, opened up the possibilities of spectators' identification with Nadia. This strategy was unquestionably successful, as the aesthetic choices of Nadia's representation did usher in marketing opportunities for business interests that simultaneously served the cultural interests of a diverse array of spectators.

There are fan sites devoted to the character Nadia hosted by young Black women who "read" the character as Black and as a positive signifier of Black girlhood and dark skin pride. Further, at anime conventions such as Anime Expo and Comic-Con, women (not girls) of the African and Asian diaspora dress up and perform as Nadia, indicating that they see her as a performative choice within the realm of fantasy that they can aesthetically re-create more easily than the white-skinned anime characters who make up the majority. As we saw in the 2004 film *Catwoman*, the racial ambiguity of the lead roles seemed to alienate target constituencies. Black interpretations of the *Catwoman* and *Wonder Woman* film adaptions concerned comic book fans because they viewed such racial departures as a divergence from the original characters, despite the actual racial fluidity in the comic book titles in which Catwoman and Wonder Woman appear. However, in the case of *The Secret of Blue Water*, the visual presentation of characters seems to have the opposite effect. Ethnic identification appears more fluid and contingent in the world of anime, where fairy-themed, anamorphic, or animated characters, rather than human bodies, portray the main protagonists.

Scholar Ami Shirong Lu provides empirical evidence of this hypothesis and marketing strategy. In her study on racial identification and anime characters, Lu concludes that while Japanese animators claim their characters are ethnically Japanese, Caucasian audiences view the same characters as white. Latino and Black viewers, comparatively, see the ambiguity of characters as an opportunity to imagine their own ethnic identities as having a place within the anime world.[24] The case is often the opposite in television and film, where racial ambiguity assuages those with an aversion to bodies of color but often fails to result in an increase in commitment and identification among racial and ethnic minorities. Anno's decision to make Nadia dark but still racially ambiguous reflects a concession to the producer's perception of the tastes of Japanese audiences. Ironically, it is precisely Nadia's racial ambiguity that situates her as a productive, transpacific, and Afroanime subject, which allows spectators to imagine points of convergence between Asian and African struggles and experiences under the auspices of European colonialism.

"The Little Fugitive": Spectacles of Technology and Transatlantic Slavery

The presentation of the Paris Universal Exposition in *Nadia: The Secret of Blue Water* moves from loose historical references regarding cultural ambivalence about nineteenth-century technological production to depicting spectacles of the Black female body. Technological production, especially mechanical technology, serves as an accessory subplot in Anno's narrative. An international world's fair presenting various countries' contributions to technology and the arts, the Paris Exposition of 1889 featured the newly erected Eiffel Tower, and displayed dioramas, crafts, trained and amateur performers, and exotic and eroticized semblances of the Third World.[25] French technological advancements and inventions, however, remained the central focus of the fair. Americanist Leo Marx writes that mechanical power and ideological presuppositions of technology constituting progress were the two entities that shaped the nineteenth-century discourse, character, and representation of technology. While Marx is critical of postmodern interpretations of technological advancement that do not account for agency in contemporary times, he embraces analyses that think more broadly about technology as a social invention.[26] *Nadia: The Secret of Blue Water* is a visual analysis of the collision of anxieties and disappointments about technological production. The show also introduces the way ideas of race, gender, and sexuality work as a cultural technology, that is, as an invention of social categories that shape interrelations between the characters.[27]

Jean furthers the show's intention to mark the relationship between mechanical production and social technologies when he says at the outset of the first episode: "So this is the Paris Exposition! Looks like the crowds are more important than the inventions!" Here, Anno directs the viewer's attention to the role the crowd plays as comakers of the meaning of technological production, and Jean's acknowledgment of this situates one of the main protagonists as cognizant of technology's cultural role. Jean's primary identity is that of a young inventor and junior scientist, but his ill-conceived inventions, submarines, and disappearing naval ships are consistently presented as symbols of tenuous or failed tools of progress. Scenes of the Paris Exposition in the beginning of the series present confident showmen who capitalize on the desire of onlookers and audiences to witness gadgets that awe and promise to transform their lives. Yet nearly all such gadgets—including aircraft and automobiles with complex, clunky structures of implausible design—stop working, crash, or explode before spectators' eyes.

As the *Nadia* series progresses to the episode "The Little Fugitive," Nadia, Jean, and additional, peripheral characters find that the sea monsters responsible for the disappearance of small boats and large ships in the ocean are in actuality submarines. Concentration on the various roles played by submarines—from vessels of scientific exploration to rescue crafts to war machines—aligns with *Twenty Thousand Leagues Under the Sea*'s fictional chronicle of the strides of advancement made by the French in the mechanization of the submarine. In Anno's reinterpretation, futuristic science seems less hopeful, and the series shows the hope for technology that characters place upon mechanization as a product of capitalism's false consciousness. Nadia admires Jean's ability to create machines and gadgets at a whim to help them survive, and she marvels at his ability to recite scientific theories to explain what seems mystical or unknown. This is seen when Jean explains the heliocentric theory as he and Nadia gaze at the stars, and she compliments his ability to teach and inform the ship crew. At the same time, Nadia questions technology's ability to solve all of their problems, and she doubts that science is the ultimate authority for explaining the unknown. When Nadia and Jean are sailing, for example, they spot an iron fleet, which, unbeknownst to them, is being navigated by jewel thieves in search of Nadia and her blue water necklace:

JEAN: A ship that floats and flies! What an incredible invention.

NADIA: (*Angrily, Nadia tightens and raises her shoulders and stomps her right foot.*) But we still have to get away from it! [Our] sailboat can't out-run that.

JEAN: Watch this. (*Jean ignites an engine that suddenly emerges from the back of the boat.*) That iron ship is too weighed down to catch up with us at this point. The foils lift [our] ship up, which lowers the water resistance. And that's the secret behind its great speed!

NADIA: (*Calmed and forgiving.*) That's remarkable.

JEAN: The original concept actually belongs to another Frenchman. I added my own improvements.

NADIA: It amazes me that a young boy can be so smart . . . you are a do-it-yourself genius!

JEAN: (*Shyly as he winks at her.*) I'm much more than that.

NADIA: (*Shyly smiling.*) You're telling me.

After the flirting, the boat begins to fill with smoke and then breaks down, and Jean admits in embarrassment, "I don't think I ever tested the engine for endurance." Nadia answers in disappointment, "Flimsy construction. I guess it's not so amazing after all."

Later, Jean shows off a flashlight that he has created, which initially allows them to explore an island at night while shipwrecked. As Jean and Nadia walk through densely planted trees, Nadia asks, while looking down at the flashlight, "So, did you make that?" Jean responds that it was one of his early inventions, and proudly continues, "The hand crank powers the generator, which charges the light belt, but it takes some work . . . too much work really." Nadia muses aloud, "[That's] pretty obvious." Jean's flashlight, of course, malfunctions, and begins to dim, while the hand mechanism to the flashlight turns out of control. Such scenarios are repeated throughout the series, often with humor and wit. Errors of mechanical production serve the humanistic intents of the narrative, which aims to situate human beings as culpable in the advancement of society—not the machines that they make. In other words, *The Secret of Blue Water*'s narrative affirms that people change and transform the world and its attendant problems, and that a moral aptitude is required in the responsible deployment of technology. The promise and perils of technology are significant to Anno's tale of nineteenth-century America, but it is his direct engagement with colonialism as it collides with historical semblances of slavery, race, and race relations that stands out as the show's most impressive accomplishment.

Historian Dana Hale informs us that prior to World War I, the French opinion of people of African descent was one of "primitiveness and backwardness," a view that was confirmed in the way Africans were represented in various public cultural forms.[28] Before the Exhibit of American Negroes at the Paris Exposition of 1900 touted the progress of Black American men and women since emancipation, Black representation at world expositions and world fairs were more a matter of spectacle than a platform for presenting the spectacular achievements of people of African descent. For Africans at the Paris Exposition of 1900, no uplifting narratives were offered, as spectacles of primitivism were abundant and transplantations of Africa became a scientific lab of amusement. Africans were indigenous objects seen in replications of "African villages," or specimens who would "dance, sing, and do manual work" before a voraciously gazing public.[29] Anno plays with such documentary facts and turns them into postmodern, critical anime fiction. His episode "The Little Fugitive" articulates French ambivalence and contradictory attraction to blackness. The narrative also informs on Nadia's African identity and its relevance to the history of slavery in the United States, to Reconstruction in the US South, and to the use of Black and African subjects as objects of sexual and racialized spectacle at freak shows, amusement parks, and world expositions. In so doing, the narrative conjures the use of African subjects such as the infamous Sarah Saartjie Baartman, otherwise known as the Hottentot Venus, who was an object of sexual spectacle at circuses in Paris in 1815.[30]

"The Little Fugitive" introduces Nadia's European boss, whom she refers to as "master." After indicating that she does not want to perform her circus routine because she fears those who wish to steal her blue water necklace will abduct her, her master asks, "Did you remember to eat your breakfast today Nadia?" When Nadia responds that she has, her master demands, "If you eat my food, you'll earn it by performing!" Nadia's working conditions and relationship to her "master" are reminiscent of the ways tenant farming and sharecropping kept people of African descent in the United States in a subordinate and dependent position in the wake of legal emancipation. That is, though Black Americans were technically free and deserving of equal pay, many were trapped in debt systems wherein their earnings did little more than keep them dependent. At the same time, obvious references to extralegal enslavement in the episode expose slavery as a global, hemispheric, and inhumane practice, and informs upon myriad forms of servitude, both psychological and economic. Nadia is technically free and not a slave but refers to her boss as "master," showing that she has psychologically internalized her subservient status when it comes to her economic survival.

In the episode and in the series, nineteenth-century US race relations are imprinted on a French context, but such postmodern and transhemispheric leaps still hearken back to aspects of nineteenth-century France. In the nineteenth century, writes Shelby McCloy, no person of African descent in France would "enjoy the social, professional, or legal position of the white race," and they would fail to have opportunities to secure any significant professional position. Although life for Blacks in France was at times better than for those enslaved, squalid living quarters were inevitable.[31] For Nadia, being a "little fugitive" represents her eventual fleeing of such conditions; in particular, her oppressive economic situation is a condition that exists as a form of legal servitude in an environment in which Black bodies are viewed as free or low-paid labor and in which the dominant power group expects gratitude from those they subjugate. Yet the use of Nadia as a circus amusement also sets the stage for and challenges the character to later emancipate her body from the racialized gaze of European audiences.

As Nadia emerges onto the stage to perform her circus routine, the audience finds mesmerizing her acrobatic ability and the racial difference signified by her skin, attire, and props. After being introduced as Princess Nadia, the young Nadia cartwheels across the stage, wearing a gold crown, a small white bra top, a short red vest, a skirt with a slit up the side, and black ballet shoes with ribbons wound around her legs. She proceeds to dance, leap into the air on a trapeze, and fall to the ground to tame wild African lions, and finally curtsies to the roaring applause of the audience. Nadia's performance embodies spectacles of primitivism similar to the plantation acts of scantily clad Africans at freak shows and at many world expositions of the nineteenth and twentieth century, as well as early twentieth-century amusement parks that staged antics that appealed to the visual appetites of white audiences. Nadia's performative mixture further displays what Americanist and film historian Lauren Rabinovitz describes as the Orientalist-inscribed inferences of the white performer Nan Aspinwall Gable's yellowface in her racial and sexual performance as Princess Omene at amusement parks in the early twentieth century. Omene's gendered and racialized performances, argues Rabinovitz, enabled attendees to experience "a voyeuristic encounter with [perceived] foreign otherness."[32]

After her performance, Nadia returns to the squalid shack where she lives, and soon learns that her master has sold her to the show's antagonist, the jewel thief Grandis, who wishes to obtain Nadia's blue water necklace. Nadia is sold at whim, just as African slaves were, underscoring that she was seen and treated as property rather than an employee with full rights of citizenship. Before the transaction is completed, however, Jean intervenes and "saves" Nadia from Grandis and her fumbling male lackeys Sanson and Hanson by whisking her away with one of his ill-conceived inventions. Despite Jean's help, Nadia asserts her intention to remain autonomous, and she again contemplates returning to her homeland as an answer to her predicament of exile and ancestral displacement:

JEAN: I can help you get away, Nadia.
NADIA: I can get away myself, and stop using my name so casually.
JEAN: Where is home?
NADIA: I don't know.
JEAN: (*Surprised.*) Really? You forgot?
NADIA: No, I've never known. (*Nadia lowers her head and sulks while her pet lion growls.*) Yes, King. He (King) thinks that I was born in Africa. And I have a feeling he could be right. But it's so far away, and it's too large. You want to go back to Africa, King, don't you?
JEAN: Africa, that is far.

Jean realizes at this moment that his entanglement with Nadia is more than just a romantic interest, and involving himself with her escape and subsequent safety would require him to give up the comfort and privilege of his white identity and his life in Paris. This becomes apparent when Jean and Nadia arrive at his home. Jean lives with his aunt and uncle, and Jean's aunt makes it clear that if he chooses Nadia he will have to shoulder the responsibility alone when she says, "Do you expect me to take in a stranger? Did you notice her skin? Who knows what trouble she'll cause. You ask me to take in some dark skin easel and her scary pet?"[33]

Jean decides to run away from home and takes Nadia with him aboard one of his seaplanes, which allows the two to temporarily elude Grandis. Of course, the plane malfunctions, and they are left adrift in the water until they are rescued by a US submarine called the *Nautilus*, navigated by Captain Nemo, his first mate, the female character Electra, and a multinational ship crew. While aboard the submarine, Nadia and Jean meet the American scientist Professor Harrington. The *Nautilus* is a metonym for the contradictory aspects of empire in movement. The American submarine saves Nadia and Jean thereby signifying freedom, but it also symbolizes war. Despite the kindness of Professor Harrington, Captain Nemo, and First Mate Electra, Nadia warns Jean not to trust the three, and suspects that their kindness masks deception. Indeed, her mistrust of authority and her suspicion are not without merit or cause. Later in the story, the spectator learns that Captain Nemo is in actuality Nadia's father, thus changing her previous identity as an orphan.

Before Nadia learns of her legacy, however, an attack on the *Nautilus* results in a shipwreck, and Nadia and Jean find themselves on an island and captives of the Klan-masked Gargoyle, the head of the menacing Neo-Atlantean force and former prime minister of Africa.[34] Like Grandis, Gargoyle seeks Nadia's blue water necklace, but he is also a supremacist seeking to control not only Africa but also the entire world and its populations, which he views as inferior. Gargoyle initially treats Nadia and Jean with kindness, but only because he feels that his conquering the world depends on Nadia relinquishing her blue water necklace. The term "blue water" is as significant as the piece of jewelry that bears its name. "Blue water" is a naval colloquialism referring to maritime forces that operate and function in the depths of the ocean while exerting control at wide latitudes and longitudes. Nadia and her blue water navigational necklace hold the power to diffuse Gargoyle's efforts; she needs only to learn how to focus and harness her power. Indeed, Nadia and her allies defeat the Klan-masked Gargoyle by the end of the series, and in so doing, Anno presents a progressive narrative that places adolescents in the position to solve adult-made catastrophes, while also offering a critique of colorism, racism, white colonialism, and supremacy. The narrative manages to do this through humor and even, at times, silly and prolonged action sequences, but these moments bode well as comic release for the more substantial and subtle messages put forth by the show's writers. *The Secret of Blue Water* illustrates the workings and interception of empire and fulfills anime's postmodern objectives, but Nadia and Jean's relationship and the sexualization of Nadia's adolescent body require further investigation.

"The First Kiss": Nadia as Postcolonial Subject and Sexual Object

In *Nadia: The Secret of Blue Water*, Nadia is often visually presented in a sexual way, and although the show would frame Jean and Nadia's relationship as innocent, it also existed on adult terms. In one scene on the submarine, Nadia is shown showering, and when Jean gazes over at her with wide eyes and lust, she hits him in the head with a readily available object. This provides a moment of comedy and sexual autonomy for Nadia, but as the show progresses, the tension between the two inevitably leads to a sexual encounter that comes in the way of a long and lingering kiss. The initial kiss occurs in the episode "The First Kiss," which Jean forgot because he was delirious at the time. It is in the episode "King, the Lonely Lion" that a more prolonged kiss between the two serves as a metaphor for sexual intercourse. Additionally, their kiss alludes to how their inferred sexual union represents a form of sexual colonialism that threatens African sovereignty, which is signaled by the reaction of Nadia's African pet King, who witnesses the kiss and mourns it with melodramatic screeching and a flowing stream of tears:

> NADIA: Without you I'd be, I—
> JEAN: I promise to take you to your birthplace someday. (*The two of them hold hands and then intimately kiss while her pet King hides behind the bushes and sobs.*)
> NADIA: Jean . . .
> JEAN: Nadia . . . that was my first real kiss . . . was it . . . your first?
> NADIA: Jean!
> JEAN: I'm curious. Was it your first?
> NADIA: (*Screaming.*) My second!
> JEAN: (*Turning a paler white.*) Your second? Who was your first?

Jean begins to list potential "kissing partners," but Nadia demands he cease his sexual interrogation, reminds him that it is rude to ask a girl such a question, and storms off. Jean sheepishly follows her. Nadia's anger increases, and she tells Jean that the two had kissed before but that he had forgotten; Jean was indeed her first "real" kiss (see plate 14).

In this case, a kiss is not just a kiss. Rather, Jean's query serves as a veiled inquiry into Nadia's virginity. At this point in the series, the two are now fifteen, and such a scenario no doubt appealed to the show's target teen market—an audience that would identify with the awkwardness of first kisses and early sexual experiences. In compliance with the show's young-adult rating, *The Secret of Blue Water* safely turns from sexual inferences to the more innocent themes of travel, adventure, Nadia's coming to know her identity, and later, marrying Jean, which justifies their future cohabitation. Early in the series, Nadia and Jean become surrogate parents to an orphaned character named Marie, thus creating a semblance of a nuclear—albeit adolescent—family. Nadia's response to the gendered framing of Jean's queries is protofeminist, and her relationship with Jean, including their eventual marriage alluded to at the end of the series by Marie, presents a progressive vision of interracial relationships to young adults. Still, the visual representation of Nadia and of female characters in anime in general surpass vague, sexual inferences.

Female characters in anime are infused with visual and narrative codes of potent, adult sexuality, and Nadia—as depicted in the show and as developed in into an action figure and pinup—does not stray from this convention. After Nadia and Jean's first meeting, Nadia is depicted in skimpy clothing marked as African or indigenous that is ill fitting or wrapped around her body in a way that makes it appear as if she is in a perpetual state of undressing. The Nadia action figure is an example of Steinberg's tripartite marketing strategy mentioned earlier, and it is also a striking example of the intent to market adolescent sexuality.[35] Wave, a Tokyo toy and hobby company, manufactures the Nadia doll as well as an impressive number of other anime action figures.[36] Wave's male action figures are commonly in combat attire, whereas the female action figures are all scantily clothed or nude, and are positioned in sexually suggestive poses. Wave's doll offers Nadia in three distinct though related poses: first, in a circus outfit, appearing to undo the outfit's belt; second, in a white peasant dress that she raises above her thighs; and third, posing simply in her undergarments. Another action figure of Nadia shows her leaning forward as her skirt appears to fly halfway off. The aspect of the character presented in these action figures provides a visual contradiction to the more progressive autonomy voiced in the narrative of *The Secret of Blue Water*. What is one to make, then, of this visual disjuncture between a postcolonial narrative and the postmodern, adolescent, anime pinup?

Art historian Elizabeth Johns argues that the sexualization of children in nineteenth-century American genre painting became a vehicle through which adults—painters and spectators alike—would displace the anxieties of their own sexuality onto children so as to diffuse such anxieties. Viewing or creating representations of innocence, emotion, and embodiment, coupled with signs of slight disrobement and suggestive sexuality acted as a process of adult sexual cleansing and purification. Young painted bodies would therefore symbolically purify spectators' adult, sexualized thoughts.[37]

Johns's observation helps to frame and possibly explain the various media and material forms in which Nadia appears. Nadia's poses, postures, skimpy clothing, and animators slight steering into "accidental" cinematic nudity in the show situates her as an anime pinup, but one that is empty of the sexual agency one might attribute to an adult female pinup. That is to say, Nadia's illustrated sexuality constitutes consentless, sexual spectacle.

Art historian Maria Elena Buszek rightfully argues that Vargas pinups of adult women and pinups from the nineteenth through the early twenty-first centuries served many purposes with their gender-bending, monstrous beauty and "entice but not invite" gazes that contradicted "come hither glances."[38] As discussed in regard to Jackie Ormes's comic strip women, Buszek's argument is a provocative analysis of adult female sexuality that shifts the discourse of sexuality away from a progressive or regressive dichotomy to explore moments of agency, gender, and sexual transgression. Yet it is difficult to attribute such sexual agency to images of adolescent girls. As disempowered subjects by age, female minors cannot "entice but not invite" in an autonomous fashion. Rather, the sexuality they are externally imbued with (as Johns writes of nineteenth-century genre art and as Anno himself admits) serves adult and largely, though not exclusively, male sexual fantasy. A visual analysis of Nadia pinup art and film stills disseminated online by fans inform upon this sexual quandary.

In regard to the gendered and sexual politics of the gaze, in a particularly revealing and symbolically powerful image Nadia is depicted in a short, bright blue wraparound skirt and a low-cut French bandeau top. The setting is an island beachfront at night, where the reflected light of the moon and stars illuminate Nadia's dark skin. Behind Nadia, Jean sits atop a rock boulder, where, unbeknownst to Nadia, he stares at her so intensely his eyes bulge. Recall that Anno seeks to convey emotions and ideas in the faces of his characters, and in this image, Jean's gaze appears to signify the idea of penile erection. Nadia's back is turned away from his gaze, a positioning that doesn't allow the adolescent characters to confront the meaning of that gaze, but their placement within the space of the frame encourages hierarchal, sexual identification. Put another way, since Jean sits above Nadia, who appears as a larger frontal image within the frame, the viewer's gaze is drawn to the adolescent female form. Similarly, in a Nadia pinup still taken from the series, Nadia is sprawled on her back on a sandy beach in her skimpy circus costume, her thighs are bare and her skirt is tangled between her legs, which emphasizes sexual anatomy.

Nadia's vest lays open across her chest, revealing slight cleavage protruding from her bandeau top. In this pinup, however, Nadia is aware of the spectators' gaze, which is signaled by her facing an imagined spectator with an impish smile. Her hands are folded under her head, thereby allowing her bare abdomen and barely covered chest to curve forward as a focal point. Such imagery is too close to the common pose of a Vargas pinup to dismiss as unrelated to the pinup genre, and the comparison adds to the adult sexual inferences of anime production and consumption.

In another print image, Nadia sits in a chair wearing a blue-and-white sailor top that falls off her shoulder, revealing her cleavage; she innocently smiles back at the spectator. This print is strikingly similar to a painting by the nineteenth-century child-theme genre artist Lilly Martin Spencer. In Spencer's 1889 painting *The Height of Fashion*, a young Black American girl wears a white dress that falls off her shoulder, suggesting perhaps eventual disrobement; the young girl holds a magnifying lens up to her right eye as she innocently smiles back at an assumed spectator. In these two images, the postures and slight disrobement insinuate sexuality, but the innocent and impish smiles deflect overt, sexual overtones.

Film stills disseminated online at anime fan sites and Nadia sketchbooks for sale are sexual as well. Both include illustrations in which Nadia is swimming underwater with her bottom undergarments seemingly absent, and frolicking in the water or bathing her pet lion in the ocean as she spreads her legs and leans over to reveal cleavage that most fourteen-year-old girls would lack. These depictions and their dissemination have a historical legacy and constitute calculated marketing. In the words of Hideaki Anno, "Some characters are made to be sexy, others not. You need to understand that Japanese animation is an industry that is, for the most part, male, and ... everything is made for their gratification. Further, it is more gratifying for us to draw this sort of character, rather than old grandmothers."[39]

Scholars of anime and girl culture appropriately pause to locate female anime characters as powerful, especially when they are involved in fighting injustice, but still argue that anime's sexual overtones remain problematic. Cultural critic Susan Napier writes that anime productions "show images of powerful women (albeit highly sexualized)," and J. Keith Vincent writes that these characters are "overtly sexualized, always intensely cute, and often a mixture of both," thereby constituting an anime formula of what Japanese psychiatrist Saitō Tamaki defines as the contradictory location of "the beautiful fighting girl." The beautiful fighting girl—one who fights criminality and injustice while being depicted as "cute and sexy"—is a trope that saturates anime. For Tamaki, the beautiful fighting girl is a phallic representation—not of a real woman but of a fictive sexual imaginary of illustrators and spectators. Vincent, drawing from Tamaki's work, explains the sexual phenomenon and spectatorship of anime in this way:

> [Female anime characters] are phallic girl[s] whose unbridled *jouissance* lends reality to the fiction spaces she inhabits ... a drawn image of a beautiful girl with no referent in reality. The beautiful fighting girl is not a reflection of sociological reality or even of a desire for a certain reality but a perverse fantasy that functions to recathect and invest with a new reality, to animate. [A female anime character is] a sexual object that threatens to dissolve into fiction [for] anime and manga makers and fans for whom the beautiful fighting girl represents an unattainable yet irresistible sexual object.[40]

Understanding a broader psychology of their production locate the girls of anime into an imaginary and fictive space for which, according to Tamaki, they never seem to leave. But do such interpretations of nuance and theoretical proffering about adolescent characters occlude the meanings behind the materialization of the anime form when performed by and consumed by adults?

Images of Nadia in anime stills and in pinup art leave little question as to the intent of producers and some anime fans to displace adult sexuality onto the character. Further, adult women who dress as Nadia in seductively posed photo shoots on websites directed at men and at conventions such as Anime Expo and Comic-Con show the powerful effect of the character on young and adult fans of anime. Nadia cosplay, as it is called in the world of comics, offers an opportunity to live out the contradictions of innocence and potent sexuality as safely depicted in an adolescent anime character. The 2012 news headlines about Anastasiya Shpagina, a nineteen-year-old Ukrainian woman who transformed herself to look like an anime character, attests to this hypothesis. Shpagina is more than simply an example of what some may consider extreme fandom-turned-obsession.[41] Anime girl performance is contiguous with the much-lauded and -criticized Harajuku girl subculture,[42] as well as the long-established tradition of adult entertainment in which women present themselves and perform as sexual objects in private schoolgirl attire. Shpagina's transformation from an average young woman to a fairy-looking-girl with large, painted doe eyes, powder-white skin, long fuchsia hair, and a corset-enhanced waist replicates the common look of female anime characters. Such fan performances of anime identity may be empowering and fulfilling for adult female fans by providing an opportunity to vicariously usurp the power of a "beautiful fighting girl." In contrast, adolescent anime pinups underscore that the appetites these illustrations are meant to fill constitute more than the insinuation of innocent flirtation.

Anno's first feature film *Love & Pop* (1998) amplifies my argument about the complex and calculated nature of anime sexuality given his similar characterization of schoolgirl prostitutes in Japan, where high-school-age teens seek sexual autonomy and economic freedom as dates for hire. *Love & Pop* presents their life as a seedy dystopia rather than as a prescriptive film that is pro–adolescent prostitution. Still, the DVD sleeve uses the following titillating caption: "Schoolgirls by day... call girls by night..." Four teens in private-school attire are pictured at the top of the DVD sleeve, while at the bottom the same teens are shown in underwear of childish prints in garish colors. The film's fantasy narrative presents young girls willing to sell their bodies for pleasure, though not always for sex, and to provide company for middle-aged men. Responsibility of the men or "Johns" is extinguished by typifying them as pitiful rubes who are controlled by manipulative teenage girls. This type of narrative framing is a common upside-down rationale of distorted predatory psychology, where an idea is posited that young girls are seducers of older men and therefore deserving of any sexual exploitation that comes their way. Such rationales underpin the sexualization of the adolescent anime form.

Taken out of context of the television show and transformed into adolescent sexualized icon, Nadia leaves the realm of empowered, self-reliant, and autonomous girlhood and lands in the realm of adult sexual fetish. Interpretations of the show and a walking through of the myriad of ways spectatorship is experienced by fans of different ages and of various ethnicities across the globe situates *The Secret of Blue Water* as an international force. Yet the more muddled area of fandom's deluge into anime body adornment and the adult world of Nadia cosplay is similar to—as discussed with the transformation and sexualization of the character Catwoman across various media forms—the visual and narrative wars that comic book and graphic novel producers have faced since the mid-twentieth century. Insofar as anime and its print sister manga are concerned, because both forms focus heavily on adolescent characters, unlike graphic novels that feature adult characters, the consumption and dissemination of anime and manga at times tips the sexual scale to adolescent exploitation. This has led to US and Canadian courts waging war against using the genre for predatory ends.

Not all anime and manga steers toward adolescent-themed sexuality; the shows on the Anime Network at times have MA (mature audience) ratings but are not categorized as pornographic. Yet the genre has crossed the line and expanded into this area. In 2008, an Iowa man was arrested after a postal inspector determined that the books that he had ordered from Japan contained obscene sexual content. Law enforcement seized his collection of over twelve thousand volumes of manga, hundreds of anime DVDs and VHS tapes, and computers. Given that it is "a crime to knowingly produce, distribute, receive, or possess with intent to distribute, a visual depiction of any kind, including a drawing, cartoon, sculpture, or painting, that is, or appears to be a minor engaged in sexual conduct," the fan was prosecuted for his collection.[43]

Similarly, in 2011, a twenty-year-old American man was arrested for the images of the manga and anime character "Magical Girl Lyrical Nanoha" that were on his laptop. Canadian customs agents searched his computer and found what they deemed pornographic images. Magical Girl, like other popular anime characters, such as Sailor Moon, wears attire that is a mix of schoolgirl and sailorgirl. The clothing on Magical Girl, Sailor Moon, and most female anime characters is drawn tight and clingy to show cleavage and figures uncommon for most prepubescent girls. The Comic Book Legal Defense Fund (CBLDF) put together a coalition to defend the man, who faced criminal charges for the possession and importation of child pornography.[44] This landmark case has led the CBLDF to advise American comics fans not to transport manga or anime images across the US border until the case is resolved. Determination of the criminality of the distribution and consumption of these images will continue to occur in a court of law, but that the man had such images in electronic form as extracted from manga into fan art shows an affinity for the character and a desire to view and store the character's sexualized imagery. Nadia's visual sexualization is thus part of a larger network of anime girl dissemination that is not just a question of psychological and theoretical explanation; when couched within the legal parameters of pornographic illustration and dissemination, it may constitute a crime.

The Secret of Blue Water and the Epistemologies of Empire

In narrative form, *Nadia: The Secret of Blue Water* remarks upon the process of empire in movement. As a character within the diegesis of the television show, Nadia, and especially her characterology and dialogue, constitutes a transpacific subjectivity that marks transnational and postcolonial subaltern agency in the face of racialization. The show contained a politically progressive narrative disseminated and consumed through global cultural circuits. Many of the show's characterizations constituted an intervention from the tendency to propagate formulaic, fetishized, and palatable narratives of Japanese cool that the business of anime fosters. Hideaki Anno's televisual dream for an African girl in some ways departed from such conventions and served as an accessible narrative regarding what psychiatrist and theorist Frantz Fanon observed as the colonial culture's tendency toward a priori or highly subjective attitude in regard to the African subject in the wake of colonialism, thereby asserting the character as an example of resistance.[45] Yet the circulation of Nadia's image and the displacement of adult sexuality onto her adolescent body represents an entanglement pertaining to how the character is also a product of an a priori logic of capitalism's propagation of sexual empire.

Following the television series, a film featuring Nadia was released in which she has left Jean to find work in London as a quasi reporter and freedom fighter. *Nadia The Secret of Blue Water: The Motion Picture* contained some brief nudity but still secured a teen rating. Fans panned the film version for its recycled footage of the television series and its disappointing treatment of Nadia and Jean's rocky romance. Market cross-fertilization and digital dissemination continues to make the show accessible to a new generation of fans, and the character's image remains a popular one that women of color emulate and fans disseminate online, thus asserting Nadia's ongoing relevance to the representation of women of African descent in sequential art. Following *The Secret of Blue Water*'s first run, in the late twentieth century through the early twenty-first century, Black women artists' and writers' work show how anime and manga are one of the biggest influences on their stylistic choices. Through an explication of their comics, and as presented in their own words, they convey how their production and consumption of comic books, graphic novels, manga, and anime eschews sexual stereotypes and helps to reconstitute identity, reform subcultural practices, and renew Black cultural politics through an interexchange of visual and music expression.

PLATES 12, 13 Film stills from Hideaki Anno, "The Girl at the Eiffel Tower," *Nadia: The Secret of Blue Water*, NHK (Japan Network), Anime Network (US and Canada Network), Gainax, ADV films, 1990–91.

PLATE 14 Film still from Hideaki Anno, "King, the Lonely Lion," *Nadia: The Secret of Blue Water*, NHK (Japan Network), Anime Network (US and Canada Network), Gainax, ADV films, 1990–91.

PLATE 15 Rashida Jones, *Frenemy of the State* #2 (2010). Courtesy of Oni Press.

PLATE 16 Afua Richardson, "Niobe" (2014). From *The Untamed*™
and © Stranger Comics. Courtesy of Afua Richardson.

PLATE 17 Afua Richardson, "Bubbles" (2013). Courtesy of Afua Richardson.

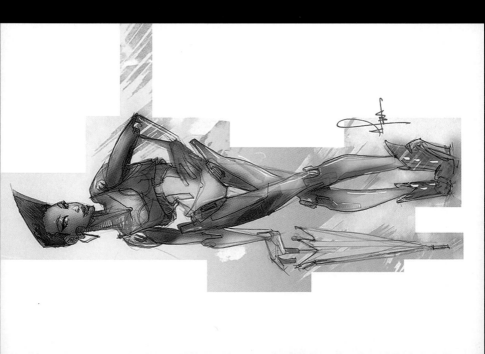

PLATE 18 Afua Richardson, "Robochique" (2013). Courtesy of Afua Richardson.

Legacy of Light
the light of day

①

PLATE 19 Nara Walker, *Legacy of Light* (2006). Courtesy of Nara Walker.

PLATE 20 Ashley Woods, *Millennia Wars* (2010). Courtesy of Ashley Woods.

PLATE 21 Ashley Woods, *Millennia Wars* (2010). Courtesy of Ashley Woods.

PLATE 22 Roberto Aguirre-Sacasa (w), Tonci Zonjic (p), *Marvel Divas* (2009).

WHERE I'M COMING FROM

Black Female Artists and Postmodern Comix

When they unearth the time capsule for the nineties ... Barbara's contribution to our times will make the Top Ten. She's a New Age storyteller. None of us is safe from [her] incisive humor, the crying shame, the truth-funny and not-so-funny-of our lives.

—Actors Ruby Dee and Ossie Davis

I'm merely holding up a mirror ... if you see something in that mirror that makes you uncomfortable, maybe it's a call for self-evaluation.

—Barbara Brandon-Croft, *People Magazine*

BARBARA Brandon-Croft was the first syndicated Black female cartoonist to publish in mainstream newspapers, and one of eight Black cartoonists syndicated as of 2013. Brandon-Croft majored in illustration at Syracuse University.[1] Her comic strip *Where I'm Coming From* (1989–2005), a *Detroit Free Press* weekly installment, reached 1.5 million readers, and gained a broader readership when it went national in 1991.[2] In the strip, Brandon-Croft animated the personal lives and social commentary of a visually diverse group of Black women: Alisha, Cheryl, Dee, Jackie, Judy, Lekesia, Lydia, Monica, Nicole, and Sonya.[3] Brandon-Croft's characters discuss romantic love; the Clinton and Bush administrations; race, color, gender, and class disparities; and human and sexual rights. In

a visual space in which women's bodies often serve as exploitive signifiers, Brandon-Croft shifts the aesthetic in comics by presenting only the heads and hands of her characters. In

5.1 Barbara Brandon-Croft, *Where I'm Still Coming From* (1994), 56.

an *Essence* magazine feature in 1990, Brandon-Croft explained her decision to use talking heads by explaining, "I don't draw bodies. Women are always thought of in terms of their bodies. You'll see heads [in my comics] because that's where my character's minds are."[4] In an interview in the *New York Times*, she stated, "We are too often summed up by our body parts . . . and black women are at the bottom of the totem pole. I'm saying 'We have opinions,' and 'Look me in the eye and talk to me.'"[5]

Brandon-Croft's comic was drawn and printed in black and white. She used thick sharp lines, pronounced yet varied ethnic features and hairstyles, and expressive, freely moving arms and hands. Her direct and didactic dialogue appears under her talking heads without callout bubbles, and her characters' voices discuss complicated cultural problems with pithy and vernacularly inflected language. Each week, readers had the opportunity to play the role of eavesdropper to the colorful conversations between Brandon-Croft's main characters and their relatives, male friends, and suitors. In many installments, however, characters speak directly to the reader. In so doing, Brandon-Croft encourages readers to invest in the knowledge she imparts, and challenges each reader to take a position on the historically situated and socially charged topic of her comic strip.

5.2 Barbara Brandon-Croft, *Where I'm Coming From*, (1993), 87.

Brandon-Croft's insightful dialogues and dialogic monologues took the topics of the day as their subject matter, paying particular attention to the power dynamics entrenched within hierarchies of race, gender, color, sexuality, and class. After the Rodney King trial and Los Angeles uprising in 1992,[6] Brandon-Croft published a single panel with the words "We *can* all get along" on a brick wall, with her character Lekesia in the corner holding a sign that reads, "when there's equal justice."[7] On the sexual politics of the military during the Clinton administration and of president Bill Clinton's "Don't ask, don't tell" policy of 1993, Cheryl and Alisha exchange thoughts on the character Dee, sharing that she is queer-identified.[8] The two joke that while coming out is a truth that will give Dee "a new lease on life," and that "the truth will set you free," they conclude that this is only true if "you're [not] about to join Clinton's military."[9] On the subject of the marginalization of diverse family structures during the Bush administration, Lekesia queries, "Family values.... I've yet to have someone explain that term to me.... Would that be valuing one family over another?" The interplay of workplace racism and sexism is also an ongoing topic for Lekesia. After her boss chastises her decision to read Black history books on her lunch break and accuses her of segregating herself, she answers, "I guess we had good teachers; the idea of segregation wasn't something *we* invented."[10]

In one strip, the characters Nicole and Cheryl discuss the insidious view that one Black woman speaks for all Black women, while at the same time remarking on the sexual assault trial of boxer Mike Tyson in 1992.[11] After Cheryl is asked by a reporter what Black women think about Mike Tyson's conviction, she tells her friend Nicole, "I [said], 'sorry, as of yet, I haven't spoken to every Black woman in America.'"[12] Brandon-Croft's character Monica takes on colorism when she divulges, "I come from a long line of 'high yellow negroes,' but is that any cause for 'my so-called sister' to say to me, 'You don't even know what it's like to be Black.'" Brandon-Croft uses Black vernacular and decries, "Ain't life a trip?" (i.e., erroneous and unpredictable) and concludes about the politics of color and race, "This is America where as far as racism is concerned . . . it doesn't matter if you're light or dark . . . it's the fact that you aren't white."[13]

Instead of providing unrealistic accounts of romantic liaisons, Brandon-Croft paints a humorous picture of heterosexual courtship. Cheryl asks Lekesia how she reconciles unabashedly flirting with men with being a feminist, and Lekesia replies with a wide smile, "I don't deny women the right to be sexy. . . . I'm just saying that is not all that we are."[14] When Judy asks Nicole how she managed to get rid of a man she was not interested in, but who was in pursuit of her, Nicole replies, "Simple. I started calling [him back]."[15] Alisha tries to fix her brother up with one of her friends but finds it an impossible task because, as her brother says over the phone, Judy is "too chunky" and Lekesia is "too headstrong." None of Judy's friends fits her brother's needs because to him female partnership means having a caretaker with sexual benefits, or, as he says, "I need a woman who can take care of the homefront when I'm gone, and take care of me when I'm home." Alisha, exasperated by her brother's shallow and antiquated idea of womanhood, responds to him with sarcasm by saying, "Well, good luck. You deserve everything you don't get!"[16] Judy, making a perfunctory follow-up call weeks after a blind date, suffers an emotional bait and switch when, after an overly formal verbal exchange, the former suitor admits that when he said "We must do this again," he was "just being polite."[17] In these strips, Brandon-Croft depicts the experiences of everyday life with a mixture of relatable, funny, and sometimes controversial topics.

Brandon-Croft's comic strip art is postmodernism at its best, given her embrace of yet break with traditional and culturally experimental comic strips. *Where I'm Coming From* draws upon the talking head approach of one of her strongest influences, *Village Voice* contributor and Pulitzer Prize–winning comic artist Jules Feiffer.[18] Like Feiffer, Brandon-Croft's profile images center the cerebral and direct the reader's eye to the character's facial and hand expressions to visually depict mood, emotion, tone, and intent. Brandon-Croft's comic strip depicts blackness in its complexity and diversity and fulfills what cultural critic bell hooks argues is the criterion for postmodern blackness: a "radical practice . . . conceptualized as a 'politics of difference' [that] incorporate[s] the voices of displaced, marginalized, exploited, and oppressed black people." hooks continues, "If radical postmodernist thinking is to have a transformative impact . . . it must be reflected in habits of being, including styles of writing as well as chosen subject matter."[19] Unlike many forms of Black popular culture, *Where I'm Coming From* does not depict the problems of cultural life in isolation; Brandon-Croft encourages critical consciousness. At the same time, she does not reduce blackness to a monolith but instead depicts it as a shifting identity composed of color, sexuality, class, and gender differences.

Though Brandon-Croft did experience mainstream success in the 1990s, some newspapers did pass on carrying the comic because, according to her, they viewed *Where I'm Coming From* as "too Black" and therefore not marketable.[20] Despite such criticism, Brandon-Croft's approach to the comic strip remained consistent throughout the years, which was similar to the midcentury defiance of Jackie Ormes. Brandon may have been inspired by the longevity of her cartoonist father, Brumsic Brandon Jr., one of the first Black cartoonists to gain mainstream syndication in the 1940s. Brandon Jr. experienced an increase in popularity in the 1960s with his socially conscious comic strip *Luther*, which focused on working-class struggles, urban blight, and civil rights. While growing up, Barbara Brandon-Croft had worked alongside her father in an apprentice role.[21] Jackie Ormes and Brandon's father made use of sequential art to forge social commentary, but, as with many Black cartoonists of an earlier era, some of the content seemed beholden to various aspects of Black respectability. In the late twentieth century, the postmodern impulse of Barbara Brandon-Croft and the Black women who came after her eliminated this constraint from their art, helping to usher in defiant and experimental frames of narratology, form, and language. As actors and activists Ruby Dee and Ossie Davis opined in the foreword to a collection of Brandon-Croft's comic strips, "She is showing and telling us about ourselves as if through a funhouse mirror."[22]

Where I'm Coming From anchors a discussion about the postmodern turn and cultural work of contemporary comix by Black women. Within the field of sequential art, the term "comix" refers to socially relevant, underground, and independent forms of comics. In the twenty-first century, Black women comix artists and writers engage with the idea of a post-Black aesthetic that does not suggest a break with historical formations of blackness in comics, graphic novels, or anime. Instead, they call into question the very idea of blackness, as well as archaic ways of seeing and understanding the process of nation making and its collision with the cultural politics of difference. Comic art by Leisl Adams, Michelle Billingsley, Rashida Jones, Rashida Lewis, Afua Richardson, Nara Walker, and Ashley Woods—most of whom are members of the comix coalition the Ormes Society—offers an artistic bricolage and new episteme of blackness.[23] This assemblage of visual and narrative parts takes on four sometimes interrelated affective and artistic forms:[24] Afroanime, Afrofuturism, Afrophantasmagoria, and Afropunk. An interweaving of these conceptual frameworks with the artist's voices, narratives, and visual framing is not to uncritically overdetermine their comix within container categories that they may not use to describe their work. Rather, it is to engage with and bracket their art in visual, theoretical, and practical terms. In so doing, I underscore the artistic efficacy, possibilities, and originality of Black women's comix and the organizing body, that is, the Ormes Society, that contributes to their visibility.[25]

The Ormes Society and Black Women's Comix

The Ormes Society is an electronic conglomeration of a large majority of Black women comic writers and artists that supports and promotes Black women's comix via the virtual cybersphere. Formed by comic artist Cheryl Lynn Eaton in 2007, the society, as an organizing body and as a website portal, serves two primary functions. First, it places Black women artists in the field of sequential art in contact with one another, thereby acting as a vital professional network. Second, the organization's website contains an ongoing archive of members' work. Though the organization's namesake was an obvious choice, in a CNN interview, Eaton explained the significance of Jackie Ormes to the field of comics and Black representation as a whole: "Finding [Ormes's] work was like opening the door to a lost world. Her work should be collected and shelved next to peers such as Will Eisner."[26] In regard to the larger cultural work of the Ormes Society and their presence on the Internet, Eaton says, "I wanted to use the organization as a way to fend off creative isolation and to build a support network of like-minded individuals. I think all of these organizations and sites . . . help to dispel the cookie-cutter stereotype surrounding female readers. . . . We don't look the same, we don't create the same work, we don't read the same comics, but we'd all like to be respected."[27]

Eaton's initiative affirms the vital role of building counterinstitutional organizations and the Internet as a viable site for the dissemination and recognition of comix. In my interviews with Black women writers and artists, all spoke to the role of the Ormes Society in their work and viewed it as a worthy venture. Of course, building counterinstitutions as a response to unequal circumstances within established institutions is not new; this has always been a constructive strategy for historically marginalized groups and aggrieved populations. Yet, with the Ormes Society's electronic reach, Twitter, Facebook, Tumblr, Instagram, Pinterest, and Blogger—all powerful social networking portals offering images and videos—have become technological conduits to disperse the women's work in a global market. Electronic posts of sample comics link back to the artists' websites, allowing readers to learn more, make purchases, and, in the case of webcomix artists, read their work online free of cost. The exposure that the society provides has allowed webcomix writer, artist, animator, and children's book author Leisl Adams (*On the Edge, Monsters Under the Bed*) to secure paid assignments: "I've actually gotten some freelance work through the site," says Adams. "It's a nice feeling to see that there are other women like me out there trying to make their living as an artist, and we can keep up with each other's work."[28] Artist Afua Richardson positions the Ormes Society within the context of the male-dominated comic book world:

> Okay, let's be real here. This is a big ole' Boys club (the comic industry) [and there are] no girls allowed unless they can play tough too. The Ormes Society is doing great work by just making these names and faces known. I know for me a BIG part of my NOT thinking that I could do comics was not seeing anyone looking like me at conventions. Lucky for me, I was a tomboy and that never bothered me. If I could believe I could do it, I did it. Though I'm not at the top of the food chain, I'm not sure I care to be. If I can encourage someone along the way, [then] doing comics is worth every sleepless night in front of the computer.[29]

The Ormes Society constitutes postmodernism in an organizational form. Sociologist Stuart Hall points out that an understanding of postmodernism as a permanent break with all aspects of modernism and traditionalism inhibits its possible use as an analytical tool or strategy that can incorporate the best of the old while it reimagines cultural forms, ideas, and politics within new epistemological frames.[30] The organizational structure of the society and the work of artists affiliated with it show that today's comix artists are standing on the shoulders of giants, from whom they get inspiration even as they forge innovative and experimental directions in the field.

Examining the work of Black women comix artists and writers means contemplating a host of difficult questions in regard to postmodern blackness, including considering whether it is too restrictive to label their work "Black" as a whole. When depictions of blackness are absent in comix by Black women, can such work qualify as aesthetically "Black?" How does what Richard Iton describes as the "Black fantastic" in popular culture offer an opportunity to see the narrative and aesthetic choices of Black women comix artists and writers as exhibiting emergent postmodernism? In what ways does an examination of comix in relationship to Afroanime, Afrofuturism, Afrophantasmagoria, and Afropunk allow for a rethinking of the interconnection between art, racial difference, politics, and creativity? I grapple with these questions through a description of the characters and of the fantastical, affective worlds that Black women artists and writers bring to life.

Afroanime is an amalgam of Black cultural politics, postmodern narratives, and the visual aesthetics of Japanese animation. Afrofuturism describes science fiction narratives with postmodern interpretations of blackness and interspecies relations. Afrophantasmagoria is a mélange of fantasy and dream imagery with hybrid identities that signify blackness and/or broader configurations of difference. Afropunk is a subcultural identity of music, visual style, and consciousness inspired by the soundscapes of punk rock, alternative soul, hip-hop, and trip-hop. Taken together, these articulated visual, narrative, and, in some cases, music and lived stylistic choices constitute Afrofusion comix. The prefix for each aesthetic form culturally contextualizes rather than limits the narrative strategies by Black women writing, drawing, and producing underground and independent comics. This is not to say that all Black women doing comix do "Black comics," something that the "Afro" prefix in my theorization of their aesthetic choices may seem to signify in essentialist haste. It is to say, however, that artists work from their diverse origins of identity and experiences that can mark, unmark, and reconfigure categories—or, more specifically, de-essentialize blackness and other identity categories—even as they inhabit, partially represent, or reject such categories. In other words, to think through their comix in terms of blackness makes the best argument for rethinking what blackness and "Black art" encompass as a whole. Black postmodern comix (BPCs) are extraterrestrial, musical, futuristic, multiracial, multinational, multiclass, insurgent, humorous, male, female, transgender, heterosexual, pansexual, queer, contradictory, and powerful; they constitute a diverse and imaginary *fantastical world*.

Richard Iton writes that the "Black fantastic" in popular culture comprises "the experiences of the underground, the vagabond, and those constituencies marked as deviant." Additionally, as a product of postmodern blackness, the Black fantastic reveals "notions of being that are inevitably aligned within, in conversation with, against, and articulated beyond the boundaries of the modern."[31] Such elements, I argue, exist within the articulated genres of Afroanime, Afrofuturism, Afrophantasmagoria, and Afropunk—an Afrofusion blend that is present in the work of Black women's comix. Exemplary of this mixture are Nara Walker's *Legacy of Light: The Light of Day* (2010) and *Songbirds* (2011), and Rashida Lewis's *Sandstorm* (2007). These three titles crystalize the attendant possibilities of a collision between Afrophantasmagoria, Afropunk, and Afroanime. Walker produces fantasy-themed manga with complex constructions of affect, gender, and sexual difference in the musical world of Afropunk, while Lewis appears to trope anime characters such as Nadia (from *Nadia: The Secret of Blue Water*) to offer a viewpoint of *Afrafemcentric*, that is to say, African and feminist liberation.[32] Leisl Adams's *Monsters Under the Bed* (2007) and *On the Edge: Tales from the Therapist's Couch* (2003) and Ashley Woods's *Millennia Wars* (2009) push the boundaries of Afrofuturism through their mixture of an implied Black aesthetic or critical consciousness with science fiction and anthropomorphic narratives. Adams uses cyborg elves and demonic animals to signify difference, affect, and mental anxiety, whereas Woods depicts planetary and human extinction using racially diverse, extraterrestrial, and elf characters to fight for their survival and for social justice.

Afua Richardson, a comic book illustrator and musician, draws curvaceous women who have Afrofuturism, Afropunk, and Afroanime cool; she contributes artwork to a host of independent comic listings, including the popular *Pilot* (2008) and *Genius* (2014) series distributed by the indie label Top Cow. Writer, producer, and actor Rashida Jones presents a plot of intrigue with riot grrrl rebellion in her politically focused and transnational comic book *Frenemy of the State* (2010)—a comic featuring an heiress whom the Central Intelligence Agency (CIA) hires as a spy. Michelle Billingsley's webcomix *Joe!* is a family themed comic. The protagonist, Joe, like Ormes's Patty-Jo, is young, mischievous, funny, and culturally profound. The work of all of these women, like that of Barbara Brandon-Croft, finds humor in "where they are coming from." Unlike Brandon-Croft, many reach beyond the depiction of the Black subject and the Black interior world to confront readers with transnational, transcultural, and transhuman subjects. Their movement across international and geographical borders, across cultural divides, and beyond human/animal/species distinctions defines these Black women artists and their postmodern comix as generative of familiar and new sequential subjects.

Absence, Presence, and Afropunk in the Comix of Rashida Jones and the Art of Afua Richardson

In an essay about visuality and affect in the catalogue for the exhibition *'Toonskin: Blackness in Sequential Art*, I explain how artists and writers constitute and reflect upon Black consciousness in a myriad of ways, including their choice to make blackness absent, present, or present through visual absence.[33] Artists represented in the exhibition reframe visual scripts of blackness even when blackness is not in the artistic productions they create. Black consciousness is an invisible designing hand or a concentrated decision to press beyond the parameters of one racial-ethnic identity to forge retractable skins of identification. The Black subject, then, is reconfigured, and artists can create new meanings and new ways of thinking through mapping and inciting a progression of feeling about how and why blackness appears and disappears in sequential art, and the possibilities in re-creating (dis)appearance. I call this process the "affective progression of blackness," or the embodied way artists layer images and visually narrate meaning through absence and presence to move spectators emotionally, thereby making sequential art anew. I maintain throughout this book that sequential art is relevant to the "structures of feeling"[34] inherent in the corporeality of a given aesthetic choice to depict or not to depict blackness. Comix creator Rashida Jones, known best as an actor, writer, producer, and the daughter of musician/producer Quincy Jones and actor Peggy Lipton, and comix artist and musician Afua Richardson are prime case studies to begin this theoretical inquiry.

Rashida Jones's *Frenemy of the State* shows nation making as a process by which a country initiates and induces its constituents into upholding its values and national agenda through aggressively seeking their consent. Jones claims to have based the main protagonist of the comix, Ariana Von Holmberg, on the US socialite Paris Hilton:

> Back when Paris [Hilton] was at her height of fame and people were just obsessed with her, I had this funny notion that she's actually some crazy genius who . . . was just conducting this elaborate anthropological study on the world. . . . That was sort of where the idea for this comic started. . . . I thought, "Wouldn't it be interesting to give somebody like Paris Hilton another layer? What if her fame is something more than just an overwhelming need to be an object of desire?" Ariana [in *Frenemy of the State*] is a little bit reluctant to be in the spotlight, and there's a sadness to that.[35]

Though coded as white, Von Holmberg could serve as Jones's visual doppelganger. Von Holmberg appears as a critique of conspicuous consumption and the socialite lifestyle. When the CIA asks Von Holmberg to spy on one of her "frenemies," Haven Douglass, and elects her as an operative, she reluctantly agrees and soon finds herself leaping out of the window of a skyscraper and traveling abroad to intervene in an illegal weapons sale between Russia and Saudi Arabia. During her first mission, as diverse onlookers below her gasp in fear, Arianna leaps from a window and lands on the pole of an American flag, and pulls herself up over the pole to safety.[36] Her maneuvering around the flag is representative of the series, as she is as much at war with what the United States represents in the comic book—that is, militarism, neoliberalism, and surveillance—as she in alignment with its avowed assets (i.e., freedom, autonomy, and democracy). In this way, "the state" is her frenemy and she is simultaneously a frenemy of the state. She holds no superpowers, nor does she have the dual identity that most comic book heroes possess. Von Holmberg is an antihero in the Catwoman tradition, drawing her strength from learned physical training and relying upon her timely sarcasm and wit to get her out of difficult situations (see plate 15).

Jones's protagonist seems reminiscent of her own status as a Black/multiracial Hollywood outsider/insider, allowing her to critique that world from the inside and from the outside. In so doing, Von Holmberg reads like a character with the subconscious one might attribute to a racial-ethnic minority, making blackness simultaneously absent and present for strategic reasons. Ariana is part of the white affluent world she inhabits, but she seems to resent much of what that world stands for, and she repeatedly questions the state's assumptions about those deemed foreign and therefore dangerous.

In the third installment of the series, Von Holmberg goes to Saudi Arabia to visit a friend and a prince whom the US government believes is harboring and trying to sell nuclear weapons. Von Holmberg doubts the prince's guilt. She critiques the harboring of weapons of mass destruction rhetoric espoused by the CIA and asserts her autonomy by assessing the situation using her own intellect rather than relying on the fear-stirring tactics of those she reports to.[37] There are essentialist moments when the story line oscillates between presenting Saudi men as clownish patriarchs and anti-American terrorists or accommodating "Americanized" capitalists, but Ariana is a complex character who plays by the rules only to subvert those rules through audacious posturing and defiant dialogue.[38] Her femaleness and her wealth lead the CIA and the men around her to underestimate her strength and her ability to problem solve, which she uses in her favor to maneuver through her undercover missions. *Frenemy of the State*'s relevance therefore derives from its imbuing the lead character with a dimensionality that runs counter to superficial appearances. Even those who seem the most innocuous, the comic title suggests, such as the socialite Ariana Von Holmberg, can act as an arm of the state while critiquing the role she plays as a mechanism of state enforcement.

Frenemy of the State's Ariana Von Holmberg serves Black presence through absence in the tradition of Afropunk cultural politics. As Rubén Ramírez Sánchez says of Afropunk subculture, "Even as Black punks choose identifications that conflict with traditional notions of Blackness, these identifications serve to reaffirm Black identity."[39] Artist Jeff Wamester draws Von Holmberg real-sized and muscular, wearing a mixture of nerd and punk clothing, and a riot grrrl sneer, and Jones, with collaborators Christina Weir and Nunzio DeFilippis, writes the protagonist as a nonconformist white Other within a dominant conformist culture. Given that Afropunk is an experience and a stance that is simultaneously part of a subcultural community and culturally distinct and conscious at the same time, Von Holmberg is a quintessential punk icon. She derives her identity from aligning herself with marginalized communities even as she embraces parts of the dominant cultural milieu. As with Frank Miller's Martha Washington, *Frenemy of the State* asks readers to complicate the role of the United States in global militarism and to question military policies abroad. Individuals, the comic shows, can be resistant to aspects of nation making that rely on demonizing segments of the world for behavior it employs, yet casts as problematic when propagated by those deemed unfit for self-government.

Afropunk encompasses a do-it-yourself (DIY) visual aesthetic that includes reappropriations of punk culture, and its ideology hinges on the political aspects of reclaiming public space via the utilization of new technologies. The art of Afua Richardson references aspects of Afrofuturism and Afropunk via her ability to visualize this aesthetic, as well as through the musicality and subcultural iconic references of her characters. In regard to the musicality of her work, Richardson says, "Music [inspires me to create]. It's my blood and bones. I've been a musician going on 20 years now—probably a professional for half that time and the visual induction music serves in my life is vital to my creation. I'm also very inspired by artists such as Hiroaki Samura, Chris Buchalo, and Claire Wendling; I've sat a great many hours staring at their work."[40] Richardson also describes her work as a mixture of "sci-fi, the occult, catastrophism, experimental biology, aliens, and monsters," but many of her sketches and commissioned artworks consist of images of Black women (see plate 16).[41]

In her sketch of the comic book and graphic novel character Storm from *X-Men*, Richardson portrays the character with a sharply cut white Mohawk, dark angular brows, and an assertive stare. Richardson uses a technique similar to that of Barbara Brandon-Croft in drawing the viewer's eye toward Storm's facial expressions and her thoughts rather than her body. In the sketch "Bubbles," Richardson presents a character with a curly pink Afro that frames her face, a matching pink eye thickly lined in black that peeks out from the curly wisps, and a large bubble pipe positioned at her lips. The woman in the image appears racially coded as Black, yet her hair and eye color are playful alternatives to the phenotypical traits associated with blackness (see plate 17).

In the sketch "Robochique," sharp, angular lines compose a woman leaning on an umbrella; she has a purple Mohawk, purple eyes, purple lips, diamond-shaped earrings, and short purple latex boots. Her clothing is a hybrid of punk and robot, asserting the character as an amalgam of Afrofuturism and Afropunk stylization (see plate 18). "Robochique" is not void of sexuality; rather, she presents a sexual posture reflective of the artist's commitment to re-ink and therefore rethink the sexuality of Black women in comics: "I want to paint eroticism how I see it—cheeky and funny and space age. I try, in my non-erotic comics, to capture that same form of appeal. Perhaps not soaked in the content of adult themes, I always want my character to be appealing. As a comic creator, you are capturing the peak or pivotal moment in your character's motion. So the most flattering pose usually ends up being the one that appears sexy, which creates the most dynamic lines and shapes."[42]

Richardson's use of assertive and strategic sexuality is complementary to that of Black female comic creators such as C. Spike Trotman, an editor who works in web and print comics, and is an activist in the Afropunk tradition.[43] Though Richardson's aesthetic choices are more subtly sexual and Afropunk than Trotman's erotic comic art, her unpredictable depictions of female characters (re)present Black presence to viewers in a way that questions and rages against imagery associated with blackness and femaleness in the popular imagination. Her colorful choices for hair, eyes, dress, and unpredictable poses align with an Afropunk and Afrofuturist stylization that seeks to present the adorned body individualistically while at the same time presenting aesthetic codes of visible blackness. Addressing the lack of Black female comic characters outside of clichés, as well as the limiting imaginary space of the Black female image in mainstream comics, Richardson shares,

> It kind of gets on my nerves the way Black women are always painted
> out [in comics] to either be these jungle bunnies, thugs, or poor beggar
> thieves with ratty hair. Yes, there is Storm, and though we are grateful
> to have her, can you name any others in mainstream comics that . . .
> speak without . . . jive talk? There is a demographic not being repre-
> sented. As far as we think we've gotten—even with a Black president
> in office symbolizing the potential of progression—in our hearts and
> minds we're still 50 meters behind the starting line—and expected to
> stay there. I've got work to do; LOTS.[44]

Jones and Richardson, through narrative or visualization, widen the terrain of national consciousness (Jones) or of the Black female image as a whole (Richardson). Not being wedded to gender or racial expectations in their creativity allows both women room for the affective progression Richardson seems to call for in the field of sequential art. That is to say, these two creators move readers into alternative spaces of identification. For both women, comix are an independent and a viable site for forging new fantastical worlds and imagery that are culturally distinct and strategic. It is indeed in the terrain of the fantastic and phantasmagoria that Black female writers and artists can paint worlds of identification that reimagine the perceived fixed categories of gender, sex, and race that popular culture often relies upon. For many of these creators, Afroanime's collision with Afrophantasmagoria and Afropunk answers the creative call of Black postmodernism and its attendant, political possibilities.

Dreaming Afrophantasmagoria and Afroanime through the Affects of Sexuality, Gender, and Everyday Life

As creative devices, phantasmagoria, manga, and anime are deliberate and pervasive aesthetic choices by Black women doing contemporary comix. Cultural critic Andrew McCann writes, "For some [phantasmagoria] refers to the marking of the pejorative space of mass culture and modern entertainment." Intervening in such assumptions, he argues that phantasmagoria "may also define a shifting medley of real or imagined figures, as in a dream, or with the mental . . . workings of the imagination itself; the relationship between the exterior and interior, spectacle and imagination."[45] Nara Walker's graphic novels *Legacy of Light* and *Songbirds* position male, female, transgender, and transracial characters within the fantasy landscape of phantasmagoria and contain an eccentric assemblage of characters that reflect optical illusions. Drawing from her major artistic influences in Japanese comics, including Moto Hagio, Shurei Kouyu, Matsuri Hino, and Chiho Saito, Walker focuses on emotion, formalism and the beauty of physical bodies. As she explains, "My stories are emotion driven so I focus on their feelings. The hardest thing I find to convey is the disconnect between a character's feelings, thoughts, actions and emotions. So many people say one thing but then do another thing."[46]

In Walker's work, characters who appear female are male; characters who appear raced simultaneously question visible signifiers of race; and didactic, visual poetry augments cyclical narratives. Visual poetry, that is, the calculated spatial arrangement of visual images and written verses to convey meaning, becomes a compelling approach to interweave stories of love, loss, and intense emotion. Walker's comix comprise a unique affect aesthetic she calls "prettyism."[47]

As an artistic method, prettyism, like anime, conjures vulnerability through the large expressive eyes and elongated bodies of the characters. Yet, Walker's prettyism contributes to the traditional aesthetic of anime in its ability to evoke melancholy through performative stillness. Walker explains that her graphic novels are "manga academy meets French Academy and a touch of American Cinema. My male characters have an androgynous look, which is styled after [shōjo, or] Japanese girls comics."[48] However, prettyism is more than the coining of an artistic style of fantasy, emotion, anime, and manga, and Walker reveals that it arose, ironically, out of early criticism of her artwork: "I love French academic art, especially the drawings of Bouguereau, Prud'hon, Ingres, and Bargue. I [also] love manga, so subconsciously I put them together. I work intuitively for the most part. [The] prettyism name came about due to complaints about my artwork being too pretty, so I just went with it. In one [art] class, I was forced to come up with an artist statement, so I officially defined prettyism a couple of years ago."[49] Like Jackie Ormes's vulnerable art student in the comic strip that began this book (see figure I.1), there is still a lack of support for Black women in the arts and in comics in contemporary times. Nara Walker's coinage of the term "prettyism" asserts that the Black fantastic is a space of invention and can serve as an intellectual contribution, artistic subversion, and signify(ing) practice. Put simply, naysayers and skeptics of Walker's vision prompted her to embrace prettyism as a formal and legitimate approach to art.

Walker's phantasmagoric world of prettyism features strikingly beautiful boys and Harajuku-style girls. Transracial coding comes in the way of darkly shaded and white skin tones, rainbow-colored hair styled in straight wisps, coarse waves, and braids; blue, green, and lavender eyes; full lips; and the minimalist facial features of anime. The bodies of Walker's characters appear in listless poses as they maneuver within and through fantastical and lustrous settings like magical marionettes. Walker's first graphic novel, *Legacy of Light*, begins with Walker's visual poetry. A black background with floral appliqués engulfs the sleeping (and inebriated) protagonist, Mezine; he is dressed in a neoromantic wide-sleeved jacket and a lace shirt. His long, straight hair lies across his face, and his full, dark-stained lips pucker. The bottom of the page reads, "Can I count you like the sands I feel slipping through my hands? I want to hold you like a ray, of some long forgotten day"—words that represent Mezine's feelings for the female coprotagonist, Star.[50] The graphic novel proceeds to tell the story of two opposing forces—angels and demons—that battle each other and, in so doing, alter the balance of their kingdoms. Drawing from a *Romeo and Juliet*–style romantic trope, the relationship trouble between Mezine and Star emanates from the latter's being an angel and the former, a demon. The laws of their kingdoms forbid interbeing relations, thus placing a strain on their relationship (see plate 19).

The story shifts in time, presenting back stories to the current antagonism between species. The unique use of panels and backgrounds intensifies the emotional effect, as characters caught between situations appear outside and in between panels. Close-ups of pensive eyes and bewildered stares appear as overlays on panels when Walker presents the introspective, interior thoughts of characters. The integration of square, hexagonal, and circular panels throughout the graphic novel creates visual diversity that inspires the reader's eye to slowly assess each page. Moving away from the theme of romance and toward the anime trope of the "beautiful fighting girl," *Legacy of Light* immerses the reader in a visual mirage in which Star's search for her brother, Nova, temporarily thwarts her focus on Mezine. Like Alice in *Alice in Wonderland*, Star maneuvers within a complicated maze of secret passages and disappearing doors, and talking animals magically appear to guide her through her journey before becoming her enemies. *Legacy of Light* ends dramatically, with a haunting poem of unrequited love describing the maddening desire and pain that Star and Mezine feel at being unable to share their lives:

> All I want is to be with you.
> No matter what you put me through
>
> . . . .
>
> My insanity increases
> As you rip me into pieces.
> I know you are the only thing that is real
> Because you are the only thing that
> makes me feel.[51]

While *Legacy of Light* centers on the love between a young man and a young woman, Walker's second graphic novel, *Songbirds*, evokes Afropunk in its musically inspired plot that involves the love between two young men: Gavin Star, a singer, and Zione Cole Tempest, a punk rock musician. Zione tries to recruit Gavin to serve as the lead singer for his alternative band, Void, which leads to the two becoming close. Gavin longs for Zione's romantic attention, and despite brief kisses and intimate moments, he remains unsure of Zione's true feelings. Like *Legacy of Light*, *Songbirds* reflects the romantic genre of *shōjo*, in which external forces play against the love and sexual relationship of two characters. *Songbirds'* narrative also reflects the subgenre *shonen-ai*, which entails suggestive sexual themes between young men. Zione's homophobic manager and brother Alan, Gavin's insecurity, and Zione's flirtation with young women threatens Gavin and Zione's relationship. At the onset of the graphic novel, Gavin describes the difficulty that the two face: "It's not like I wanted this . . . but from the moment I saw him, it was over. I just wanted to be with him, no matter what. I really didn't know what that would come to mean. . . . I knew there would be obstacles from society, because we're both guys, which bothered me a lot more than him. Zione doesn't care what people think."[52]

Race also becomes a visually implied but unspoken obstacle between the two: Zione has a generous, muscular build, dark skin, lavender-brown eyes, and unruly, densely curled hair that falls to his midback, whereas Gavin has blue eyes, straight, wispy hair that hugs his ears, and a slender, modest physique. The two appear as aesthetic and as ethnic opposites. Yet *Songbirds'* primary focus is the sexual coming-of-age and angst of teenagers, and the graphic novel moves beyond the typical love story to address the marginalization and ostracization of teenage boys who do not fit hegemonic forms of masculinity and sexuality. It delves further into the psychology of characters who displace their sexual anxieties onto the main protagonist, Gavin, and considers the long-term effects of sexual trauma on adolescent sexual development. Heterosexual male characters seem fixated on defining Gavin as gay because of his beautiful, tailored face and effeminate posture, and they pejoratively refer to him as "transgendered trailer trash" in order to patrol and cajole their own class, heterosexual, or undisclosed homosexual identities. Those who taunt Gavin are the same characters who in private make unwanted sexual overtures toward him. For example, at the climax of *Songbirds*, a "heterosexual" (and perhaps latent homosexual) classmate, Larkin, sexually forces himself upon Gavin after their school prom, which triggers Gavin's memory of his uncle sexually abusing him as a child:

LARKIN: Hey Gavin, I could give you a ride somewhere ...

GAVIN: No thanks.

LARKIN: (*In a nervous chuckle.*) Even in a tux you look like a girl.

GAVIN: Look Larkin, I'm busy. Fuck off.

LARKIN: (*Moving close to Gavin and caressing his genitals.*) What's the
big deal? You're into guys. Let's go back to my truck.

GAVIN: (*Gavin attempts to leave.*) Get off me!

LARKIN: Where the fuck do you think you are going? You little bitch.

GAVIN: (*Narration to reader.*) This is just like before, with my
uncle. ... I'm not sure what happened next, but I kept thinking
of my uncle ...[53]

Walker's unique poetic aesthetic and the visually implied racial and sexual diversity of characters contribute much to the field of comics. She reimagines *shōjo* comix from a US cultural perspective, and both graphic novels encompass a queer textuality of transgression via an illustration of interspecies (*Legacy of Light*) or same-sex (*Songbirds*) desire. The novels' target market, young women, get to consider normative and nonnormative representations of love, romance, and sexuality; neither depiction is hierarchized, and therefore both are affirmed as equal choices among a spectrum of possibilities. The two novels also conclude with the lead and coprotagonists not ending up together, thus defying absurd romantic traditions in which lovers eventually and easily overcome their cultural and sexual conflicts. Cultural critic Andrea Wood's analysis of sexuality and manga is relevant to understanding the effect of Nara Walker's Afro-phantasmagoric worlds. Referring to the lucrative genre of what she calls "boy love manga" for girls, Wood explains the cultural work of and the relationship between the genre of *shōjo*, the narrative of *shonen-ai*, and its 70 percent female readership: "The gender representations and sexuality visualized in [*shonen-ai*] challenge and trouble the belief that these categories are ontologically coherent, contained, and one-dimensional. For as Eve Sedgwick argues, 'queer' involves 'the openness of possibilities, gaps, overlaps, dissonances, and resonances ... of meaning [that occur] when the constituent elements of anyone's gender, of anyone's sexuality aren't made ... to signify monolithically. In other words, [*shonen-ai*] is not simply queer because it depicts homoerotic love stories between men, but rather because *they ultimately reject any kind of monolithic understanding of gender or sexual identity.*"[54]

If *Legacy of Light* and *Songbirds* work as Afrophantasmagoric and Afroanime texts that create queer dreams for straight girls, Rashida Lewis's self-published *Sand Storm* is an Afroanime inverted mirror of *Nadia: The Secret of Blue Water* or a Black American dream for an African girl. Lewis's protagonist in *Sand Storm* is an Egyptian princess named Anumari, and, as is the case with Nadia, Anumari embarks on a journey to fulfill her role as African princess and leader of her people. Nadia and Anumari are also visual mirror images. Anumari has blue-black coarse hair, dark brown skin, and a muscular yet curvaceous figure, and she wears a bright yellow bandeau top with a short wraparound skirt. Anumari's sexual imagery, however, is more potent. Her skin-tight top barely covers her breasts, and her skirt comes down only a centimeter below her genital region. The character also has crossover components with DC Comics' and Marvel's Black and African female characters. Like the *Justice League of America*'s Vixen, Anumari is an African superheroine who specializes in ass kicking. As with *X-Men*'s Storm and *Wonder Woman*'s Nubia, Anumari functions as a goddess-type character who leads her people through dangerous battles and vies for power. Volume one of the five-part series begins in ancient Egypt, where Anumari combats an army of African men who wish to dethrone her from leadership. The melodramatic narration contextualizes the story within a familiar superhero trope: a lone individual fights evil to save a nation and to save himself or herself from the persecution of a lawless mob:

> NARRATOR: Seems as though she'd been running most all her life. But no amount of running will keep her from her destiny.
> ANUMARI: I cannot continue to run. I am moving further away from my people. Never in all my days could I have imagined this. I do not wish to fight . . . my own people. But I am left with no alternative.
> MALE WARRIOR: (*Leading a charging mass of armed men.*) Large bounty for anyone that takes her![55]

Unlike *Wonder Woman*'s Nubia and the *Justice League*'s Vixen, Anumari's battle with an army of men is not fought alone; male members of her tribe help her in conquering tribesmen who seek to neutralize her power. Lewis writes, "Creating [*Sand Storm*] was a way for me to visualize what was happening in my own life. I definitely believe I am a feminist. My characters aren't shallow, and for me, that's where the line is drawn. In *Sand Storm*, Anumari faces criticism and prejudice from her male advisors. [Criticism] pushes me to do more, because I want to see more girls [in comics]."[56]

Typical of characters in sequential art, Anumari is an orphan, but her siblings and extended family form a familial network that both support and obstruct her efforts. Her sister conspires against her but also encourages her bravery and the rejection of victimhood, and her cousin, Lady Ahknamnen, fights alongside Anumari while evoking the baadasssss personas of 1970s Blaxplocomics. "If any man . . . wishes to challenge my right to combat," warns Ahknamnen, "I am not quite as eloquent as my cousin. I will simply kill him and clean my boots with his skin. Any questions?"[57] Aiming to create a relatable heroine and therefore reaching beyond the sound bites of sexism, primitivism, and the African patriarchal buffoonery of *Wonder Woman* and *Vixen: Return of the Lion*, Lewis explains what makes *Sand Storm* different from mainstream comics with similar themes. *Sand Storm*, she clarifies, "is about a young girl trying to find her place in a male dominated Egyptian culture. After her father's death, she is anointed to the throne, but her father's high priest defected and vowed to remove her from power by any means necessary. The book is filled with fantasy, beautiful art, and most importantly, strong African characters that I can relate to."[58]

As a product of Afroanime, *Sand Storm* merges Afrafemcentric cultural politics with the visualosity of anime. Lewis's African landscape is a pertinent though quiet setting that allows the stunning anime-inspired artwork and dialogue—sometimes spoken in Swahili—to serve as the focus. This approach carries over into other forms of *Sand Storm* media as well. In 2012, Lewis expanded the *Sand Storm* franchise by producing an animation short and a multiplayer online video game, *Sand Storm Revelation*, which features *Sand Storm*'s primary characters and allows players to enter into and fight Anumari's battles. Part anime and part Black liberation theology, *Sand Storm Revelation* is a new iteration of gaming in regard to its profemale narrative with a Black female lead. At the same time, Lewis's visual depictions of women in the comix and in the game mimic the popular and exaggerated anatomies of female characters seen in most sequential art media, requiring fans to negotiate or find pleasure in such imagery alongside what they find culturally compelling about the title. Fan comments appear at the end of individual issues of *Sand Storm*: "The main character is beautiful *and* realistic"; "It's about time we have a female hero like this. Beautiful, captivating and above all REAL"; "What you are doing is phenomenal. We need more work coming from women."[59] Though one might consider the inclusion of fan letters selective propaganda, the mostly male responses to *Sand Storm* purport to embrace its feminist consciousness, while not denying their physical attraction to the beauty of the main protagonist. Those who write of the character's realness seem to refer to Anumari's strength, humanity, and vulnerability as envisaged through her dialogue and interaction with other supporting characters—the same type of narrative intimacy that readers appreciated in their assessment of Ed Brubaker's and Mindy Newell's versions of the *Catwoman* graphic novel. As responses to *Sand Storm* affirm, for Afrofans and for readers of comics in general, consumption of sequential art is neither passive nor remedial; rather, it is highly participatory, sometimes critical, and complex.

Anime and its print counterpart, manga, also influence the narrative and visual framing of contemporary webcomix by Black women. Artists and writers of webcomix use an anime-inspired aesthetic to depict the sentiments and playful aspects of anime and manga while creating stories that are relevant to the diversity of Black experiences. Webcomix artist and writer Leisl Adams (*On the Edge* and *Monsters Under the Bed*) describes this process and explains her influences as a combination of Disney and manga. Adams discloses, "I grew up on Disney movies, and grew up wanting to work at Disney, then in high school I got really into anime, so I guess my style ended up being a bit of both."[60] Citing western comic influences such as Mohammad "Hawk" Haque, Cheeks Galloway,[61] and Mike Knanick, webcomix artist Michelle Billingsley shares that an Afroanime aesthetic allows her to push artistic boundaries into emotional realms: "I describe my artwork as zany, fun, with a bit of anime. To me, [anime and manga are] the same style. One is on the screen, while the other is on paper. What I find appealing are the facial expressions. I'm a fan of *The Avatar*, and it amazes me how I can feel the happiness or pain just by the look on a character's face. I push myself to have exactly that with my comic."[62]

Billingsley's *Joe!* presents characters who operate within the public realm of education and the private sphere of the home. She works in color and in black and white, and while her illustrations focus on reenacting emotion through facial expressions, as in anime and manga, her work is distinct and unique for its circular spheres of multiple scale and for her use of round edges to depict characters and settings. Far from being a positive portrayal in the traditional sense, her lead protagonist Joe is more than precocious—he is a menace. Weekly installments show

Joe disrespecting his teacher and school administrators, taunting his siblings at home, and being the ultimate mischievous youngster. However, his mischief making does not translate into a narrow representative vacuum. One main aspect of the webcomix centers on how Joe's parents, Jon and Kathy, choose to enact appropriate discipline and handle his shenanigans. The two manage to keep a sense of humor while doing so, and they allude to "adult" topics:

> KATHY: This is what I'm talking about Jon, your influence on Joe.
> JON: (*While reading the newspaper.*) I'll talk to him as soon as I finish reading . . .
> KATHY: Jon, if you hold off one more minute on talking to that boy, I'll hold off on something too. Catch my drift?
> JON: Joe! Daddy needs a word with you![63]

Popular culture and political events make their way into *Joe!* in a humorous way. Billingsley admits that engaging with serious topics through humor without diminishing them is a delicate balance. With a keen attention to the ways humor can provide what cultural critic Janice Radway refers to as "equipment for living,"[64] Billingsley emphasizes the profundity in funny: "I feel it is important to focus on humor. We all go through trials and tribulations through life. I want my comic to make someone smile or laugh aloud if they're having a bad day."[65]

As part of the comix revolution, webcomix place the responsibility for creativity, production, and circulation in the hands of the writers and artists themselves, thus taking the comic forms out of the hands of newspaper executives and comic conglomerations. Billingsley's choice to create a webcomix instead of a newspaper comic is therefore strategic and financial, as the Internet medium reaches a broad audience, brings her closer to her fan base, allows for self-publication, and keeps her free from censorship. At the same time, Billingsley finds that fan response is not always satisfying in regard to commentary about the content of the work: "Webcomics have no rules. I can write and draw whatever I want. An audience for webcomics can be different because readers are only a click away from interacting with the artist. I can definitely reach more readers. Readers have contacted me about my comic. So far, there hasn't been anything they disapproved of. The responses I usually get are about how good the art is. I appreciate it, but I would like to hear more about the writing."[66]

Collectively, comix by Walker, Lewis, and Billingsley show how cultural borrowing does not close off the capacity for innovation. In *Legacy of Light* and *Songbirds*, broad engagement with difference point to the ways cultural production can contribute to the project of Black postmodernism. *Sand Storm* exemplifies how portrayals of Africa and African characters can traverse oversimplified signification to affirm readers' sense of what Africa and Africaness, at least from a Black perspective, means to them as diasporic and racialized subjects in the United States. *Joe!* resists a dichotomy of good and bad and embraces an approach in which the imperfections of Black characters can serve as teaching moments. Phantasmagoria and the postmodern impulse of Afroanime in Black women's comix assert how aesthetic mixtures make the genres within sequential art new. Leisl Adams's webcomix and the graphic novels of Ashley Woods not only find inspiration in anime and manga but also combine their shared inspiration with horror and science fiction to spawn characters in "other worldly" stratospheres of emotion, redemption, and desire.

Spawning Afrofuturism and Affective Anthropomorphism in *Millennia Wars* and *On the Edge*

Black women writers and artists in comix reach beyond the present and the past to create futuristic settings that demonstrate the potential of depicting what is yet to come. Cultural critic Alondra Nelson, in her discussion of Afrofuturism in technoculture, science, medicine, and popular culture, exposes the unproductive aspects of what she describes as "colorblind mythotopias" in futuristic narratives. Such creative devices appear to present various cultures that operate in stratospheres free of hierarchy, where difference is visually abundant. Yet, the subjects that occupy spaces of difference rarely engage in direct or indirect discussions about the racialization of their bodies. In a mythotopia, such representations may seem, and in some ways are, liberating as an aspirational vision. However, one might ask what additional emancipatory elements may arise from narratives in which forms of difference appear and act within narrative discourse and exist as a cultural struggle that characters actively negotiate. Scholars, writers, and artists working within the expansive narrative paradigm of Afrofuturism assert that racial, gender, sexual, and class difference does and will continue to matter—even if on different terms and in varying ways—in the future. As Nelson argues, Afrofuturism illustrates how blackness and additional, intersectional aspects of difference are essential to understanding how the multiplicity of identities are a part of our "living past, retained in the present and carried into the future."[67]

Ashley Woods's *Millennia War* intermixes the experiences of everyday life, visual semblances of the pastoral, and futurism as the backdrop for a "race war" between humans and elves (see plate 20).[68] The graphic novel aims to create relatable experiences for readers. "Growing up," says Woods, "I have seen many movies and played many video games where the characters leave a lasting impression on me. I can relate to them and I become involved in the world they live in. I want to create that same experience for my readers. I also draw inspiration from the people around me. Every one of my characters in *Millennia Wars* has . . . traits similar to those people and even me."[69]

In *Millennia Wars*, human hunters accidentally kill Nadia, the wife of an Elvaan king, thus causing a war between the two camps. Given their advanced weaponry and genocidal tactics, the humans assert victory and kill many elves, pushing the Elvaan race near extinction. Those of the Elvaan community who remain emigrate from the United States to their ancestral home of Zano to begin anew. The plot jumps ahead a thousand years and introduces the human Asian/American Hayashi family. Saya Hayashi has been promoted to captain in the Federation Army and soon faces deployment. The family is afraid for her, and their fears have merit: enemies capture Saya during a mission in the Uba Forest and the army classifies her as missing in action. Saya's sister Hannah and an ethnically diverse group of friends—Lydia, Tomiko, Roman, and Julius—set out to find her. Along the way, humans become elves (Lydia), enemies become allies (rescuer Taija), and assumed allies become foes (Tomiko). Rather than a mythotopia of the future, the conflict between humans and elves is based on a history of colonialism and cultural misunderstanding, and the shifting alliances and betrayals of the supporting characters serve as examples of the negotiation of shifting identities and contradictory behavior that thwarts the possibility of sustained freedom for either camp (see plate 21).

Millennia War, presents the complications of war and racism between irrational and rational grievances that lack nuanced understanding between and within species; it also shows the enemies and factions that arise from the subterfuge and grudges of the few in power, and the savior delusions of the powerful. Woods also draws characters who operate under the auspices of quests for freedom and the freeing others. Ironically, despite their rhetoric of freedom, it is these same freedom-bound characters who engage in dictatorial grabs for power that escalate into violence, death, and genocide.

Woods's Afrofuturistic graphic novel is a textual and visual intervention. The narrative shows that there are no true victors in war: the novel ends decades after the humans' supposed victory with all of the antagonisms and contradictions still in place. Avoiding mythotopic science fiction narratives where the roots of colonialism are subject to abstraction or are absent altogether, *Millennia War* shows the making of empire as being dependent on technologies of power and invention. Drawing a parallel to recent military malfunctions in the material world, in the novel's subsequent battles, the humans' advanced weaponry eventually fails precisely because it is a human invention, susceptible to imperfection, and a product of neoliberalism and the privatization of combat resources for profit. Difference among humans and within the Elvaan species is varied; neither group is overly romantic nor held up as a paragon of virtue. *Millennia War* presents a visual recoding of race rarely seen in comics, where all characters, whether Elvaan or human, appear ethnically diverse without replicating nebulous multiculturalism, cultural demonization, or fetishistic Otherness. Woods discloses that the diversity among characters is both conscious and unconscious, and while her strongest characters are female, she is particularly aware of the repercussions of erroneous depictions of Black American men in film and in comics:

> The main characters in *Millennia War* all exist together from different creeds and backgrounds. After working on the books for the past couple of years, I've become aware about the message I send to readers. I don't really approve of how black males are portrayed in movies and in comics so my character Julius is how I would like to see them more often in other movies and comics. He's very smart, likes to read, and can even decipher some forms of hieroglyphics. I don't want him to follow the stereotype of the hothead or troubled person in the group. I hope my readers have noticed these things about him.[70]

Webcomix artist and writer Leisl Adams has the same concerns about depictions of Black women and class. She says she is "sick of seeing giant-breasted women in comics. Not just Black women, but any women. And I don't think all Black women need to be depicted coming from 'stereotypically Black' neighborhoods. It would be nice to see something that I can relate to, a girl coming from a boring middle-class suburb."[71]

Woods and Adams thus both see race and gender in comics as a representational concern, but while *Millennia War* is about a war between species, Leisl Adams's *On the Edge: Tales from the Therapist's Couch*, is about cross-species interaction and the war of the mind. Alice, the strip's protagonist, is a police officer who lives with her roommate Negs (a nickname for Negative). Negs is a wise-cracking demon who makes his living as a psychiatrist; he is humorous but he often hurts and confuses Alice and his patients with a mixture of cruelty and "tough love" therapy. Though depicted as a separate character, Negs is an extension of Alice's own psyche and he helps to create a phantasmagorical world that allows Alice to bifurcate, perform, and critique unresolvable parts of her emotions and the anxieties she has about her identity and life choices. Alice and Negs live in a futuristic setting in which elves, ethnically diverse humans, demons, and cats are equal species who interact with, love, and fight each other on a daily basis.

On the Edge, like Nara Walker's *Legacy of Light*, uses *Alice in Wonderland* as a reference point. Adams consciously employs anime conventions and blends them with what she describes as Western comics. Her mixture of phantasmagoria and futurism is "based [on a central question]: 'if the devil had to get a job, what would it be?' My answer was that he would be a therapist. The story combines that with my take on *Alice in Wonderland* in a 'what if she grew up there' scenario."[72] Adams has experienced depression and sought counseling in her own life, and the webcomix seems in part generative of some of her ideas about therapy and the psychology of the mind. In regard to her aesthetic choices, Adams explains, "I think a lot can be said without words, just through body language, expressions and tone or colour. I love the challenge of telling a story without using too many words. I think it comes naturally for me. People give too much credit to the writing in a comic sometimes. That said, I find writing a tougher challenge for myself. Keeping the story moving and interesting for 100 pages is hard; I'm very bare bones and to the point most of the time."[73]

Elsewhere, Adams confesses that the inspiration for Negs came while in therapy, when she "drew a picture of what [she] thought 'depression' would look like."[74] Her choice to attribute human characteristics to animals, demons, and elves serves as affective anthropomorphism. These characters are literary and visual tools to make emotions visceral through

otherworldly species or animals who are human-like. Informing upon the personal aspects of the anthropomorphic choices in

her work, Adams says, "I decided to put Cat-people in *On the Edge* because I had a cat and I wondered what it would be like if he could talk."[75] Giving human characteristics to animals is a long-standing device of sequential art, but rather than presenting the blackface minstrelsy animals of Disney and Warner Brothers' early and objectifying animation ventures (Mickey Mouse, Bugs Bunny, and Tom and Jerry, for example), Black women's comix use animals as posthuman subjects with agency.

The visual appearance of *On the Edge*'s characters intensifies their meaning as transgressive tools. The issues Adam takes up in regard to depression and anxiety trouble and unease readers, but also encourage reflection and contemplation. Negs, as a demon and the personification of the devil, has red skin, large eyes, horns, a protruding stomach, tail, and sharp, pointed teeth. His short stature, half grin, half sharp-tooth growl, and mean-spirited advice situate him as a complex part of Alice's subconscious that, once detached from her own body, she can both resent and understand. Negs is therefore a Cartesian device for Alice that allows her to engage in self-loathing and self-reflexivity at the same time, as we see in a scene where Alice sighs despairingly and slouches against a table, and Negs asks her what is wrong. "I feel so alone," she replies. Negs grins at her and responds, "I'm here!" and Alice retorts angrily, "That's the problem."[76] Race does not appear as a struggle for the protagonist, but her appearance performs useful gender work. Alice is ethnically marked as white, and has brown short hair with bangs, and a slender, nearly waiflike physique, which makes her profession in law enforcement a powerful statement that counters occupation essentialism based on gender and body type.

The webcomix's title, *On the Edge*, represents a desire to contain and explain extreme emotions—the characters are literally on the edge emo-

5.4 Leisl Adams, *On the Edge: Tales from the Therapist's Couch* (2013), 13. Courtesy of Leisl Adams.

tionally, and Negs pushes the boundaries of appropriate behavior in the name of curing their psychological woes. Negs's medical negligence calls into question the efficacy and reliability of therapy to solve emotional problems. One edition of the comic strip illustrates Negs's "new" invention for helping his clients and reveals that he (and Alice's subconscious) have psychologically warped and dangerous tendencies:

> NEGS (*Proudly with chest and stomach puffed out and hiding a noose tie behind his back before placing it around his neck.*): Wanna see my new invention?
> ALICE (*Horrified.*)
> NEGS (*Grinning widely.*): Noose ties! They'll be all the rage in a few months!
> ALICE: Don't you think that will be a bit discouraging for your clients?
> NEGS (*Yanking the noose tighter.*): Hell no![77]

Similarly, when a patient calls Negs on the phone and declares that s/he wants to kill himself, Negs appears to show concern but then finishes with shocking advice: "WAIT, WAIT. Ok, go get a plastic bag."[78]

On the Edge's topical choices are sometimes more benign, particularly when depicting Alice at work as a police officer or when referencing her relationship troubles. Negs and Alice therefore exist within a future that is not without its fun and humor but, as with *Millennia War*, not mythotopic or utopic either. The story exists within a futuristic fantasy world created by the mind, and Negs's core role is as an applicable psychological device. It is through this mind-produced world of extremes—where negative thinking becomes a demonic monster to hate, separate, and ultimately conquer by realizing its counterproductive properties—that Adams's work presses the boundaries of Afrophantasmagoria and Afrofuturism. Alice has created an environment in which her troubled mind seeks to make sense of and grapple with her inner demons. Her agency thus comes from naming and bringing her depression to life in order to purge herself of it and of the social anxiety that threatens her well-being. However, *On the Edge* is not prescriptive and does not offer a pseudopsychological discourse of healing. Instead, through Negs, it presents the difficult work of therapeutic healing and its narratives attempt to create shared registers of affect and emotional relationality. In so doing, *On the Edge* may allow a variety of racial ethnic readers to experience the intense feelings that arise from coping with isolation, fear, depression, and happiness. It is also indicative of the commonly adopted idea of Black popular culture being *by* and *for*, as opposed to only being *about*, issues that seem to conspicuously reference the Black diaspora. Indeed, Adams (as with Rashida Jones's *Frenemy of the State*) illuminates the representative problems and expands the term "Black comix"; she disentangles the idea that Black characters should exist as the primary or only vehicle to explore the Black subconsciousness. Black consciousness can exist within the realm of creation making and critique, where for Black women artists and writers, Black absence and presence serve strategic purposes.

The Tricky Art of Comix and the Art World

In cultural critic Michele Wallace's essay "Why Are There No Great Black Artists?' The Problem of Visuality in African-American Culture," Wallace reveals a set of problematics for questioning why recognition of the artistic legacy of people of African descent—and particularly of Black women—is rare.[79] Tethered to the false and Eurocentric standards of the white art world, artists such as Elizabeth Catlett, Faith Ringgold, Betty Saar, Emma Amos, Kara Walker, Rene Cox, Annie Lee, and Karin Turner do not hold the same place in the elite, artistic imaginary as do white artists. All of these artists have received critical acclaim, but the art world is no different from the larger hegemonic structure of which it is a part. Put simply, the great artists in the elite artistic imaginary are men, such as Pablo Picasso, Vincent van Gogh, Jackson Pollock, and Rembrandt van Rijn. The former camp holds the place of well-known Black female artists in the Black public sphere and within progressive art and museum fields, while the latter camp—who are all male and overwhelmingly European—hold the place of the "real" great artists in culturally supremacist minds. Many of the aforementioned Black women artists use humor and various aspects of a sequential art aesthetic, that is, penciling, simple to sophisticated lines, bold color, and references to everyday Black life and history or depictions of spaces of subversion. Wallace's question, then, is rhetorical. There *are* many great Black artists, but the gatekeepers of the art world, as well as the Black conservative sphere beholden to safe and respectable images, work as an ideological bloc that makes the idea of a "great" Black female artist seem like an oxymoron.

In a 2012 article in the *Los Angeles Times*, "Women in Comics and the Tricky Art of Equality," writer Noelene Clark reports on a parallel problem in the field of comics, where women in general lack visibility compared with their male counterparts. Though comics are a mass-produced form, they mirror the masculinist and racist discourses of the larger art world. Clark and the white female artists and writers she discusses and interviews for her story (Sarah Oleksyk, Faith Erin Hicks, Lora Innes, Jessica Abel, Alison Bechdel, and Ann Nocenti) report that they are tired of addressing the issue of women in comics. Instead, these women want to move on to discussing their art rather than the legitimacy of their presence. Comics journalist and former editor for Disney and DC Comics Heidi MacDonald also doubts the utility of a seemingly passé "women in comics" approach to comic scholarship: "Outside the world of Marvel and DC, women are just doing it, and it's awesome. They're succeeding or failing on the content of their work. I think the time has come to stop saying, 'Oh, my God, there are women in comics!' and just be like, 'Here's some really cool stuff.' And really just talk about the work and not the issue, because it's just not an issue the way it used to be."[80]

MacDonald is wise to encourage a discussion that moves beyond the issues of inclusion and inequality and analyzes the work of female comic artists. Clark's concentration on white female artists, journalists, and characters may suggest a new era for white women in comics, but she reinscribes the invisibility of Black female artists, writers, and characters at the same time through her exclusion of their voices. The names Sarah Oleksyk (*Regular Show*), Faith Erin Hicks (*Demononlogy 101*), Lora Innes, (*The Dreamer*), Jessica Abel (*Life Sucks*), Alison Bechdel (*Dykes to Watch Out For*), and Ann Nocenti (*New Mutants*) do not register as being a part of the historical lexicon of comics as do the names Frank Miller (*Batman*), Milton Caniff (*Terry and the Pirates*), Stan Lee (*X-Men*), Robert Kanigher (*Wonder Woman, Justice League of America, Green Lantern*), and William Moulton

Marston (*Wonder Woman*). The tricky art of equality, then, still exists across racial and ethnic groups when it comes to the comic art of women as a whole. Clark's *Los Angeles Times* piece embodies the problem that cultural critic Michele Wallace exposes, thereby underscoring that an analysis of Black women's presence, or lack thereof, and of their work in the comics field reveals a differentiated and larger historical and contemporary artistic milieu in which Black women continue to reside and struggle to thrive.

The story of contemporary Black female comix artists is certainly one of struggle, but it is also a story of tenacity and creativity. Black women in comics do not allow mainstream acceptance or invitations to work for large comic book companies to determine their presence in the field. They create opportunities to self-publish, work through independent distributors, and sell or display their work on the Internet. Their influences vary from US mainstream comics to Black popular culture and alternative music subcultures to Japanese manga and anime. With trailblazers such as Jackie Ormes and Barbara Brandon-Croft as a point of reference and departure, the Black women who comprise the Ormes Society write and draw comix to illustrate that "where they are coming from" is a postmodern and sundry terrain. This terrain is not limited to artists in the Ormes Society. Rashida Jones and other Black female comix artists—such as Jennifer Crute, Viga Victoria, and Juliana Smith—all use the medium of comics to mix traditional comic forms with postmodern sensibilities by drawing intersectional points of identification and experience.[81] Crute's coming-of-age comix *Jennifer's Journal* is the female counterpart to Billingsley's *Joe!*; Victoria's Afropunk and Afroanime mixture in *Viga Love's Comics* is concomitant with Walker's print work and Adams's *On the Edge*; and Smith's *(H)afrocentric* is a brilliant examination of Black college life as it intersects with the cultural politics of our neoliberal and neoconservative era. These diverse and unexpected spaces of contestation—of gender, race, sexuality, color, and class—as well as the pursued points of relationality from which they work to build the comix revolution is perhaps best concluded by artist Afua Richardson. Of her work Richardson says, "A Southeast Asian antagonist; a West African demi god; an 'all American' thug; a Native American doctor (no feathers). I hope . . . to blur those lines together. [And] as for gender—well, . . . everyone likes to see a chick that's a badass."[82]

CONCLUSION

Comic Book Divas and the
Making of Sequential Subjects

BLACK CAT: Our line of work can be . . . so isolating.

PHOTON: Please, you want to talk isolation? Try being a black woman in this business.

—*Marvel Divas*

WITH an arched torso, hands behind her back, and wearing a skintight black catsuit zipped down to her abs, Black Cat (Felicia Hardy) balances herself on a fire-flamed disc as her long white hair curls around her left shoulder and large, protruding breast tissue. Firestar (Angelica Jones) stands next to Black Cat; her red hair blows forward into the air, her red cat mask frames her piercing blue eyes, and fire erupts from her yellow form-fitting spandex body suit. Wearing a silver spandex catsuit that accentuates her small waist, a black leather jacket that falls around her large breasts, and gold combat boots, the character Photon (Monica Rambeau) stands to the right of Firestar. Photon wears black mid-length dreadlocks tamed by a sliver headband; her full lips pucker and her brown eyes stare directly forward. Beneath the three is Hellcat (Patsy Walker), who balances on her knees and toes with her thighs sprawled open. A black waistband sits below her hips, and her black thigh-high boots, black leather gloves, and black cat mask provide dark accents to her yellow spandex cat suit. Hellcat stares forward with a daring taunt to her eyes as her arms appear to hold back impending flames. The fire erupting behind the four suggest that these "divas" represent a dubious mixture of potent sexuality, power, and danger that is typical of the cover art of Marvel Comics' 2010 adult-themed series *Marvel Divas* (see plate 22). This cover art is in stark contradiction to the content and visual images within the book. The same characters on the cover are pictured pages later in modest clothing with short hair, glasses, and wearing business or casual attire.

The book begins by introducing Patsy Walker/Hellcat, a New York City writer preparing to celebrate the publication of her new tell-all book of her sexual exploits and former romantic relationships. The graphic novel proceeds to explain how the four superheroines became friends, making intertextual references to HBO's popular television series *Sex and the City*. Like the four coprotagonists in *Sex and the City*, Hellcat, Firestar, Photon, and Black Cat attend movies, talk of trips to Paris, drink designer cocktails at trendy nightclubs, and talk graphically about dates, sex, and men. Unlike the HBO series and DC's similarly constructed title *Gotham City Sirens*, however, *Marvel Divas* is not white-centric. Photon/Monica Rambeau is a Black female character who has a legitimate back story and is an integral part of the series. *Divas* does not relegate Monica Rambeau to the role of sidekick or cliché; rather, the character often makes direct references to racism, the Black community she comes from (New Orleans), and how the politics of gender and race shape her superheroine life as Photon and her everyday life experiences as Monica Rambeau.

In a flashback, *Divas* shows Photon channeling energy to help address, as she frankly tells her three friends, "the mess white people left behind" in New Orleans post- Katrina.[1] We later see Rambeau frolicking in bed with a male lover, and afterward joking about how she handles clingy male suitors.[2] Photon/Rambeau is neither the asexual nor the hypersexual character of the Golden Age of comics, nor is she a product of 1970s Blaxplocomics. Rambeau traverses contemporary, interracial mythotopias in which Black characters exist in popular culture as forms of difference that negate the power and the politics of difference. In addition to addressing the politics of race through Monica Rambeau/Photon, *Divas* takes on a serious tone and the relationship between the four women deepens when Angelica Jones announces to her three friends that she has breast cancer.

Marvel Divas is thus unique for its ability to frankly discuss how race and sexual relations affect its Black protagonist, and it stands out for its depiction of white and Black women who maintain a working and social relationship without ignoring issues related to racism. Indeed, when the white Black Cat tells the Black Photon that superhero life is isolating, and Photon replies that it is even more isolating for a Black female superhero, she is alluding to the world of real-life Black women.

The cover art of *Marvel Divas* and its competing title by DC Comics, *Gotham City Sirens*, have become direct-marketing strategies to appeal to readers interested in stories about and images of women.[3] Both books steer away from the intergender superhero collective of the Avengers and the Suicide Squad, to an all-female ensemble, with female forms posing seductively on their covers. Such representations are no different from the way comic book conglomerates have historically depicted women in general: with large breasts, impossibly small waists, and ample derrieres. Upon the release of *Marvel Divas*, there was little discussion of the book's contents or of its atypical and transformative depiction of a Black female colead. Instead, the title and the sexy cover dominated the discourse.[4]

Writer Hortense Smith critiques the book's replication of *Sex and the City*'s propagation of consumerist culture and romantic narratives and places *Marvel Divas* within a context of mass media's portrayal of women, writing with sarcasm, "Oh, awesome! Now I can find the same stupid Carrie Bradshaw bullshit that has invaded every aspect of my life from television to magazines to the Internet since 2000 in a comic book, too! Because I don't care about how awesome superheroines are when they're out kicking ass! I just want to know what they're like when they're having some hot sudsy fun and talking about shoes and boys!"[5] In response to the book's naysayers, *Divas* writer Roberto Aguirre-Sacasa asked the following questions in an interview about the title, suggesting, perhaps, that many of the book's critics had not read it and were only responding to the cover and online blather: "If you're [a] Marvel reader and truly feel we're sexist, then why are you reading our books?" He continues, "Perhaps you're not a Marvel reader, [and] if that's the case, I'm not quite sure what you're criticizing if you don't read our books?"[6] Aguirre-Sacasa also directly addressed the book's cover art, rationalizing that "comics are . . . a part of the entertainment business . . . and the cold hard truth is that if we were to launch *Marvel Divas* with a 'quiet cover,' I guarantee you the book would be canceled before it hits the shelves."[7] The narrative and ensuing visual imagery in

Marvel Divas is a case of the old adage "don't judge a book by its cover," as well as an example of marketing ploys that encourage readers to purchase a book precisely because its cover is enticing.

Reflecting upon the sexual imagery of women in comics is a worthwhile pursuit. Yet I want to push the rhetorical boundaries of the "cover wars" to argue that in the case of *Divas*' Monica Rambeau and other adult characters, the cultural work of the title in relationship to proffering a Black female character as a sequential subject is worth addressing. Throughout this book, I broaden the discourse on sexuality, gender, and race while being mindful of the cultural havoc and limits of representation as a whole. *Black Women in Sequence* is thereby the means through which I unpack the multiple meanings and purposes that sexual imagery yields for female characters of African descent, and how race, class, color, and gender collide in the Black female form. Gathering various forms of sequential art—comic strips, gags, comic books, graphic novels, anime, and moving-image media such as gaming, television, and film—enables the exploration of the multiple and contradictory ways producers and consumers imagine the Black female body.

Seeing Black women as sequential subjects moves conversations about representation and inclusion to a critical terrain where the complexities of narrative and visuality collide, to imagine spaces where the fictive lives, ideas, and historical images of Black women matter. There are certainly erroneous depictions of women of African descent in popular culture, which require attention and alteration, including the exploitation and sexualization of the adolescent form as seen in *Nadia*. Yet, calls for positive or desexualized vestiges of blackness, though well-intentioned, risk foreclosing the artistic possibilities of visual culture. Offering the idea of Black women as sequential subjects interrogates problematic characterizations of difference while insisting upon the way those same characterizations are pregnant with possibilities. *Black Women in Sequence* examines the process by which Black women metaphorically remark upon or remake ideas of the self, the nation state, and belonging within the nation. As cultural critic Herman Gray reminds us, thinking through "the politics of representation as an analytic identifies discourses and social conditions where culture has been deployed and representations of blackness enlisted to shore up ideas of the nation and national identity and, more importantly, what it means to belong to the nation."[8]

I heed Gray's call for critical inquiry, his speculations about representational discourse in cultural studies, and his suggestion to engage with issues related to the political economy and the contours of national belonging. I therefore present the idea of Black women as sequential subjects to argue that women of African descent are semiotic referents for social relations and discourses about culture, national politics, and difference. This idea coheres in the way mainstream characters such as Nubia, Storm, and Vixen embody writers' fear and fascination with Africa in relation to the United States' national imaginary, international policies, and the culture wars of the past and present. At the same time, characters such as Martha Washington offer readers an opportunity to consider Black women's essential and autonomous role in US nation making. These characters, and their Black women artists and writers, show, as did Barbara Brandon-Croft's comic strip women, that Black women's minds are formidable, intellectual tools of protest and invention. Jackie Ormes's Black cultural front comics are particularly attuned to Black women's ideas and activism in nation making; for Ormes, re-inking the nation meant imbuing working- and middle-class characters with political voices. Ormes's comic strips and gags of the 1930s and later are part of a larger movement that coupled the popular arts with activism to form a cultural front of political dissent.

In both a national and an international context, characters who shore up racial ambiguity and reflect racial fluidity, such as Catwoman's changing racial trajectories and the multiple ways that viewers and writers see sexuality and racial relations through the adolescent anime character Nadia, prove that cultural production, in this case sequential art, is a puissant site. The transnational circulation of Japanese culture, especially manga and anime, influences Black women who create sequential art today, thus showing that their work is not bound by one cultural or national artistic force. More than cultural borrowing or appropriation, fusing varied forms of Black consciousness and cultural styles, as envisaged through Afropunk, Afroanime, Afrofuturism, and Afrophantasmagoria, with the stylistic and narrative cues of Japanese comics has opened up transnational terrains for Black women comic artists and writers. Women in the Ormes Society illustrate how elves, demons, animals, and posthuman subjects can push national and ethnic boundaries of identification.

Black Women in Sequence: Re-inking Comics, Graphic Novels, and Anime accompanies work in popular culture that insists upon the sophistication and relevance of de-essentialized formations of identity across space and time, thereby also advancing the conversation on the spatiotemporality of cultural productions expended in everyday life. Instead of arguing that forms of sequential art are equal to or as legitimate as what cultural gatekeepers deem elite forms of literature and art, I have let the work that writers and artists produce and that spectators and readers consume make a more meaningful argument. Sequential art performs a unique type of cultural work by navigating, surpassing, and remaking genres, by coupling images with text, and by distilling complex ideas into truncated panels or images for active wide readership or consumerism. As an Americanist and cultural theorist engaged in interdisciplinary inquiry, and one who is committed to the creation and use of analytical frames to understand all modes of cultural phenomenon, I see sequential art as a medium capable of magnifying sites of cultural struggle over forms of difference that are in an ongoing state of becoming and transformation. More powerful than the container categories that the labels often afforded to women in sequential art seem to suggest, that is, as divas, sirens, sheroes, or antiheroes, a sequential subject constitutes an imagined body and space fraught with representational ambiguity, cultural and political potential, and pleasure.

NOTES

(a) artist
(c) colorist
(e) editor
(i) inker
(m) musician
(p) penciler
(w) writer

Preface

Epigraph: Mat Johnson, "The Geek," in *Black Cool: One Thousand Streams of Blackness*, ed. Rebecca Walker (Berkeley: Soft Skull Press, 2012), 16.

1   In previous decades, the label *fanboy* was at times thought of as a pejorative description of young boys and young men who were readers of and participated in the culture of comics. Fanboys were comic-book-obsessed "geeks" who lacked maturity, and were sometimes distinguished from a cadre of self-perceived mature and discerning comic book and graphic novel readers. Today, some embrace the term, and there has been an additional emergence of derivative identities such as *fangirl* (or *fangyrl/grrrl*), which signifies being an active reader, viewer, participant, and sometimes cocreator of comic art.

2   *Cosplay* refers to fans dressing up in the attire of comic book, graphic novel, and anime characters.

3   The term *netnography* refers to the undertaking of ethnographic research on the Internet, in virtual worlds, and in gaming. As Robert Kozinets asserts, the netnographer is particularly concerned with the Internet's influence

on social worlds, and adapts and creates methods of participant/observation relevant to those worlds. Robert V. Kozinets, *Netnography: Doing Ethnographic Research Online* (London: Sage Publications 2010).

4   Mat Johnson, "The Geek," 11–18.

5   Rebecca Wanzo, "Black Nationalism, Bunraku and Beyond: Articulating Black Heroism and Cultural Fusion in Comics," *Multicultural Comics: From Zap to Blue Beetle*, ed. Frederick Aldama et al. (Austin: University of Texas Press, 2010), 94.

6   These music subcultures were and are not free from segregation or racism. Mahon argues that while the racial struggle of Black Americans exists in these sites, they still found ways to carve spaces and alternative identities that asserted the Black roots of rock and refused the essential, mainstream logics of Black identity. See Maureen Mahon, *The Right to Rock: Black Cultural Politics and the Black Rock Coalition* (Durham, NC: Duke University Press, 2004). Also see Greg Tate, "Of Afropunks and Other Anarchic Signifiers of Contrary Negritude," in *From Bourgeois to Boojie: Black Middle Class Performances*, ed. Vershawn Ashanti Young, with Bridget Harris Tsemo (Detroit: Wayne State University Press, 2011), 155–58.

7   Here, "articulation" refers to the coupling of two seemingly contradictory elements that under the right circumstances can yield new and at times progressive and transgressive meanings. See Stuart Hall and Lawrence Grossberg, "On Postmodernism and Articulation: An Interview with Stuart Hall," in *Stuart Hall: Critical Dialogues in Cultural Studies*, ed. David Morley and Kuan-Hsing Chen (London: Routledge, 1996), 115.

8   On young feminist identity, or riot grrrl culture and popular media, see Lisa Darms, ed., *The Riot Grrrl Collection* (New York City: The Feminist Press, 2014); Maria Elena Buszek, *Pin-up Grrrls: Feminism, Sexuality, Popular Culture* (Durham, NC: Duke University Press, 2006); and Trina Robbins, *From Girls to Grrlz: A History of Women's Comics from Teens to Zines* (New York: Chronicle Books, 1999).

Introduction

Epigraph: *The Butterfly*, in *Hell Rider* #1, Gary Friedrich (writer), Ross Andru (cartoonist), Jack Abel and Mike Esposito (illustrators), Skywald Publications, 1971, 2.

1   Friedrich would later create *Ghost Rider* for Marvel, which in 2007 was made into a film starring Nicholas Cage.

2   Storm was the first "major" African female superhero, appearing first in 1976, but her African American predecessors are the Butterfly, who came onto the scene in 1971, and Nubia, who appeared in *Wonder Woman* in 1973.

3   A back-up feature appears at the end of a main title, a sort of minicomic

book within the larger comic book that provides the story of a supporting character.

4   Although the term "political economy" refers generally to the economics of government, I use the term in a post-Marxist sense, which expansively refers to the interrelationship of politics, culture, economics, consumption, distribution, flexible income, and one of the most powerful ideological state apparatuses, that is, the State.

5   By "economies of scale" I mean a process of production wherein companies or the State produce goods at a low cost but with a high profit margin.

6   Hewetson wrote in an interview shortly before his death, "Our issues were selling well, and some sold out. Such returns as we received were shipped overseas, mainly to England, where they sold out completely.... When Marvel entered the game with countless [black-and-white horror] titles gutting [*sic*] the newsstand, their distributor was so powerful they denied Skywald access to all but the very largest newsstands, so our presence was minimal and fans and readers simply couldn't *find* us.... The Waldmans [Israel and business manager Hershel Waldman] and I had a business lunch with our distributor in the fall of '74 and we were given very specific information about the state of affairs on the newsstands—which had nothing to do with ... Skywald's solid readership base." See Richard J. Arndt, "The Complete Skywald Checklist [including] a 2003 Interview with Archaic Al Hewetson!" EnjolrasWorld.com, December 2, 2010, archived from the original July 16, 2011, accessed April 19, 2012, http://web.archive.org/web/20110716140104/ http://www.enjolrasworld.com/Richard%20Arndt/The%20Complete%20 Skywald%20Checklist.htm.

7   John Jennings and Damien Duffy (cocurators), *Out of Sequence: Underrepresented Voices in American Comics*, Krannert Art Museum, University of Illinois, October 24, 2008–January 4, 2009. See also the special issue of *MELUS* 32, no. 3 (Sept. 2007) on multiethnic identity and graphic novels.

8   See Jean-Paul Gabilliet, *Of Comics and Men: A Cultural History of American Comic Books* (Jackson: University Press of Mississippi, 2009); Danny Fingeroth, *Superman on the Couch: What Superheroes Really Tell Us about Ourselves and Our Society* (New York: Continuum International Publishing Group, 2004); Bradford W. Wright, *Comic Book Nation: The Transformation of Youth Culture in America* (Baltimore: The Johns Hopkins University Press, 2003); and Matthew Pustz, *Comic Book Culture: Fanboys and True Believers* (Jackson: University Press of Mississippi, 2000).

9   Jeff Yang, *Secret Identities: The Asian American Superhero Anthology* (New York: The New Press, 2009).

10   Héctor Fernández L'Hoeste and Juan Poblete eds., *Redrawing the Nation: National Identity in Latin/o American Comics* (New York: Palgrave, 2009), 16.

11   Ann Merino, "The Bros. Hernandez: A Latin Presence in Alternative U.S. Comics," in *Redrawing the Nation: National Identity in Latin/o American*

Comics, ed. Héctor Fernández L'Hoeste and Juan Poblete (New York: Palgrave, 2009), 253.

12 Brannon Costello and Qiana J. Whitted, eds., *Comics and the U.S. South* (Jackson: University Press of Mississippi, 2012).

13 Richard King, "Alter/native Heroes: Native Americans, Comic Books, and the Struggle for Self-Definition," *Cultural Studies ↔ Critical Methodologies* 9, no. 2 (Apr. 2009): 214–23.

14 Contemporary analyses on comic books and their male audiences include Jeffrey Brown, *Black Superheroes, Milestone Comics, and Their Fans* (Jackson: University Press of Mississippi, 2001); Christopher Lehman, *The Colored Cartoon: Black Representation in American Animated Short Films* (Amherst: University of Massachusetts Press, 2008); Rod Lendrum, "The Super Black Macho, One Baaad Mutha: Black Superhero Masculinity in 1970s Mainstream Comic Books," *Extrapolation* 46, no. 3 (Fall 2005): 360–72; and Adilifu Nama, *Super Black: American Pop Culture and the Black Superheroes* (Austin: University of Texas Press, 2012). Also see Sheena C. Howard and Ronald L. Jackson II's edited anthology *Black Comics: Politics of Race and Representation* (New York City: Bloomsbury Academic, 2013).

15 See Trina Robbins, *From Girls to Grrlz: A History of Women's Comics from Teens to Zines* (New York: Chronicle Books, 1999); Lillian S. Robinson, *Wonder Women: Feminisms and Superheroes* (New York: Routledge 2004); Jeffrey Brown, *Dangerous Curves: Action Heroines, Gender, Fetishism, and Popular Culture* (Jackson: University Press of Mississippi, 2011). Also see Sherrie A. Inness, ed., *Action Chicks: New Images of Tough Women in Popular Culture* (New York: Palgrave Press, 2004); Mike Madrid, *The Supergirls: Fashion, Feminism, Fantasy, and the History of Comic Book Heroines* (Minneapolis: Exterminating Angel Press, 2009). Articles that mention the work of Black female characters include Jennifer D. Ryan, "Black Female Authorship and the African American Graphic Novel: Historical Responsibility in 'ICON: A Hero's Welcome,'" *Modern Fiction Studies* 52, no. 4 (Winter 2006): 918–46; Anna Beatrice Scott, "Superpower vs. Supernatural: Black Superheroes and the Quest for Mutant Reality," *Journal of Visual Culture* 5, no. 3 (Spring 2006): 295–314.

16 On this term and process, see José David Saldívar, *Trans-Americanity: Subaltern Modernities, Global Coloniality, and the Cultures of Greater Mexico* (Durham, NC: Duke University Press, 2012). Saldívar explains that the process of Americanity reveals a cross-genealogy of the ways the Americas engaged in a struggle regarding the perceived provincialism of Europe; European hegemony and social hierarchies built upon culture and society; a foundation for capitalism; and the building and maintenance of colonialism and empire.

17 See Russ Castronovo and Susan Gillman, eds., *States of Emergency: The Object of American Studies* (Chapel Hill: University of North Carolina Press, 2009), 1–16.

18 Several authors argue for the inclusion of comic book studies in academia while outlining the various methods for making arguments about comics as a whole. Among the most significant recent contributions are Rocco Versaci, *This Book Contains Graphic Language: Comics as Literature* (New York: Continuum Press, 2007); Jeet Heer and Kent Worcester, *A Comics Studies Reader* (Jackson: University Press of Mississippi, 2008); and Jeet Heer and Kent Worcester, *Arguing Comics: Literary Masters on a Popular Medium* (Jackson: University Press of Mississippi, 2005).

19 Henry Jenkins, "Introduction," *Critical Approaches to Comics: Theory and Methods* (London: Routledge Press, 2011), 6.

20 Neil Cohn, "The Limits of Time and Transitions: Challenges to Theories of Sequential Image Comprehension," *Studies in Comics* 1, no. 1 (Fall 2010): 134.

21 On the comparison between the graphic novel and the comic book, see Charles Hatfield, "Whither the Graphic Novel," in *Alternative Comics: An Emerging Literature* (Jackson: University Press of Mississippi, 2005), 152–63; and Heer and Worcester, "Introduction" to *Arguing Comics*, vii–xix.

22 Throughout this book, I connect sequential art forms to reality by pointing out the contradictions between the social worlds that the artifact aims to represent. On the graphic novel as a form of metafiction, see Paul Atkinson, "The Graphic Novel as Metafiction," *Studies in Comics* 1, no. 1 (Fall 2010): 112.

23 I therefore address the psychoanalytic subjectivity of writers, artists, and readers; the poststructuralist turn toward the multiple meanings and referents of visual and narrative components; the post-Marxist explanation of the interplay between difference, capital, markets, and commodity circulation; the social construction and materiality of identity and politics under the advent of colonialism; and the politics of everyday life and reading practice. Theoretical interventions on the Black female body, history, performance, visual culture, and popular culture also act as models to present the analytical constructs of form, context, and movement spurred by these fields. The following are methodological and theoretical influences: Stuart Hall's writing as anthologized in David Morley and Kuan-Hsing Chen, *Stuart Hall: Critical Dialogues in Cultural Studies* (London: Routledge, 1996); Janice Radway, "Interpretive Communities and Variable Literacies: The Functions of Romance Reading," in *Rethinking Popular Culture*, ed. Chandra Mukerji and Michael Shudson (Berkeley: University of California Press, 1991), 465–86; Lisa Lowe, *Immigrant Acts: On Asian American Cultural Politics* (Durham, NC: Duke University Press, 1996); Paul Gilroy, *The Black Atlantic: Modernity and Double Consciousness* (Cambridge, MA: Harvard University Press, 1993); Paul Gilroy, *Postcolonial Melancholia* (New York: Columbia University Press, 1996); Paul Gilroy, *Darker Than Blue: The Moral Economies of Black Atlantic Culture* (Cambridge, MA: Harvard University Press, 2010); George Lipsitz, *American Studies in a Moment of Danger* (Minneapolis: University of Minnesota Press, 2001); George Lipsitz, *Footsteps in the Dark: The*

Hidden Histories of Popular Music (Minneapolis: University of Minnesota Press 2006); Daphne A. Brooks, *Bodies in Dissent: Spectacular Performances of Race and Freedom, 1850–1910* (Durham, NC: Duke University Press, 2006); Jayna Brown, *Babylon Girls: Black Women Performers and the Shaping of the Modern* (Durham, NC: Duke University Press, 2008); and Kimberly Springer, *Living for the Revolution: Black Feminist Organizations, 1968–1980* (Durham, NC: Duke University Press, 2005).

24 Understanding the cultural work of comics in this context relies on the recognition that the nodes of American politics and participation change over historical time; they are varied and contradictory within political movements, parties, and thought. Black female characters embody this broad spectrum. As sequential subjects, their agency and political possibilities challenge the binary idea that a character, action, or political movement is progressive and subversive, or mostly retrograde and complacent. As Antonio Gramsci's theorization of forming a historic bloc that intercedes in key portions of the havoc of hegemony, and Foucault's illustration of the discursive way power is seized and dispersed, remind us, the utopian idea of a complete revolution or a massive upheaval of power in real life or in cultural production misunderstands how politics and power works. See Antonio Gramsci, *Selections from the Prison Notebooks* (New York City: International Publishing Company, 1971); Michel Foucault, *Discipline and Punish: The Birth of the Prison* (New York City: Vintage Books, 1995).

25 *The Life and Times of Martha Washington in the Twenty-first Century*, Frank Miller (w), Dave Gibbons (i), Angus McKie (c), Diana Schutz, editor (Milwaukie: Dark Horse Comics, 2010).

26 See Jeffrey Brown, *Black Superheroes, Milestone Comics, and Their Fans* (Jackson: University Press of Mississippi, 2001); Adilifu Nama, *Super Black: American Pop Culture and the Black Superheroes* (Austin: University of Texas Press, 2012).

27 Miller, *Life and Times of Martha Washington*, 12.

28 Ibid.

29 Ibid.

30 Ibid., 17.

31 Ibid., 21.

32 Ibid., 58.

33 On whiteness as compensation in social relations, see David Roediger, *The Wages of Whiteness: Race and the Making of the American Working Class* (New York City: Verso Press, 1999).

34 Campbell's work is especially noteworthy for its progressive depiction of sexuality(ies) and punk subcultures. See Ross Campbell, *Wet Moon* (Portland: Oni Press, 2005), and *The Abandoned* (Northridge: TokyoPop Press, 2006).

35 Michael Denning, *The Cultural Front: The Laboring of American Culture in the Twentieth Century* (New York City: Verso, 1998); Bill Mullen, *Popular Fronts:*

Chicago and African-American Cultural Politics, 1935–46 (Urbana: University of Illinois Press, 1999).

36 On other aspects of Ormes, see Nancy Goldstein, *Jackie Ormes: The First African American Woman Cartoonist* (Ann Arbor: University of Michigan Press, 2008); and Edward Brunner, "'Shuh! Ain't Nothin' to It': The Dynamics of Success in Jackie Ormes's *Torchy Brown*," *MELUS* 32, no. 3 (Sept. 2007): 25–50.

37 For theoretical explorations of Catwoman, see Phillip Orr, "The Anoedipal Mythos of Batman and Catwoman," *Journal of Popular Culture* 27, no. 4 (Spring 1994): 169–82; and Prisilla Walton, "A Slippage of Masks: Dis-guising Catwoman in *Batman Returns*," in *Sisterhoods: Across the Literature/Media Divide*, by Deborah Cartmell et al. (London: Pluto Press, 1998).

38 The work of Herman Gray on semiotics and the sign of blackness in 1980s television is an influence on my interpretation. See Herman Gray, *Watching Race: Television and the Struggle for Blackness* (Minneapolis: University of Minnesota Press, 1996).

39 "Constructive engagement" refers to a political policy during the Reagan administration that limited but did not end US business dealings with Africa, while making rhetorical proclamations about supporting the end of apartheid. See Christopher Coker, *Constructive Engagement and Its Critics* (Durham, NC: Duke University Press, 1986).

40 Harry Elam et al., *Black Cultural Traffic: Crossroads in Global Performance and Popular Culture* (Ann Arbor: University of Michigan Press, 2008).

41 Jeffrey Brown, *Black Superheroes, Milestone Comics, and Their Fans* (Jackson: University Press of Mississippi, 2001); Rod Lendrum, "The Super Black Macho, One Baaad Mutha: Black Superhero Masculinity in 1970s Mainstream Comic Books," *Extrapolation* 46, no. 3 (Fall 2005): 360–72.

42 See Graeme McMillan, "Marvel Boss: We're Not Sexist, Just Loud," May 5, 2009, accessed April 20, 2014, http://io9.com/5239963/marvel-boss-were-not-sexist-just-loud.

43 *The Butterfly*, in *Hell Rider* #1, Gary Friedrich (w), Ross Andru (p), Jack Abel and Mike Esposito (i), 1971, 2.

Chapter 1. Re-inking the Nation

Epigraphs: The Jackie Ormes profile appears in "Achievements," *One Tenth of a Nation*, 1953, American Newsreel Company, archived on YouTube, accessed 17 January 2015, https://www.youtube.com/watch?v=gmdHOkBISHA. Federal Bureau of Investigation, Freedom of Information/Privacy Acts, release, "Subject: Zelda Jackson Ormes" (Washington, DC: US Department of Justice, 1948–58). The report contains no page numbers. Italics in both epigraphs are mine.

1   The Dusable Museum of African American History, Chicago. The precise date of the illustration is unknown.

2   On the work and themes of Pablo Picasso, see John Richardson, *A Life of Picasso: The Triumphant Years, 1917–1932* (New York: Knopf, 2010).

3   On McGruder's comic strip and his subsequent animated series, see Deborah Elizabeth Whaley, "Graphic Blackness/Anime Noir: Aaron McGruder's *The Boondocks* and the Adult Swim," in *Watching while Black: Centering the Experience of Black Television Audiences*, ed. Beretta Smith Shomade (New Brunswick, NJ: Rutgers University Press), 187–204.

4   Ormes's FBI report claims that she was born in 1914. FBI release, "Subject: Zelda Jackson Ormes."

5   Nancy Goldstein, *Jackie Ormes: The First African American Woman Cartoonist* (Ann Arbor: University of Michigan Press, 2008), 184.

6   FBI release, "Subject: Zelda Jackson Ormes."

7   There is some speculation in the historical record about whether Ormes actually served as a sports reporter. Goldstein, *Jackie Ormes*, 184.

8   Alice Fahs, *Out on Assignment: Newspaper Women and the Making of Modern Public Space* (Chapel Hill: University of North Carolina Press, 2011), 17.

9   Ibid., 26–29.

10 See Patrick S. Washburn, *The African American Newspaper: Voice of Freedom* (Evanston, IL: Northwestern University Press, 2006), ix. Italics mine.

11 Trina Robbins, "Women in Comics," in *Out of Sequence: Underrepresented Voices in American Comics*, ed. John Jennings and Damian Duffy (Urbana-Champaign, IL: Krannert Art Museum, 2008), 56–57.

12 Maria Elena Buszek, *Pin-up Grrrls: Feminism, Sexuality, Popular Culture* (Durham, NC: Duke University Press, 2006), 96.

13 Bill Mullen, *Popular Fronts: Chicago and African-American Cultural Politics, 1935–1946* (Urbana-Champaign: University of Illinois Press, 1999), 2–3.

14 Erik S. McDuffie, *Sojourning for Freedom: Black Women, American Communism, and the Making of Black Left Feminism* (Durham, NC: Duke University Press, 2011), 5.

15 Throughout this chapter, I at times use the terms "popular front" and "cultural front" interchangeably. The Popular Front, in part, viewed culture and cultural production as a site for disseminating and acting upon the messages of their broad-based alliance. Thus, I see comics by leftist activists and artists as a form of cultural production that was an arm, or tool, of the Popular Front.

16 Steven Loring Jones, "From 'Under Cork' to Overcoming: Black Images in the Comics," in *Ethnic Images in the Comics*, ed. Charles Hardy and Gail F. Stern, Philadelphia: Museum of the Balch Institute for Ethnic Studies, September 15–December 20, 1986, 21–30.

17 Christopher Lehman, *The Colored Cartoon: Black Representation in American Animated Short Films, 1907–1954* (Amherst: University of Massachusetts Press, 2007).

18 Jones, "From 'Under Cork' to Overcoming," 21–30.

19 Angela M. Nelson, "Middle-Class Ideology in African-American Postwar Comic Strips," in *From Bourgeois to Boojie: Black Middle-Class Performances*, ed. Vershawn Ashanti Young (with Bridget Harris Tsemo) (Detroit: Wayne State University Press, 2011), 177.

20 Ibid., 186.

21 Edward Brunner, "'Shuh! Ain't Nothin' to It': The Dynamics of Success in Jackie Ormes' *Torchy Brown*," *MELUS* 32, no. 3 (Sept. 2007): 25.

22 Ibid.

23 On the *Amos 'n' Andy* controversy in the public sphere and the Black intellectual and activist response to the show, see Melvin Patrick Ely, *The Adventures of Amos 'n' Andy: A Social History of an American Phenomenon* (Charlottesville: University of Virginia Press, 2001).

24 Christine Stansell, *Sex and Class in New York City, 1789–1860* (Urbana-Champaign: University of Illinois Press, 1987), xii.

25 Angela Davis, *Blues Legacies and Black Feminism: Gertrude "Ma" Rainey, Bessie Smith, and Billie Holiday* (New York: Vintage, 1999), 66.

26 Goldstein, *Jackie Ormes*, 37.

27 The biography of Joe Louis recounts his contribution to sports in the face of the US racialist order. See Chris Mead, *Joe Louis: Black Champion in White America* (Mineola, NY: Dover Publications, 2010).

28 On African Americans in the Depression as the topic intersects with communism and activism, see Robin D. G. Kelley, *Hammer and Hoe: Alabama Communists during the Great Depression* (Chapel Hill: University of North Carolina Press, 1991).

29 Erik S. McDuffie, *Sojourning for Freedom*, 91–92.

30 James Smethurst, "SNYC, *Freedomways*, and the Influence of the Popular Front in the South on the Black Arts Movement," *Reconstruction: Studies in Contemporary Culture* 8, no. 1 (2008), accessed 1 March 2013, http://reconstruction.eserver.org/Issues/081/smethurst.shtml.

31 See Robin D. G. Kelley, *Race Rebels: Culture, Politics, and the Black Working Class* (New York: Free Press, 1996); Angela Davis, *Women, Race, and Class* (New York City: Vintage, 1983), 222.

32 Alice Childress, *Like One in the Family: Conversations on a Domestic's Life* (Boston: Beacon Press, 1986).

33 See Trudier Harris, *From Mammies to Militants: Domestics in Black American Literature* (Philadelphia: Temple University Press, 1982); Mary Helen Washington, "Alice Childress, Lorraine Hansberry, and Claudia Jones: Black Women Write the Popular Front," in *Left of the Color Line: Race, Radicalism, and Twentieth Century Literature of the United States*, ed. Bill Mullen and James Smethurst (Chapel Hill: University of North Carolina Press, 2003), 183–204.

34 Mullen, *Popular Fronts*, 48.

35 Nancy Goldstein writes that Ormes was not the only Black cartoonist to portray an attractive domestic in the *Defender*; comic artists Jay Jackson

and Wilbert Holloway would also depict domestics in a similar manner. Goldstein, *Jackie Ormes*, 75.

36 As cultural critic Gena Caponi explains, within Black vernacular speech practice, to "signify is to repeat, revise, reverse, or transform what has come before, continually raising the stakes in a kind of expressive poker, as in 'I'll see your insult and raise you one more.' Signifyin(g) is inherently dialogical, to use Mikhail Bakhtin's word, always existing within a relationship with an other." See Gena Caponi, *Signifying, Sanctifyin' and Slam Dunking: A Reader in African American Expressive Culture* (Amherst: University of Massachusetts Press, 1999), 22.

37 Bill Mullen, *Popular Fronts*, 5, 126.

38 Mullen, *Popular Fronts*, 5.

39 See Mary Anderson, "The Plight of Negro Domestic Labor," *Journal of Negro Education* 5 (Jan. 1936): 66–72; David Katzman, *Seven Days a Week: Women and Domestic Service in Industrializing America* (Urbana-Champaign: University of Illinois Press, 1981); Erik S. McDuffie, "Esther V. Cooper's 'The Negro Woman Domestic Worker in Relation to Trade Unionism': Black Left Feminism and the Popular Front," *American Communist History* 7, no. 2 (Dec. 2008): 203–9; L. S. Kim, *Maid for Television: Race, Class, and Gender on the Small Screen* (New York City: New York University Press, 2013); and Katherine Van Wormer et al., *The Maid Narratives: Black Domestics and White Families in the Jim Crow South* (Baton Rouge: Louisiana State University Press, 2012).

40 Jodie Kim, *Ends of Empire: Asian American Cultural Critique and the Cold War* (Minneapolis: University of Minnesota Press, 2010).

41 Buszek, *Pin-up Grrrls*, 3. See also Joanna Frueh, *Monster/Beauty: Building the Body of Love* (Berkeley: University of California Press, 2001).

42 From here on I quote from the FBI release, "Subject: Zelda Jackson Ormes."

43 Also known as the Alien Registration Act of 1940, the Smith Act required foreign-born and noncitizen adults residing in the United States to register with the US government and made any verbal and material schemes by such individuals to overthrow the US government subject to criminal penalties.

44 FBI release, "Subject: Zelda Jackson Ormes."

45 McDuffie, *Sojourning for Freedom*, 162.

46 "ISAs" refer to institutions that uphold and transmit the values of the state to secure the hegemony of the state. See Louis Althusser, "Ideology and Ideological State Apparatuses," *Lenin and Philosophy, and Other Essays*, trans. Ben Brewster (London: New Left Books, 1971), 127–88.

47 Goldstein, *Jackie Ormes*, 85.

48 "Code switching" refers to moving back and forth between Black vernacular language and standard English speech, whereas "code meshing" refers to an integration of vernacular and English that is a more fluid, and less

compartmentalized, form of speech. Patty-Jo exhibits both forms; in some gags and ads her speech is entrenched in heavy vernacular and even exaggerated stump speech. At other times, her speech is more fluid. Her speech is certainly indicative of her young age—she has not yet developed a full vocabulary—but given the implied location of her school, it seems that her speech pattern also represents an ongoing venture to mix vernacular speech and standard English for Ormes's Black audience, one that would vary in terms of class and speech patterns. For more on code switching and code meshing for Black Americans as it intersects with class, see Vershawn Young, "'Nah, We Straight': An Argument against Code Switching," *JAC* 29, nos. 1–2 (2010): 40–49.

49 Jay David, *Growing Up Black: From Slave Days to Present: Twenty-five African Americans Reveal the Trials and Triumphs of Their Childhoods* (New York: Harper Collins Publisher, 1971).

50 Goldstein, *Jackie Ormes*, 85.

51 See Debra J. Rosenthal, *A Routledge Literary Sourcebook on Harriet Beecher Stowe's Uncle Tom's Cabin* (New York: Routledge, 2003), 31; Henry Louis Gates and Kwame Anthony Appiah, eds., *Africana: Arts and Letters: An A-to-Z Reference of Writers, Musicians, and Artists of the African American Experience* (Philadelphia: Running Press, 2005), 544; Sophia Cantave, "Who Gets to Create the Lasting Images? The Problem of Black Representation in *Uncle Tom's Cabin*," in *Approaches to Teaching Stowe's* Uncle Tom's Cabin, ed. Elizabeth Ammons and Susan Belasco (New York: Modern Language Association of America, 2000), 93–103.

52 On the Patty-Jo doll, see Debbie Behan Garrett, "Jackie Ormes' Patty-Jo and Other Black Terri Lee Dolls," *Doll Castle News* (Mar.–Apr. 2008).

53 The doll test, though initiated by psychologists Kenneth and Mamie Clark, was replicated in later studies. The original test, however, helped shape decision making in *Brown v. Board of Education*. Ann DuCille treats the psychological impact of representation and dolls in her seminal book *Skin Trade* (Cambridge: Harvard University Press, 1996).

54 Buszek, *Pin-up Grrrls*, 311–54.

55 Maurice Horn, "Torchy Brown," *100 Years of American Newspaper Comics* (New York: Random House, 1996); Trina Robbins, *A Century of Women Cartoonists* (Northampton, MA: Kitchen Press, 1993).

56 Mullen, *Popular Fronts*, 3.

57 Lawrence's strip later became a comic book published by Dell Comics in 1972, and a film starring the actor Pam Grier in 1975. For brief mention of this character, see Jennifer D. Ryan, "Black Female Authorship and the African American Graphic Novel: Historical Responsibility in ICON: A Hero's Welcome," *Modern Fiction Studies* 52, no. 4 (2006): 918–46. *The New Yorker* published an article and an interview with the creator of *Friday Foster* in 1970, describing the lead character as a "pretty black girl making her way

in the white world" and a "gorgeous hip black chick." The comic's creator was inspired to write the strip given the dearth of images of Black Americans in the funny papers. Lawrence shared in the interview that he turned to the comic section and "was running my eye down the page and I suddenly said to myself, 'God, here's a page full of nothing but white faces!' It struck me as very wrong." See Anthony Hiss, "Friday Foster," *New Yorker*, March 21, 1970, 33–34.

Chapter 2. Black Cat Got Your Tongue?

Epigraphs: *The Many Faces of Catwoman*, directed by Jeffrey Lerner (Burbank, CA: DC Comics and Warner Brothers Pictures, 2005), DVD. A. D. Collier, "Halle Berry Is 'Purrrfect,' as She Cracks the Whip in Movie *Catwoman*," *Jet*, July 26, 2004, 56–61.

1   *Eartha Kitt: Femme Fatale,* Marc Shapiro (w), Felipe Montecinos and Ricardo Ayala (a), Felipe Montecinos (i), Bluewater Publications, February 6, 2013.

2   Laura Hudson, "There's a Lot of B*tching about Catwoman in 'Arkham City,'" *Comics Alliance*, October 20, 2011, accessed October 25, 2011, http:// comicsalliance.com/catwoman-arkham-city/.

3   Caniff's engagement with Orientalist motifs provides a context to understand the Cat's/Catwoman's development throughout the 1940s as a refraction of the Depression era and, later, World War II America's antagonism with China and Japan, and its ambivalence about the growing autonomy of women and their place in the workforce and in the public sphere. It is also telling that Caniff's work was available in military newspapers, thus underscoring his work's use to further patriotic and military agendas. On the work of Caniff, see Robert C. Harvey, ed., *Milton Caniff: Conversations* (Jackson: University Press of Mississippi, 2004). On Orientalism, see Edward Said, *Orientalism* (New York: Pantheon, 1978). On the Dragon Lady caricature in popular culture, see Sonia Shah et al., eds., *Dragon Ladies: Asian American Feminists Breathe Fire*, (Boston: Beacon Press, 1999).

4   Wonder Woman, Liberty Belle, and Black Canary were popular superheroines who were advocates for American patriotism and social justice against "the forces of evil" during World War II and thereafter. After the Golden Age of comics, there was a resurrection of these characters in a variety of mediums, including other comic books, television, and animation series. On women comic book characters of this era and after, see Lillian S. Robinson, *Wonder Women: Feminisms and Superheroes* (New York: Routledge, 2004); Trina Robbins, *From Girls to Grrlyz: A History of Women's Comics from Teens to Zines* (New York: Chronicle Books, 1999); and Sherrie Inness, ed., *Action Chicks: New Images of Tough Women in Popular Culture* (New York: Palgrave Press 2004).

5   Michael Uslan et al., *Catwoman: Nine Lives of Feline Fatale* (New York: DC Comics Press, 2004), 4.

6   "The Cat," *Batman* #1, Bob Finger (w), Bob Kane (p), Jerry Robinson (i), National Comics Publications (DC Comics), August–September 1940.

7   For a discussion of homoeroticism in the *Batman* series in the post–World War II years, see Chris York, "All in the Family: Homophobia and Batman Comics in the 1950s," *International Journal of Comic Art* 2, no. 2 (Spring 2000): 1000–1010. Other discussions of Batman and sexuality include Andy Medhurst, "Batman, Deviance and Camp," in *The Many Lives of the Batman: Critical Approaches to a Superhero and His Media*, ed. Roberta E. Pearson and William Uricchio (New York: Routledge, 1991); Marti Joe Morris, "Batman & Robin: 'Crime Fighting Duo' or 'Ambiguously Gay Duo?'" *Pop: A Critical Analysis of Pop Culture Matters*, a University of Idaho graduate student journal, accessed June 6, 2005, www.webpages.uidaho.edu/pop/Bat%20 Man.htm; and Freya Johnson, "Holy Homosexuality Batman! Camp and Corporate Capitalism in *Batman Forever*," *Bad Subjects* #23, December 1995, accessed June 6, 2005, http://bad.eserver.org/issues/1995/23/johnson.html.

8   On the relationship between blackness and comic book production, see Frederik Stomberg's visually stimulating *Black Images in the Comics: A Visual History* (New York: Fantagraphic Books, 2003).

9   The Comic Book Codes were a set of self-governing rules (or form of censorship) instituted by the Association of Comics Magazine Publishers in the wake of and in response to psychiatrist Frederic Wertham's claims about the negative effects of comic book reading on children, and US Senate hearings on juvenile delinquency (spearheaded by Senator Carey Estes Kefauver of Tennessee). The hearings, which cited Wertham as a reputable source, singled out comic books for their sexual and violent content. As a result, many titles retired characters and story lines that had direct and indirect sexual themes. On marriage and sexuality, for example, the Comic Book Codes held that: "(1) Divorce shall not be treated humorously nor represented as desirable. (2) Illicit sex relations are neither to be hinted at nor portrayed. Violent love scenes as well as sexual abnormalities are unacceptable. (3) Respect for parents, the moral code, and honorable behavior shall be fostered. A sympathetic understanding of the problems of love is not a license for morbid distortion. (4) The treatment of love-romance stories shall emphasize the value of the home and sanctity of marriage. (5) Passion or romantic interest shall never be treated in such a way as to stimulate the lower and baser emotions. (6) Sex perversion or any inference to same is strictly forbidden."

For an analysis of the Comic Book Codes, see Amy Kiste Nyberg, *Seal of Approval: The History of the Comics Code* (Jackson: University Press of Mississippi, 1998), 166–69. Nyberg includes the 1954 version of the codes in her appendices.

10   Readership of comics went from 50 percent female in the 1950s and '60s to 10 percent female by the late 1980s. Statistics on gender identity and comic

book reading appear in Shirley Biagi et al., *Facing Difference: Race, Gender, and Mass Media* (Thousand Oaks, CA: Pine Forge Press, 1997), 249.

11 Fredric Wertham, *Seduction of the Innocent* (New York: Rinehart, 1954).

12 The title of this section and this dialogue is from *Batman* #197, Gardner Fox (w), Bob Kane (p), Chic Stone and Sid Greene (i), National Comics Publications (DC Comics), December 1967.

13 "The Cat," *Batman* #1, Bob Finger (w), Bob Kane (p), Jerry Robinson (i), National Comics Publications (DC Comics), August–September 1940.

14 Quoted in Mila Bongco, "The Dark Knight Returns," *Reading Comics: Language, Culture, and the Concept of the Superhero* (New York: Garland, 2000), 154.

15 For a brief synopsis of Catwoman in the *Batman* comics, see Uslan et al., *Catwoman*, 5–6.

16 Stanley Ralph Ross, "Scat, Darn Catwoman," *Batman*, season 2, episode 75, directed by Oscar Rudolph, aired January 25, 1967, 20th Century Fox and Warner Brothers Television Distribution, prod. code 9743-Pt. 2.

17 "The Case of the Purr-Loined Pearl," *Batman* #210, Frank Robbins (w), Irv Novick (a), Joe Giella (i), National Comics Publications (DC Comics), March 1969.

18 The section head title comes from a phrase of dialogue from the Catwoman character in a *Batman* story that ran in "Catwoman Sets Her Claws for Batman," *Batman* #197, Gardner Fox (w), Frank Springer (p), Sid Greene (i), National Comics Publications (DC Comics), December 1967.

19 Lee Meriwether played Catwoman in *Batman: The Movie*.

20 For an analysis of stereotypes as it applies to Black comic book characters, and the counterproduction of Black comic book writers, see Marc Singer, "Black Skins/White Masks: Comic Books and the Secret of Race," *African American Review* 36, no. 1 (Spring 2002): 107–20.

21 See *The Many Faces of Catwoman*.

22 Stanley Ralph Ross, "Catwoman's Dressed to Kill," *Batman*, season 3, episode 108, directed by Sam Strangis, aired December 14, 1967, 20th Century Fox and Warner Brothers Television Distribution, prod. code 1717.

23 hooks uses the term "white-supremacist-capitalist patriarchy" in many of her writings, but the phrase appears in relationship to race and visual culture in her introduction to the book *Reel to Real: Race, Sex, and Class at the Movies* (New York: Routledge, 1996).

24 On the perception and reception of fans to the fluid masculinity of male characters in *Batman*, see Chris York, "All in the Family: Homophobia and Batman Comics in the 1950s"; Medhurst, "Batman, Deviance and Camp"; Morris, "Batman & Robin"; Johnson, "Holy Homosexuality Batman!"

25 John Nichols, "Eartha Kitt: An Anti-War Patriot," *The Beat* (blog), *The Nation*, December 26, 2008, accessed January 2, 2008, http://www.thenation.com/blogs/thebeat/391930/eartha_kitt_an_anti_war_patriot.

26 For a discussion of Eartha Kitt's transnational importance as a performer and activist, see Jayna Brown, *Babylon Women: Black Women Performers and the Shaping of the Modern* (Durham, NC: Duke University Press, 2008).

27 Stonewall riots were a series of interventions and protests around law enforcement's discriminatory singling out of gay clubs in New York City (Greenwich Village). Kitt's mixture of Catwoman camp and nightclub performer situated her as a popular culture icon in queer representation. On the convergence of popular culture, the public spheres, and queer history, see Corey Creekmur and Alexander Doty, *Out in Culture: Lesbian and Queer Essays on Popular Culture* (Durham, NC: Duke University Press, 1995).

28 Morris, "Batman & Robin."

29 "A Town on the Night," *Batman* #392, Doug Monich (w), Tom Mandrake (a), National Comics Publications (DC Comics), February 1986.

30 Jeffrey Brown, "Gender, Sexuality, and Toughness: Bad Girls of Action Film and Comic Books," in Inness, *Action Chicks*, 47–74.

31 Mila Boncgo, "The Dark Night Returns," *Reading Comics: Language, Culture, and the Concept of the Superhero* (New York: Garland, 2000), 151–76.

32 "The Ed Brubaker Interview," *Comics Journal* #263, October/November 2004, 59.

33 "Her Sister's Keeper," *Catwoman* #1–4, Mindy Newell (w), J. J. Birch (a), Michael Blair (i), National Comics Publications (DC Comics), May 1991.

34 The section head is a phrase of dialogue from the Catwoman character in a Batman story that ran in Edmond Hamilton's *Detective Comics*. See "The Jungle Cat Queen," *Detective Comics* #211, Edmond Hamilton (w), Dick Sprang (a), Charles Paris (i), National Comics Publications (DC Comics), September 1954.

35 Peter Travers, "Bat Girls on the Line," *Rolling Stone*, no. 634–35, July 9, 1992, 109.

36 Priscilla Walton, "A Slippage of Masks: Dis-guising Catwoman in *Batman Returns*," *Sisterhoods: Across the Literature/Media Divide*, ed. Deborah Cartmell et al. (London: Pluto Press, 1998), 200.

37 *Catwoman*, directed by Pitof, with Halle Berry, Benjamin Pratt, Sharon Stone, DC Comics & Warner Brothers Pictures, 2005. Also notable is that DC Comics is owned by Warner Brothers Pictures; thus, their interests are likely mutually constitutive.

38 Andrew Guy Jr. discusses fans' response to the film and interviews with fans in "A Real Catfight: Comic Book Fans Get Catty When Filmmakers Mess with Catwoman," *Houston Chronicle*, sec. 1, July 23, 2004, 1.

39 Ibid.

40 Aldore D. Collier, "Halle Berry Is 'Purrrfect' as She Cracks the Whip in Movie *Catwoman*," *Jet*, July 26, 2004, 56–61.

41 The original airdate of this *Oprah Winfrey Show* episode was May 25, 2004.

42 *Catwoman: The Movie and Other Cat Tales*, Chuck Austen (w), Jim Lee (a), Adam DeKraker (i), National Comics Publications (DC Comics), 2004.

43 *Catwoman* cost $100 million to make, and earned $39.6 million at the box office, resulting in a loss of approximately $60 million for Warner Brothers. *Catwoman* was the first action film of this magnitude and budget to feature a lead Black female actor. The release date of the film was July 23, 2004, and the release date of the special edition DVD was June 7, 2005.

44 On the legitimacy of cyber forums in cultural studies, see David Silver et al., *Critical Cyberculture Studies* (New York: New York University Press, 2006); Karen Hellekson and Kristina Busse, eds., *Fan Fiction and Fan Communities in the Age of the Internet* (New York: MacFarland, 2006).

45 George Lipsitz, "Against the Wind: Dialogic Aspects of Rock and Roll," *Time Passages* (Philadelphia: Temple University Press, 2001), 99–132.

46 I conducted the audience study as a participant and as an observer on the DC Comics message board. Given the nature of electronic media as an open forum that all users may access and respond to, the following excerpts are treated as quotations from a public Internet forum rather than as a "controlled experiment" conducted by an academician working with human subjects. Thus, from here on I am citing from the message board by use of scholarly documentation rather than presenting the voices as interviewees. The threads were generated in July 2005 and were archived at DC Comics' Catwoman message board site (now defunct) at http://dcboards .warnerbros.com/web/forum.jspa?forumID=29208977. Responses appear in Deborah Elizabeth Whaley, "Black Cat Got Your Tongue? Catwoman, Blackness, and the Alchemy of Postracialism," *Journal of Graphic Novels and Comics* 2, no. 1 (2011): 17–20.

47 Vixen is an African female superhero character discussed in chapter 3.

48 Comment on "Catwoman's Ethnicity," DC Comics' Catwoman message board site (now defunct).

49 Avid reader responses differ from the opinions of moviegoers and television enthusiasts presented in a Netflix survey of three hundred subscribers to the video rental franchise. In the Netflix survey, Halle Berry was the most popular Catwoman, garnering 31.9 percent of the vote; Julie Newmar, 13.8 percent; Eartha Kitt, 13.1 percent; Lee Meriwether, 0.3 percent; and "Other," 5 percent. Moviegoers ranked Catwoman the third-most-relatable graphic novel character, after Batman and Spiderman. A summary of these survey findings can be found in Guy, "A Real Catfight."

50 Jeffrey Brown makes this assertion about the relationship between the gender of the reader and the comic book text in *Black Superheroes, Milestone Comics, and Their Fans* (Jackson: University Press of Mississippi, 2001), 97.

51 Comment on "Male and Female Readers of Catwoman," DC Comics Catwoman message board site (now defunct).

52 Comment on "Is Catwoman a Feminist?" DC Comics' Catwoman message board site (now defunct).

53 Ed Brubaker, e-mail to author, June 17, 2006.

54 These statistics come from my interviews with five comic book retailers in Tucson, Arizona, whose answers were consistent about the title's readership.

55 The riot grrrl movement began among young women in the early 1990s and integrated punk rock and cultural politics relevant to third-wave feminists between the ages of fourteen and thirty. On the riot grrrl and third-wave feminist movement, see Maria-Elena Buszek, "'Oh! Dogma (Up Yours!)': Surfing the Third Wave," *thirdspace* 1, no. 1 (July 2001), accessed June 21, 2006, http://www.journals.sfu.ca/thirdspace/index.php./journals/article/viewArticle/buszek/6. On the relationship between the riot grrrl movement and women comic book characters, see Robbins, *From Girls to Grrlyz*.

56 "Relentless," *Catwoman Secret Files* #12–19, Ed Brubaker (w), Cameron Steward (a), Matt Hollingsworth (i), National Comics Publications (DC Comics), January 2005.

57 "Wilde Ride," *Catwoman Secret Files* #20–24, Ed Brubaker (w), Cameron Steward (a), National Comics Publications (DC Comics), February 2005.

58 "Union," *Gotham City Sirens* #1, Paul Dini and Guillem March (w), J. G. Jones (a), Ian Hannin and Raul Fernandez (i), National Comics Publications (DC Comics), June 2009.

Chapter 3. African Goddesses, Mixed-Race Wonders, and Baadasssss Women

Epigraphs: "Amazons and Apes," *Wonder Woman* #8, Doselle Young (w), Brian Denham (p), John Sibal (i), National Comics Publications (DC Comics), September 1999, 37. "Catacombs," *X-Men* #169, Chris Claremont (w), Paul Smith (p), Bob Wiacek (i), National Comics Publications (Marvel Comics), May 1983. "The Vixen: Is a Lady Fox," *Vixen* #1, Geary & Carla Conway (w), Bob Oskner (p), Vince Colletta (i), National Comics Publications (DC Comics), August–September 1978.

1 The *Wonder Woman* film project has been under way for more than a decade, but as of 2015, no actor has been named to play the role of Diana Prince/Wonder Woman. However, actor Gal Gadot will portray Wonder Woman in the 2016 film *Batman v. Superman: Dawn of Justice*.

2 Elisabeth Rappe, "The Geek Beat: All the World Is Waiting for You!" moviefone.com, November 18, 2008, accessed November 30, 2008, http://news.moviefone.com/2008/11/18/the-geek-beat-all-the-world-is-waiting-for-you/.

3 Geoff Boucher, "Beyoncé Wants to Lasso the Role of Wonder Woman," *Hero Complex: Pop Culture Unmasked*, *Los Angeles Times* online, November 7, 2008, accessed November 30, 2008, http://latimesblogs.latimes.com/herocomplex/2008/11/beyonc-wants-to.html.

4 Elisabeth Rappe, "The Geek Beat!"

5 Berbers are the indigenous peoples of North Africa west of the Nile Valley.

For an explication of the Berbers, see Michael Brett and Elizabeth Fentress, *The Berbers: The Peoples of Africa* (New York: Wiley-Blackwell, 1997).

6 I borrow this phrasing from bell hooks, "Eating the Other," *Black Looks: Race and Representation* (Boston: South End Press, 1992), 21–40.

7 For a history of the character Wonder Woman, see Les Daniels, *Wonder Woman: The Complete History* (San Francisco: Chronicle Books, 2000); and Les Daniels, *The Life and Times of an Amazon Goddess* (San Francisco: Chronicle Books, 2004).

8 *Ms. Magazine* 1, no. 1 (July 1972); *Ms. Magazine* 17, no. 4 (Fall 2007); *Ms. Magazine* 19, no. 1 (Winter 2009). Wonder Woman was also on an issue of *Ms.* in the late 1990s: *Ms. Magazine* 8, no. 1 (July–Aug. 1997).

9 "War of the Wonder Women!" *Wonder Woman* 32, #206, Cary Bates (w), Hedo Colletta (p), National Comics Publications (DC Comics), June–July 1973, 5.

10 Daniels, *Life and Times*, 132–33. Daniels opines that the Black sister of Wonder Woman was a good idea in theory but as written had representative flaws.

11 For example, Genesis 2:7 reads, "The Lord God formed man of the dust of the ground, and breathed into his nostrils the breath of life; and man became a living soul." While life begins with man in this passage, Polynesian (Māori) myth asserts that the god of the forest breathed life into clay, thereby creating woman. Gender notwithstanding, a connection to Greek mythology's Prometheus molding man from clay seems most applicable to Kanigher's narrative of the wonder woman births. For an insightful discussion of the use of African religion—real and imagined—in comic books in general, see Nicholas Yanes, "A History of African American Religion in Comic Books," in *Unionist Popular Culture and Rolls of Honour in the North of Ireland during the First World War, and Other Diverse Essays*, ed. Nannete Norris (New York: Mellen Press, 2012), 39–58.

12 "Mystery of Nubia," *Wonder Woman* 32, #205, Robert Kanigher (w), Don Heck and Bob Oksner (p), National Comics Publications (DC Comics), March–April 1973, 7.

13 Nell Irvin Painter, *Sojourner Truth: A Life, a Symbol* (New York: W. W. Norton, 1997).

14 "War of the Wonder Women!" *Wonder Woman* 32, #206, Cary Bates (w), Hedo Colletta (p), National Comics Publications (DC Comics), June–July 1973, 15.

15 Ibid.

16 "War of the Wonder Women!" *Wonder Woman* 32, #206, Cary Bates (w), Hedo Colletta (p), National Comics Publications (DC Comics), June–July 1973, 16.

17 "Mystery of Nubia," *Wonder Woman* 32, #205, Robert Kanigher (w), Don Heck and Bob Oksner (p), National Comics Publications (DC Comics), March–April 1973, 4; "War of the Wonder Women!" *Wonder Woman* 32, #206, Cary Bates (w), Hedo Colletta (p), National Comics Publications (DC Comics), June–July 1973, 23.

18 "Three Hearts," *Wonder Woman* 154, #154, Doselle Young (w), John McCrea (p), George Freeman (i), National Comics Publications (DC Comics), March 2000.

19 *Final Crisis* 1, #7, Grant Morrison (w), Doug Mahnke (p), Doug Mahnke, Tom Nguyen, Drew Geraci, Christian Alamy, Norm Rapmund, Rodney Ramos, and Walden Wong (i), Alex Sinclair, Tony Avina, Pete Pantazis (c), National Comics Publications (DC Comics), March 2009.

20 "War of the Wonder Women!" *Wonder Woman* 32, #206, Cary Bates (w), Hedo Colletta (p), National Comics Publications (DC Comics), June–July 1973, 2, 4.

21 Wilson Morales, "An Interview with Halle Berry," blackfilm.com, accessed June 10, 2009, http://www.blackfilm.com/20060505/features/halleberry.shtml.

22 Len Wein refers to Stan Lee's intents in Len Wein et al., "Introduction," *The Unauthorized X-Men: SF and Comic Writers on Mutants, Prejudice, and Adamantium* (San Francisco: Benbella Books, 2006), 1–8. See also Stan Lee et al., *Comics Creators on X-Men* (London: Titan Books, 2006).

23 The Suez Crisis refers to the 1956 struggle for occupation of and access to the Suez Canal. At the time, president Gamal Nasser of Egypt declared the Suez Canal a national right of the territory, thereby creating anxiety among Britain, France, and Israel concerning maritime access to the canal. This led to offense tactics among all three countries, most notably the deployment of British troops in Egypt. International pressure, including United States and United Nations intervention, stalled these efforts, leading the three countries to withdraw. As many revisionist accounts assert, the access and traffic of natural resources such as oil fueled the conflict, including the expelling of Britain's oil. What is significant about the choice to frame the narrative around the Suez Crisis in the comic is that it posits the United States as the savior of the region and is thus in alignment with US patriotic comics. The inclusion does provide an interesting precursor to the global conflict over oil and subsequent attempts at US empire. On this conflict, see *The Suez Crisis*, ed. Anthony Gorst and Lewis Johnman (London: Routledge, 1997); Keith Kyle, *Britain's End of Empire in the Middle East* (London: I. B. Taurs, 2002); and Steven Freiberger, *Dawn over Suez: The Rise of American Power in the Middle East, 1953–1957* (Chicago: Ivan R. Dee, 2007).

24 Anna Beatrice Scott, "Superpower vs. Supernatural: Black Superheroes and the Quest for Mutant Reality," *Journal of Visual Culture* 5, no. 3 (Spring 2006): 295–314.

25 "Welcome to the X-Men Rogue," *Uncanny X-Men* #171, Chris Claremont (w), Walt Simonson (p), Glynis Wein (i), National Comics Publications (Marvel Comics), December 1983.

26 W. E. B. Du Bois, *The Souls of Black Folk* (New York: Oxford University Press, 2007); "Binary Star!" *Uncanny X-Men* #164, Chris Claremont (w), Dave Cockrum (p), Janine Casey (i), National Comics Publications (Marvel Comics), December 1982.

27 Ibid.

28 Ibid.

29 *Storm*, Jerome Eric Dickey (w), David Yardin and Lan Medina (p), Jay Leisten and Sean Parsons (i), National Comics Publications (Marvel Comics), 2007.

30 Ibid.

31 William Jelani Cobb refutes the accuracy of what some refer to as the "Willie Lynch Internet Hoax" of the early 1990s. See Cobb's "William Lynch Is Dead 1212–2003," in *The Devil and Dave Chappelle and Other Essays* (New York City: Basic Books, 2007), 261–66; and Manu Ampim, *The Death of the Willie Lynch Speech* (Baltimore: Black Classic Press, 2013). Other accounts of Lynch that claim that the narrative is real are either self-published books or smaller press books available at outlets such as Amazon.com. See Lawanda Staten, *How to Kill Your Willie Lynch* (self-published by Lawanda M. Staten, 1997); Kashif Malik Hassan-el, *The Willie Lynch Letter and the Making of a Slave* (Chicago: Frontline Distribution International, 1999); Marc Sims, *Willie Lynch: Why African-Americans Have So Many Issues!* (self-published by Marc Sims, 2004); and Alvin Morrow, *Breaking the Curse of Willie Lynch: The Science of Slave Psychology* (Saint Louis: Rising Sun Publications, 2003).

32 Rebecca Housel, "Myth, Morality, and the Women of the X-Men," *Superheroes and Philosophy* (Chicago: Open Court Press, 2005), 81.

33 "The Vixen: Is a Lady Fox," *Vixen* #1, Geary and Carla Conway (w), Bob Oskner (p), Vince Colletta (i), National Comics Publications (DC Comics), August–September 1978.

34 On Pam Grier films, including the iconography of her film posters as creating a montage of content and violence, see Christopher Sieving, "She's a Stimulatin', Fascinatin', Assassinatin' Chick! Pam Grier as Star Text," *Screening Noir* 1, no. 1 (2005): 9–31.

35 Rod Lendrum, "The Super Black Macho, One Baaad Mutha: Black Superhero Masculinity in 1970s Mainstream Comic Books," *Extrapolation* 46, no. 3 (Fall 2005): 369.

36 "Destiny's Children," *Superman and Vixen*, special issue, *Justice League of America* #68, Jerry Conway (w), Curt Swan (p), Murphy Anderson (i), National Comics Publications (DC Comics), March 1984.

37 "Blood and Snow," *Suicide Squad* #11, John Ostrander (w), Luke McDonnell (p), Bob Lewis (i), National Comics Publications (DC Comics), March 1988.

38 For a political and ethnographic analysis of the Ethiopian Civil War and the struggle for succession by Eritrean nationalists between 1961 and 1991, see Tricia Redeker Hepner, *Soldiers, Martyrs, Traitors, and Exiles: Political Conflict in Eritrea and the Diaspora* (Philadelphia: University of Pennsylvania Press, 2009). On the postwar effects on Eritrean human rights in the region, see David O'Kane and Tricia Redeker Hepner, eds., *Biopolitics, Militarism,*

and *Development: Eritrea in the Twenty-first Century* (New York: Berghahn Books, 2009).

39 On this policy, see Christopher Coker, *Constructive Engagement and Its Critics* (Durham, NC: Duke University Press, 1986).

40 "How Green Was My Dallie?" *Justice League of America Task Force* #8, Peter David (w), Sal Velluto (p), Jeff Albrecht (i), National Comics Publications (DC Comics), December 1994.

41 CW Seed is the digital online site for the American television broadcasting network CW. See http://www.cwseed.com.

42 "Predators," *Vixen: Return of the Lion* #1, Willow Wilson (w), Cafu (p), Santiago Arcas (i), National Comics Publications (DC Comics), December 2008, cover.

43 Ibid.

44 "Risen," *Vixen Return of the Lion* #4, Willow Wilson (w), Cafu (p), Santiago Arcas (i), National Comics Publications (DC Comics), March 2009.

45 "Three Hearts: Part 2," *Wonder Woman* 154, #155, Doselle Young (w), John McCrea (p), George Freeman (i), National Comics Publications (DC Comics), April 2000, 13.

46 Ann DuCille, "Discourse and Dat Course: Postcoloniality and Afrocentricity," *Skin Trade* (Cambridge, MA: Harvard University Press, 1996), 120–35.

47 On this comic book, see Jeffrey Brown, *Black Superheroes, Milestone Comics, and Their Fans* (Jackson: University Press of Mississippi, 2001). Brown mentions Rocket only briefly. There is a thorough analysis of the character in Jennifer D. Ryan, "Black Female Authorship and the African American Graphic Novel: Historical Responsibility in ICON; A Hero's Welcome," *Modern Fiction Studies* 52, no. 4 (2006): 918–46.

48 Tricia Rose, "Foreword," *Black Cultural Traffic: Crossroads in Global Performance and Popular Culture* (Ann Arbor: University of Michigan Press, 2008), vi.

49 For a discussion of comics as social objects, see Charles Hatfield, *Alternative Comics: An Emerging Literature* (Jackson: University Press of Mississippi, 2005). In Jeffrey Brown's groundbreaking ethnography on readers of comics, parents of young readers note that despite their faults in representation, Black characters in comic books provide children with heroes to look up too. See Jeffrey Brown, *Black Superheroes*.

Chapter 4. Anime Dreams for African Girls

Epigraph: *Nadia: The Secret of Blue Water*, directed by Hideaki Anno; Hideaki Anno, Toshio Okada, Akio Satsukawa, Kaoru Umeno, and Hisao Okawa (w); Shiro Sagisu and Ukihiro Takahashi (m), NHK (Japan Network), Anime Network (US and Canada Network), Gainex (pro), ADV Films, 1990–91.

1 *Nadia: The Secret of Blue Water*, directed by Hideaki Anno; Hideaki Anno, Toshio Okada, Akio Satsukawa, Kaoru Umeno, and Hisao Okawa (w); Shiro

Sagisu and Ukihiro Takahashi (m), NHK (Japan Network), Anime Network (US and Canada Network), Gainex (pro), ADV Films, 1990–91. The show aired April 15, 1990, to March 16, 1991.

2 Jules Verne, *Twenty Thousand Leagues Under the Sea*, translated by F. P. Walter (Paris: Hetzel Publishers, 1870). The connection between *Nadia* and *Twenty Thousand Leagues* is confirmed in interviews with Anno, on the jacket of the DVD box set, and in the DVD credits.

3 Trica Danielle Keaton et al., "Introduction," in *Black France-France Noire: The History and Politics of Blackness* (Durham, NC: Duke University Press, 2012), 2–3.

4 Jodi Kim, *Ends of Empire: Asian American Critique and the Cold War* (Berkeley: University of California Press, 2010), 6.

5 All section titles in this chapter are taken from the show's episode titles.

6 Roland Kelts, *Japanamerica: How Japanese Culture Has Invaded the US* (New York: Palgrave, 2007), 72.

7 See Marc Steinberg, *Anime's Media Mix: Franchising Toys and Characters in Japan* (Minneapolis: University of Minnesota Press, 2012), viii; and Thomas Lamarre, *Anime Machine: A Media Theory of Animation* (Minneapolis: University of Minnesota Press, 2009), xiv.

8 Ibid. *Speed Racer* is also discussed in Kelts, *Japanamerica*, 11, 15–16, 21, 184.

9 Kelts, *Japanamerica*, 69–73.

10 See the Digital Hollywood University website, accessed January 15, 2013, http://www.dhw.ac.jp/en/.

11 Ibid.

12 Kelts, *Japanamerica*, 69–73.

13 A transcript of the interview with Anno was printed in *Animerica* 4, no. 9 (1996), accessed January 20, 2013, http://web.archive.org/web/20020606012703/http://masterwork.animemedia.com/Evangelion/anno.html.

14 On neoliberalism, identity, politics, and cultural production, see Pierre Bourdieu, "The Essence of Neo-liberalism," *Le Monde Diplomatique* online, December 1998, accessed September 5, 2003, Mondiplo.com, http://mondediplo.com/1998/12/08bourdieu; George Lipsitz, *American Studies in a Moment of Danger* (Minneapolis: University of Minnesota Press, 2001); Stephen Steinberg, "The Liberal Retreat from Race in the Post Civil Rights Era," in *The House That Race Built,* ed. Wahneema Lubiano (New York: Vintage, 1998), 13–47; Melvin Thomas, "Anything But Race: The Social Science Retreat from Racism," *Perspectives* 6, no. 1 (Winter 2000): 79–96; Adolph Reed Jr., "The 2004 Election in Perspective: The Myth of the Cultural Divide and the Triumph of Neoliberal Ideology," *American Quarterly* 57, no. 1 (Mar. 2005): 11; and Deborah Elizabeth Whaley, "Spike Lee's Phantasmagoric Fantasy and the Black Female Imaginary in *She Hate Me,*" *Poroi: An Interdisciplinary Journal of Rhetorical Analysis and Invention* 7, no. 2 (2011), 13.

15 Yasuhiro Takeda, *The Notenki Memoirs: Studio Gainax and the Men Who Cre-ated Evangelion* (Houston: A. D. Vision, 2005), 130–31.

16 The award is based on the number of fan votes.

17 Interview with Hideaki Anno, *AnimeLand* #32, May 1997, 19–21.

18 "Narratological grammars" inform on the theoretical implications and reception of narrative. "Visual grammars" refer to the structural rules of visual composition.

19 For a discussion of the visual aspects of anime and postmodernism, see Deb-orah Elizabeth Whaley, "Graphic Blackness/Anime Noir: Aaron McGruder's *The Boondocks* and the Adult Swim," in *Watching While Black: Centering the Experience of Black Television Audiences*, ed. Beretta Smith Shomade (New Brunswick: Rutgers University Press), 187–204.

20 "Interview with Hideaki Anno," *NewType*, January 2013.

21 "Interview with Hideaki Anno," *NewType*, June 1996.

22 Though Nadia is not originally from France, it would be quite probable for her to be a native Parisian, as Africans had been present in France (a long-standing free and educated population) long before the historical moment depicted in the series. See Shelby McCloy, *The Negro in France* (Lexington: University of Kentucky Press, 1961).

23 Though many online fan sites on Tumblr and Blogger allude to this, espe-cially those that argue for Nadia's blackness, no such sketch of Nadia with tightly coiled hair exists in online image databases. Still, tvtropes.com lists in its review of common anime tropes of the show that "in early production art, a later version of Nadia has textured hair which the designers admitted they liked, but found difficult to animate." No accompanying citation exists to corroborate the sketch's existence. See the tvtropes.com website, accessed February 17, 2013, http://tvtropes.org/pmwiki/pmwiki.php/Anime/NadiaTh eSecretOfBlueWater?from=Main.NadiaTheSecretOfBlueWater.

24 Amy Shirong Lu, "What Race Do They Represent and Does Mine Have Any-thing to Do with It? Perceived Racial Categories of Anime Characters," *Ani-mation: An Interdisciplinary Journal* 4, no. 2 (July 2009): 169–90.

25 For a discussion of world's fairs, see Paul Greenhalgh, *Fair World: A History of World's Fairs and Expositions from London to Shanghai 1851–2010* (Chi-cago: University of Chicago Press, 1993); Robert Rydell, *All the World's a Fair: Visions of Empire at American International Expositions, 1876–1916* (Chicago: University of Chicago Press, 1993); Lauren Rabinovitz, *Electric Dreamland: Amusement Parks, Movies, and American Modernity* (New York: Columbia University Press, 2012), 48–51.

26 See Leo Marx, *Machine in the Garden: Technology and the Pastoral Ideal in America* (London: Oxford University Press, 1964); and Leo Marx, "The Idea of Technology and Post Modern Pessimism," in *Does Technology Drive His-tory? The Dilemma of Technological Determinism*, ed. Merit Rowe Smith and Leo Marx (Cambridge, MA: The MIT Press, 1999), 237–57.

27 For a discussion of gender and race as a technology, see Teresa de Lauretis, "Rethinking Women's Cinema: Aesthetics and Feminist Film Theory," *Technologies of Gender: Essays on Theory, Film, and Fiction* (Bloomington: Indiana University Press, 1987), ix.

28 Dana Hale, *Races on Display: French Representations of Colonized Peoples, 1886–1940* (Bloomington: Indiana University Press, 2008), 24.

29 Ibid., 34.

30 Ibid., 24. See also Deborah Willis, ed., *Black Venus 2010: They Called Her "Hottentot,"* (Philadelphia: Temple University Press, 2010).

31 McCloy, *Negro in France*, 64.

32 Lauren Rabinovitz, "Urban Wonderlands," in *Electric Dreamland: Amusement Parks, Movies, and American Modernity* (New York: Columbia University Press, 2012), 48–51.

33 Given the context, writers were likely using the less common definition of "easel," which, according to Dutch usage, refers to the ass of a donkey.

34 On Atlantis as a symbol, see Richard Ellis, *Imagining Atlantis* (New York: Vintage Books, 1999).

35 *Nadia* the videogame, released concurrently with the television series, had a rudimentary platform that resembled games played on Atari machines in the 1980s. Though in Japanese, it was made available to the US market by the Japanese distributor Namco (which had by then bought Atari Games).

36 See the Hobby Search website, accessed September 9, 2012, http://www.1999.co.jp/houki_e.asp?Typ1_c=101. The action figures are also available at Amazon.com.

37 Elizabeth Johns, "Full of Home Love and Simplicity," *American Genre Painting and the Politics of Everyday Life* (New Haven, CT: Yale University Press, 1995), 172–73.

38 Maria Elena Buszek, *Pin-up Grrrls: Feminism, Sexuality, Popular Culture* (Durham, NC: Duke University Press, 2006), 2–3.

39 "Interview with Hideaki Anno," *AnimeLand* #32, May 1997.

40 J. Keith Vincent, "Translator's Introduction: Making It Real: Fiction, Desire, and the Queerness of the Beautiful Fighting Girl," in *Beautiful Fighting Girl*, ed. Saitō Tamaki (Minneapolis: University of Minnesota Press, 2011), xi.

41 Rebecca Adams, "Anastasiya Shpagina Turns Herself into Real-Life Anime Girl," *Huffington Post*, October 10, 2012, accessed October 15, 2012, http://www.huffingtonpost.com/2012/10/01/anastasiya-shpagina-anime-cartoon-pictures-photos-surgery_n_1929012.html.

42 "Harajuku subculture" refers to the style and culture that emanate from the Japanese shopping district of Harajuku. Journalist MiHi Ahn describes the style of dress that young women adopt as a "mix of seemingly disparate styles and colors [where] vintage couture can be mixed with traditional Japanese costumes, thrift store classics, Lolita-esque flourishes and

cyber-punk accessories." See MiHi Ahn, "Gwenihana," *Salon*, April 9, 2005, accessed May 20, 2013, http://www.salon.com/2005/04/09/geisha_2/.

43 Brad Rice, "Man Arrested for Manga Collection?" *Japanator*, October 11, 2008, accessed May 20, 2013, http://www.japanator.com/post.phtml?pk=8753. In this case, the jury was asked to weigh: "(a) whether the average person, applying contemporary community standards would find that the work, taken as a whole, appeals to the prurient interest; (b) whether the work depicts or describes, in a patently offensive way, sexual conduct specifically defined by the applicable state law; and (c) whether the work, taken as a whole, lacks serious literary, artistic, political, or scientific value."

44 According the CBLDF website, "The Comic Book Legal Defense Fund was founded in 1986 as a 501(c)3 nonprofit organization dedicated to the preservation of First Amendment rights for members of the comics community. They have defended dozens of Free Expression cases in courts across the United States, and led important education initiatives promoting comics literacy and free expression." Comic Book Legal Defense Fund website, accessed May 20, 2013, is at http://cbldf.org/f-a-q/.

45 See Frantz Fanon, *Toward the African Revolution* (New York City: Grove Press, 1967), 7.

Chapter 5. Where I'm Coming From

Epigraphs: Ruby Dee and Ossie Davis, foreword to *Where I'm Coming From*, Barbara Brandon-Croft (Kansas City: Andrews and McMeel, 1993), 5. Barbara Brandon-Croft, "Talking Heads: Cartoonist Barbara Brandon Hears the Voices of Nine Opinionated Black Women," *People* 36, no. 5 (Feb. 10, 1992): 104.

1 Sheila Rule, "The Girls Talking, with a Black Perspective," *New York Times*, July 19, 1992, 16. On the work of Brandon-Croft, also see Dawne E. V. Simon, "Barbara Brandon: A Womanist in Syndication," *Ms. Magazine* 4, no. 2 (Sept.–Oct. 1993): 85; Scott Markie Robson, "New Strip on the Block," *Guardian*, Feb. 12, 1992, 17; David Astor, "Where She Came from to Get Syndicated," *Editor & Publisher* 124, no. 47 (Nov. 1991): 38.

2 "A Look at Barbara's Life's Work," Black History Month Profile: Barbara Brandon-Croft, *Fort Bend Herald*, February 3, 2012, accessed February 5, 2012, http://www.fbherald.com/article_b6c2c7b8-4d08-11e1-9316-0019bb2963f4.html?mode=story.

3 There were twelve reoccurring characters in *Where I'm Coming From*.

4 Amy Linden, "Barbara Brandon: A Comic Strip About Us," *Essence Magazine* 7, no. 5 (Mar. 1990): 14.

5 Sheila Rule, "The Girls Talking," 16.

6 The LA uprising was a series of protests, often termed "riots," in response to four police officers being acquitted of beating a Black male civilian, Rodney

King, even though the beating was videotaped and considered by many to be an example of excessive police force.

7 Barbara Brandon-Croft, *Where I'm Still Coming From* (Kansas City: Andrews and McMeel, 1994), 56.

8 President Clinton initiated this policy in the United States for the US military, which held that lesbian, gay, and bisexual individuals in the military would not face inquiries into their sexuality, and that such individuals would not divulge their sexual preferences. This policy was overturned in 2010.

9 Brandon-Croft, *Where I'm Still Coming From*, 26.

10 Barbara Brandon-Croft, *Where I'm Coming From* (Kansas City: Andrews and McMeel, 1993), 17.

11 Mike Tyson was convicted of raping an eighteen-year-old woman.

12 Brandon-Croft, *Where I'm Coming From*, 53.

13 Ibid., 87.

14 Brandon-Croft, *Where I'm Still Coming From*, 6.

15 Ibid., 57.

16 Ibid., 44.

17 Ibid., 7.

18 Jules Feiffer is an American cartoonist (and playwright and screenwriter), best known for his comic strip *Feiffer* that featured inked talking heads with tightly written dialogue and captions. For more on his work, see his memoir, *Backing into Forward* (Chicago: University of Chicago Press, 2012).

19 bell hooks, "Postmodern Blackness," in *The Norton Anthology: Theory and Criticism*, ed. Vincent B. Leitch (New York: W. W. Norton & Company, 2001), 2480.

20 "A Look at Barbara's Life's Work," *Fort Bend Herald*.

21 Nancy Goldstein, "Correcting the Historical Record," *Jackie Ormes: The First African American Woman Cartoonist* (Ann Arbor: University of Michigan Press, 2008), 185.

22 Dee and Davis, "Foreword," *Where I'm Coming From*, 5.

23 All of the artists listed here—except Rashida Jones—are members of the Ormes Society.

24 I use the term *affect* as a critical analytic to reflect the precognitive intensities of emotional, visceral, and embodied forces that drive subjects (i.e., humans and posthumans) to feel, transform, and act. Rather than being simply synonymous with emotion per se, Jasbir Puar and Ann Pellegrini propose affect as "the body as well as emotion's *trace effect*. This conception of affect poses a distinction between sensation and the perception of the sensation. Affect, from this perspective, is precisely what allows the body to be an open system, always in concert with its virtuality, [and] the potential of becoming." On theories of affect see Melissa Gregg and Gregory J. Seigworth eds., "Introduction," *The Affect Theory Reader* (Durham and London: Duke University Press, 2010); Ann Cvetkovich, *Depression: A Public Feeling*

(Durham and London: Duke University Press, 2012), 4; Jasbir Puar and Ann Pellegrini, "Affect," *Social Text* 27, no. 3 (Fall 2009): 35–38.

25 Container categories leave out and suppress information, whereas a bracket methodology works from both ends of a spectrum to explain something anew.

26 Will Eisner, an American cartoonist, is sometimes referred to as the "father of the graphic novel" and is noted for his series *The Spirit*, which ran from 1940 to 1952. See Michael Schumacher, *Will Eisner: A Dreamer's Life in Comics* (New York: Bloomsbury, 2010).

27 See Erika D. Peterman's interview with Eaton, "African-American Women Take on the Comic Book Industry," CNN online, November 28, 2011, accessed March 13, 2013, http://geekout.blogs.cnn.com/2011/11/28/african-american-women-take-on-the-comic-book-industry/.

28 Leisl Adams, interview by Deborah Elizabeth Whaley, August 26, 2009.

29 Afua Richardson, interview by Deborah Elizabeth Whaley, September 15, 2009.

30 See Lawrence Grossberg's interview with Stuart Hall in Lawrence Grossberg, "History, Politics and Postmodernism: Stuart Hall and Cultural Studies," in *The Stuart Hall Reader*, ed. David Morley and Kuan-Hsing Chen (London: Routledge, 1996), 151–73.

31 Richard Iton, *In Search of the Black Fantastic: Politics and Popular Culture in the Civil Rights Era* (Oxford: Oxford University Press, 2008), 16.

32 Manthia Diawara explains Afrafemcentric as a discourse and political position aimed at empowering Black women. See his chapter "Black American Cinema: The New Realism," in *Black American Cinema*, ed. Manthia Diawara (New York: Routledge, 1993), 5.

33 Deborah Elizabeth Whaley, "Celluloid Masks and Retractable Skins: Transforming the Scales of Blackness in Sequential Art," foreword to *Toonskin*, exhibition catalogue, curated by Kenya(Robinson), ArtSPACE, New Haven, Connecticut, Saturday, May 11, 2013–Saturday, June 29, 2013, 8–9.

34 I employ here a common phrase associated with the work of Frederic Jameson on affect. See Fredric Jameson, "Postmodernism, or the Cultural Logic of Late Capitalism," *New Left Review*, no. 146 (1984): 53–92.

35 Eric Spitznagel, "Rashida Jones Is All about Hot Chicks Kicking Ass!" *Vanity Fair*, December 17, 2009, accessed January 10, 2014, http://www.vanityfair.com/online/oscars/2009/12/rashida-jones-is-all-about-hot-chicks-kicking-ass.

36 *Frenemy of the State* #2, Rashida Jones, Christina Weir, and Nunzio Defilippis (w), Jeff Wamester (a), Rob Ruffolo (c), Douglass E. Sherwood (i) (Portland: Oni Press, 2010).

37 *Frenemy of the State* #3, Rashida Jones, Christina Weir, and Nunzio Defilippis (w), Jeff Wamester (a), Rob Ruffolo (c), Douglass E. Sherwood (i) (Portland: Oni Press, 2010).

38 On Orientalism, or Western representation of the East as the fabricated, threatening Other, see Edward Said, *Orientalism* (New York City: Vintage, 1979).

39 Rubén Ramírez Sánchez, "Marginalization from Within: Expanding Co-cultural Theory through the Experience of the Afro Punk," *Howard Journal of Communications* 19, no. 2 (2008): 89–104.

40 Afua Richardson, interview by Deborah Elizabeth Whaley, September 15, 2009.

41 Ibid.

42 Ibid.

43 C. Spike Trotman is the founder of Iron Circus Comics (an independent publishing outlet founded in 2007); author of the webcomic *Templar, Arizona*; and contributor to the titles *Poorcraft* and *Smut Peddler*. For examples of her work, see the artist's website at http://ironcircus.com/.

44 Afua Richardson, interview by Deborah Elizabeth Whaley, September 15, 2009.

45 Andrew McCann, "Textual Phantasmagoria: Marcus Clarke, Light Literature, and the Colonial Uncanny," *Australian Literary Studies* (University of Queensland) 21, no. 2 (Oct. 2003): 137. Phantasmagoria constitutes a space in which subjects, specters, and optic productions (such as visual images and icons) disappear and reappear, thereby conjoining fantasy with reality, animate objects, and inanimate objects. On the term "phantasmagoria," also see Margaret Cohen, "Walter Benjamin's Phantasmagoria," *New German Critique* 48, no. 87 (Sept. 1989): 93–94; Caroline Evans, *Fashion at the Edge: Spectacle, Modernity, and Deathliness* (New Haven, CT: Yale University Press, 2008), 89.

46 Nara Walker, interview by Deborah Elizabeth Whaley, August 13, 2009.

47 Ibid.

48 Ibid.

49 Ibid.

50 Nara Walker, *Legacy of Light* (Raleigh, NC: Lulu Press, 2006).

51 Ibid.

52 Nara Walker, *Songbirds* (Raleigh: Lulu Press, 2011).

53 Ibid.

54 Andrea Wood, "'Straight' Women, Queer Texts: Boy-Love Manga and the Rise of a Global Counterpublic," *Women's Studies Quarterly* 34, nos. 1–2 (Spring–Summer 2006): 397. Italics mine.

55 *Sand Storm* #1, Rashida Lewis (w), Keith Lovely (a), (c), (i), Rashida Lewis, New Wave Enterprise Publishers, November 2007.

56 Christa Babson-Thomas, "Pow! Splat! Women Muscle into the Macho World of Comics," accessed June 5, 2013, http://journalism.nyu.edu/publishing/archives/livewire/archived/comics/.

57 *Sand Storm* #3, Rashida Lewis (w), Keith Lovely (a), (c), (i), Rashida Lewis, New Wave Enterprise Publishers, August–September 2007.

58 Interview by Talib Byson, accessed August 15, 2009, http://www.black superhero.com.

59 Lewis, *Sand Storm #3*.

60 Leisl Adams, interview by Deborah Elizabeth Whaley, August 26, 2009.

61 Sean "Cheeks" Galloway is the artist and designer of *Spiderman*.

62 Michelle Billingsley, interview by Deborah Elizabeth Whaley, August 18, 2009.

63 See Michelle Billingsley's webcomic *Joe!*, accessed August 1, 2009, http:// joefunnies.com.

64 Janice Radway, *A Feeling for Books: The Book-of-the-Month Club, Literary Taste, and Middle-Class Desire* (Chapel Hill: University of North Carolina Press, 1999).

65 Michelle Billingsley, interview by Deborah Elizabeth Whaley, August 18, 2009.

66 Ibid.

67 Alondra Nelson, "Afrofuturism," special issue, *Social Text* 71, no. 3 (2002): 7. See also the Afrofuturist novel by Black male writer Thelonious Legend, *Sins of the Father* (Chicago: The Legend Books, 2014), which centers on the experiences of young Black women as superheroines.

68 Ashley A. Woods, *Millennia War: The Graphic Novel*, vol. 1, printed in the USA, 2010, available in print-on-demand at http://www.indyplanet.com/ front/product/49067/.

69 Ashley Woods, interview with Deborah Elizabeth Whaley, August 10, 2009.

70 Ibid.

71 Leisl Adams, interview by Deborah Elizabeth Whaley, August 26, 2009.

72 "Sketch Maven Comic Artist Profiles: Leisl Adams," accessed June 10, 2013, http://www.sketchmaven.com/cms.php?content=Leisl_Adams.

73 Leisel Adams, interview with Deborah Elizabeth Whaley, August 26, 2009.

74 D. M. Cunningham, "Hanging on the Edge with Leisl Adams," accessed June 10, 2013, http://literaryasylum.blogspot.com/2010/07/hanging-on-edge-with-leisl-adams.html.

75 Ibid.

76 Leisl Adams, *On the Edge: Tales from the Therapist's Couch* (San Bernardino, CA: Flat Foot Publishers, 2013), 13.

77 Ibid., 10.

78 Ibid., 13.

79 Michele Wallace, "'Why Are There No Great Black Artists?' The Problem of Visuality in African-American Culture," in *Black Popular Culture*, ed. Gina Dent (Boston: Beacon Press, 1994), 333–47.

80 Noelene Clark, "Women in Comics and the Tricky Art of Equality," *Los Angeles Times*, July 21, 2012, accessed September 12, 2013, http://herocomplex .latimes.com/2012/07/21/women-in-comics-you-cant-keep-a-good-creator-down/#/9.

81 For visual examples of these artists' work, see Jennifer Crute's illustrations on her website, crutecomics.com, and her indie comic *Jennifer's Journal: The Life of a SubUrban Girl*, vol. 1 (Raleigh, NC: Lulu Press, 2014); webcomic artist and illustrator Viga Victoria's website at http://blip.tv/vigalovescomics; and Juliana Smith's digital comic on her website (H)afrocentric, accessed July 20, 2014, http://hafrocentric.com/.

82 Afua Richardson, interview by Deborah Elizabeth Whaley.

Conclusion

Epigraph: *Marvel Divas*, Roberto Aguirre-Sacasa (w), Tonci Zonjic (a), June Chung and Jelena Kevic Djurdjevic (i), National Comics Publications (Marvel Comics), 2010.

1   *Marvel Divas*, Roberto Aguirre-Sacasa (w), Tonci Zonjic (a), June Chung and Jelena Kevic Djurdjevic (i), National Comics Publications (Marvel Comics), 2010.

2   Ibid.

3   *Gotham City Sirens*, Paul Dini (w), Guillem March (a), Jose Villarrubia (i), National Comics Publications (Marvel Comics), 2009.

4   The sexy cover war of *Marvel Divas* and DC's *Sirens* is discussed in Graeme McMillan, "Marvel Boss: We're Not Sexist, Just Loud," May 5, 2009, accessed April 20, 2014, http://io9.com/5239963/marvel-boss-were-not-sexist-just-loud; Hortense Smith, "Marvel Divas: Because Nothing Says Superhero Like 'Hot Sudsy Fun,'" *Jezebel*, April 11, 2009, accessed April 20, 2014, http://jezebel.com/5207676/marvel-divas-because-nothing-says-superhero-like-hot-sudsy-fun#c; Matt Duarte, "Sirens and Divas: A Comparison," *Weekly Crisis*, August 3, 2009, accessed April 20, 2014, http://www.theweeklycrisis.com/2009/08/sirens-and-divas-comparison.html.

5   Hortense Smith, "Marvel Divas: Because Nothing Says Superhero Like 'Hot Sudsy Fun.'"

6   McMillan, "Marvel Boss."

7   Ibid.

8   Herman Gray, "Culture, Masculinity, and the Time after Race," in *Toward a Sociology of the Trace*, ed. Herman Gray and Macarena Gómez-Barris (Minneapolis: University of Minnesota Press, 2010), 88.

INDEX

A

Cartoon Network, US, 116, 124

Cat, 69

Catlett, Elizabeth, 176

Catwoman (2004 film), 69, 81–85, 131, 200n43, *plate7*; apology in, 83; reviews of, 83–84, 199n38

Catwoman (graphic novel series), 22, 68, 70, 83–93, *plate7*; and DC message board, 85–92; readership of, 92; as soft-core porn, 92. *See also titles of graphic novels*

Catwoman (in *Arkham City*), 68–69

Catwoman (in *Batman*), x, 22–23, 65–66, 69–80, 73*fig.*, 90, 144, 157, 183; disappearance from comic book, 71, 72; and feminism, 70, 74–75, 80, 82–83, *plate5*; as hairdresser, 70, 79, 83; as jewel thief, 70, 79, 83; Kitt as, x, 65, 75–79, 82, 87, 200n49; and matrimony, 71–75, 73*fig.*, *plate4*

Catwoman (in *Batman Returns*), 81–82

Catwoman (in *Batman: The Movie*), 198n19

Catwoman (in graphic novels), 65–66, 70, 79–81, 168

Catwoman (in *The Dark Knight Rises*), 68

Catwoman: Copy Cat (2005 film short), 85

"Catwoman Dressed to Kill" (*Batman* television program), 76, 78

Catwoman: Her Sister's Keeper (Newell), 81, 83, *plate6*

Catwoman message board (DC Comics), 85–92, 200n46

Catwoman: Nine Lives (2005 film short), 85

Catwoman: The Game (video game), 69

"Catwoman: The Movie and Other Cat Tales," *plate7*

Cecilia Reyes (in *X-Men*), 21

charitable organizations, 44

chastity, 124

Cheryl (in *Where I'm Coming From*), 147, 149–50

Chicago (Ill.): Cabrini-Green housing projects, 17–18; Chicago Renaissance, 47; Chicago South Side, 47, 54–55; Council of the Arts, 55; Modern Book Store, 56; South Side Community Art Center, 47; Sutherland Hotel, 47

Chicago Defender, 33, 35, 37, 45–47, 50*fig.*, 52*fig.*, 193n35

Chicago Tribune, 65, 111

Childress, Alice, 45–46

child starvation, 115

Chinese, 23

Christmas, 62

CIA (Central Intelligence Agency), 156–58

cigarettes, 45, 52–53, 52*fig.*

circumcision, 116, 118

Civil Right Act (1964), 100

Civil Rights Congress (CRC), 55–56

civil rights movement, xi, 18, 21–22; and Catwoman, 23, 70; and Ormes, 36, 44–45, 57, 59–60, 62

Claremont, Chris, 110

Clark, Kenneth and Mamie, 62, 195n53

Clark, Noelene, 177–78

Clark doll test, 177

classism, 44, 63

class status, 11, 17, 26, 182; and Brandon-Croft, 147, 149, 151; and Catwoman, 77, 85; class equality, 101; and comix, 164, 170, 172, 178; elite artistic spheres, 28–31, 29*fig.*, 30*fig.*, 176–77; and Ormes, 28–32, 29*fig.*, 30*fig.*, 36, 38, 40, 44, 49, 52–53, 57, 63, 194n48; socioeconomic class, 53

Claw (in *Hell Rider*), 6

Felicia Hardy (in *Marvel Divas*), 179, *plate20*
femininity: and Catwoman, 76; and Ormes, 41–42, 53
feminism, 26, 63; Black feminist thought, 101; and Brandon-Croft, 150; and Catwoman, 70, 74–75, 80, 82–83, 85, 90–91, 201n55, *plate5*; and comix, 155, 166–68; and DC message board, 85, 90–91; feminist liberation, 155; misconceptions of, 91; and Nadia, 140; and Nubia, 101, 103–4, 120; and Obama, 98–99; protofeminist, 140; pseudofeminism, 101; and Storm, 108; third-wave feminism, 201n55; and Vixen, 118; and Wonder Woman, 98–99, 101, 103–4
Fernandez, Peter, 125
fetishism, 10, 96, 118, 144, 146, 172
film, 10, 11, 13–15, 182; blaxploitation era, 16, 21, 111; and Catwoman, 22–23, 65, 70, 79, 81–85; and comix, 162; and Nadia, 132, 141–42, 146; and Speed Racer, 125; and Vixen, 111. *See also titles of films*
film shorts, 85
Final Crisis (comic book), 103, *plate8*
Finger, Bill, 69
Firestar (in *Marvel Divas*), 26, 179–80, *plate20*
First Amendment, 209n44
"The First Kiss" (anime), 139
flag, American, 57–58, 58*fig.*, 157
flashlights, 134
Florence Johnston (in *The Jeffersons*), 46
foreign policy, US, 60–61
Foucault, Michel, 190n24
Fox, Gardner, 111, *plate4*
Foxy Brown (film), 111
France, 122–24, 128–30, 132–37, 207n22; French Academy, 162

freak shows, 135–36
Freedom (leftist newspaper), 46
freedom fighters, 17, 20, 75, 116, 146. *See also names of freedom fighters*
Free Expression cases, 209n44
Free Speech and Headlight, 33
Frenenemy of the State (Jones), 156–59, 176, *plate15*
Friday Foster (1975 film), 111, 195n57
Friday Foster (comic book), 111
Friday Foster (comic strip), 65, 111, 195n57
Friedrich, Gary, 3–4, 5*fig.*, 6, 186n1, *plate1*
Frueh, Joanna, 53
Fushigino umi no Nadia. See *Nadia: The Secret of Blue Water* (anime series)
futurism, 170–71, 173–75. *See also* Afrofuturism

G

Gable, Nan Aspinwall, 136
Gadot, Gal, 201n1
gags, 13–14, 31, 182–83; and Ormes, 36, 46–47, 53–54. See also *Candy* (Ormes); *Patty-Jo 'n' Ginger* (Ormes)
Gainax, 127
Galloway, Sean "Cheeks," 168, 213n61
Gargoyle (in *Nadia: The Secret of Blue Water*), 122, 138
Gavin Star (in *Songbirds*), 164–65
gay rights, 78–79, 199n27
gays, 149, 164–65, 210n8. *See also* queers
gaze: and Africa, 97, 136; and Catwoman, 92; and Nadia, 136, 141–42; and Ormes, 43; pornographic gaze, 92; racialized gaze, 136; and racial passing, 43; and sexual politics, 141–42

geek power, xi

gender discrimination, 32–33, 40–41, 100

gender relations, 9, 11, 16, 19–20, 182–84; and Africa, 97, 99–101, 103, 110, 114, 116, 118–20; and Black cultural traffic, 120; and Black migration, 40–41; and Brandon-Croft, 147, 149–51; and Catwoman, 68–70, 74–75, 77–79, 81, 84–85, 88–92, 200n50; and comix, 155, 161–68, 170, 172–74, 176–78; and DC message board, 85, 88–92; gender equality, 101; gender-exclusive products/consumers, 88; gender identity, 88, 92, 197n10; gender inclusivity, 92; gender norms, 40, 74; gender politics, 34, 38, 68–69, 91; gender wars, 23–24, 100–101; intergender relations, 100; and *Marvel Divas*, 180–82; and Nadia, 122–24, 132, 136, 141; and Nubia, 99–101, 103, 120, 202n11; and Omene, 136; and Ormes, 34, 36, 38, 40–42, 63; and Ormes Society, 153; and Rocket, 119; and Storm, 110; and Vixen, 114, 116, 118

General Manitoba (in *Vixen*), 113

Genesis, 99, 202n11

Genius (Richardson), 156

genocide, 171–72

genre painting, American, 140–42

Ghost Rider (Friedrich), 3, 6, 186n1

Giant X-Men (comic book), 107

Gibbons, Dave, 17

Gibson, Charles Dana, 33

Gibson Girl, 33–34

Gillespie, Dizzy, 47

"The Girl at the Eiffel Tower" (anime), 128–29, 133, *plate12*, *plate13*

Girls to Grrlz: A History of Women in Comics from Teens to Zines (Robbins), 10

glass ceiling: and Berry as Storm, 106; and Ormes, 32

globalization, 97, 124–26, 146, 153

Goldstein, Nancy, 47, 58–60, 65, 193n35

Gone with the Wind (1939 film), 49

Goolah (in *Wonder Woman*), 101

Gorgon (in *Eartha Kitt: Femme Fatale*), 67–68, *plate3*

Gotham City Sirens, 93, 180–81

Gramsci, Antonio, 190n24

Grandis (in *Nadia: The Secret of Blue Water*), 137–38

graphic novels, 3, 7, 8, 13–15, 17, 19–20, 22, 144–46, 182; and Africa, 23, 97; and Catwoman, 65–66, 70, 72, 79–93, 168; and comix, 152, 161–65, 168, 170–72; Eisner as "father" of, 152, 211n26; and Storm, 96, 108–10, *plate9*, *plate10*; and Vixen, 111–13, 112*fig.*, 116, 118, *plate11*. *See also titles of graphic novels*

Gray, Herman, 182–83, 191n38

Great Depression, 44–45, 193n28, 196n3

Greek mythos, 96, 99, 202n11

Green Lantern, 16, 177

Grier, Pam, 111, 195n57, 203n34

Growing Up Black (David), 59

Guy, Andrew Jr., 199n38

H

(H)afrocentric (Smith), 178

Hagio, Moto, 161

Hale, Dana, 135

Hall, Stuart, 154

Halloween, 54, 55*fig.*

Hannah Hayashi (in *Millennia Wars*), 171

Hanson (in *Nadia: The Secret of Blue Water*), 137

Haque, Mohammad "Hawk," 168

Jones, Quincy, 157

Jones, Rashida, 152, 156–58, 160, 176, 178, 210n23, *plate15*

Jones, Steven Loring, 37

jouissance, 143

Judy (in *Where I'm Coming From*), 147, 150

Julie Madison (in *Batman*), 72

Julie Storm (in *Hell Rider*), 6

Julius (in *Millennia Wars*), 171–72

Jump Start (Armstrong), 64

Jungle Tales, 16

Justice League of America (JLA), III, 113–15. See also *Justice League of America (JLA)*

Justice League of America (JLA), 23, 93, 96, 113–16, 122, 177; and comix, 166; *JLA Taskforce*, 115; *JLA Unlimited*, 115–16

K

Kane, Bob, 69, 71, 74

Kanigher, Robert, 98–104, 102*fig.*, 105*fig.*, 177, 202n11

Karon (in *Catwoman*), 89

Kathy (in *Joe!*), 169

Katrina (hurricane), 180

Keaton, Trica, 123

Kefauver, Carey Estes, 197n9

Kelley, Robin D. G., 45

Kelts, Roland, 125–26

Kenya, 107, 122, 130

Kenyah (in *Wonder Woman*), 101

Kim, Jodi, 48, 123

King (in *Nadia: The Secret of Blue Water*), 129, 137

King, Martin Luther Jr., 107

King, Richard, 10

King, Rodney, 25, 148*fig.*, 149, 209n6

"King, the Lonely Lion" (anime), 139, *plate14*

Kirby, Jack, 106–7

Kitt, Eartha: and *Batman*, x, 65, 75–79, 82, 87, 200n49; blacklisting of, 78; and DC message board, 86–87; and *Eartha Kitt: Femme Fatale* (Shapiro), 67–69, *plate3*; and gay rights, 78–79, 199n27; and White House luncheon, 78

Knanick, Mike, 168

Knievel, Evel, 4

Knowles, Beyoncé, 94–95

Korean War, 56, 61–62

Kouyu, Shurei, 161

Kozinets, Robert, 185n3

Kwesi (in *Vixen: Return of the Lion*), 116, 118

L

Lady Rawhide, 80

Lamarre, Thomas, 124

Larkin (in *Songbirds*), 164–65

Latinas/os, 9–10; and Catwoman, 23, 66, 81–84, 86–87, 93; and Nadia, 132; and Wonder Woman, 95

Lawrence, Jim, 65, III, 195n57

Lee, Annie, 176

Lee, Stan, 106–7, 177, 203n22

Left, US, 35–36, 45–47

Legacy of Light: The Light of Day (Walker), 155, 161–66, 170, 173, *plate19*

Lehman, Christopher, 10–11

Lekesia (in *Where I'm Coming From*), 147, 148*fig.*, 149–50

Lendrum, Rod, 113

lesbians, 40, 78–79, 91, 149, 210n8

"A Letter t' Home" (Ormes), 39–40

Lewis, Rashida, 7–8, 152, 155, 166–68, 170

L'Hoeste, Héctor Fernández, 9, 11

Liberty Belle, 10, 69, 196n4

Liesten, Jay, *plate9*, *plate10*

Nadia (*cont.*)
with animals, 122–23, 129, 136–37,
139; father of, 138; and language,
130; and lions, 122–23, 129, 136–37,
139, 142; magic necklace ("blue
water") of, 122–23, 133, 135, 137–38;
and origin myth, 122–23, 130; and
pinups, 124, 140–44; and sexuality,
122, 124, 128–30, 132, 134–46, 166,
183, *plate12*, *plate13*, *plate14*; and
slavery, 134–37; as trapeze artist,
122, 136–37, 140
Nadia (video game), 208n35
Nadia: The Secret of Blue Water
(anime series), 24, 121–46, 183; and
business of anime, 124–27, 131,
140, 142; and comix, 155, 166; "The
First Kiss," 139; "The Girl at the
Eiffel Tower," 128–29, 133, *plate12*,
plate13; "King, the Lonely Lion,"
139, *plate14*; "The Little Fugitive,"
133, 135–36; and narratological/
visual grammars, 127–31, 141–42,
207n18
*Nadia The Secret of Blue Water: The
Motion Picture*, 146
Nama, Adilifu, 10–11, 17
Namco, 208n35
Napier, Susan, 142
Nasser, Gamal, 203n23
nationalism, 16–18; and Catwoman,
92; Eritrean nationalism, 115,
203n38; and Nadia, 128–30;
national belonging, 128–30, 182–
83; and Nubia, 96–97, 101, 120; and
Rocket, 119; and Storm, 97, 107,
110, 120; and Vixen, 97, 115, 118–20.
See also patriotism
national security: and Nubia, 96; and
Ormes, 31; and Vixen, 114–15, 118;
and Wonder Woman, 103
nation making, 8–11, 16–17, 26,
183; and Africa, 97, 99–101; and

comix, 152, 157, 159; and Martha
Washington, 19–21, 159; and
Nubia, 99–101; and Ormes, 57, 65
Nautilus (submarine), 137–38
Nazis, 113
Negro People's Front, 47
Negro question, 56, 66
Negs (in *On the Edge*), 173–76, 174*fig.*,
175*fig.*
Nelson, Alondra, 170–71
Nelson, Angela M., 37–38
Nemo, Captain (in *Nadia: The Secret of
Blue Water*), 137–38
Neo-Atlantean force (in *Nadia: The
Secret of Blue Water*), 138
neoconservatism, 178
neoliberalism, 8, 25, 126, 157, 172, 178
Nerds of Color, x
Netflix survey, 200n49
netnography, x, 185n3
Newell, Mindy, 80–81, 83–84, 168,
plate6
Newmar, Julie, 74–76, 78, 87, 200n49
New Mutants (Nocenti), 177
New Orleans (La.), 180
newspaper comics, 7, 25, 31, 36, 51. *See
also titles of newspaper comics*
newspapers, Black, 22, 32–33, 37–39,
46, 62, 65. *See also titles of Black
newspapers*
newspapers, mainstream, 64, 147, 151
newswomen, Black, 22, 32–33,
65, 192n7. *See also names of
newswomen*
New Woman, 34
New York Times, 148
Nicole (in *Where I'm Coming From*),
147, 149–50
Nietzsche, 92
9/11 terrorist attacks, 31
"9066" (Tsuei), 9
Niobe (in *The Untamed*), *plate16*
Nippon Hōsō Kyōkai (NHK), 126

social relations (*cont.*)
  148; and Catwoman, 75; and Nadia, 123–24, 132–33; and Nubia, 100, 120; and Ormes, 41, 44; and Storm, 109, 120; and Vixen, 113, 120
Songbirds (Walker), 155, 161–66, 170
Sonya (in *Where I'm Coming From*), 147
Soul of Black Folks (Du Bois), 107
sounding (verbal dueling), 46
South, US, 9–10, 38–42, 44, 58, 61, 135
South Africa, 115
space rates, 32
Spain, 129
spatiotemporality, 11–12, 14, 183; and Ormes, 40. *See also* historical contexts
spectacle, 122, 132, 135–36, 141, 161
spectators, 31, 184; and anime, 127, 130–33, 136, 138, 140–44; and Catwoman, 65–66, 78–79; and comix, 156; and genre painting, 140–41; and Nadia, 127, 130–33, 136, 138, 140–44; and Omene, 136; and Ormes, 42, 50–51, 53, 60; queer spectators, 78–79; and Vixen, 111, 115
Speed Racer (*Mahha GōGōGō*), 124–25
Spencer, Lilly Martin, 142
Spiderman, 21, 213n61
spies, 83, 156
The Spirit (Eisner), 211n26
Stansell, Christine, 40
Star (in *Legacy of Light*), 163, *plate19*
Steinberg, Marc, 124–25, 140
stereotypes, x, 7, 8, 9, 37, 60, 65; and Catwoman, 76, 87, 90–91; and comix, 146, 153, 172–73; mammy stereotype, 37, 45, 53, 62, 76; Sapphire stereotype, 46, 53, 62, 76
Stonewall riots, 78, 199n27
Storm (graphic novel), 96, 108–10, *plate9*, *plate10*

Storm (in *X-Men*), 17, 23–24, 84, 93, 96–97, 104, 106–10, 120, 122, 183, 186n2; and comix, 159–60, 166; as leader, 108, 110; and origin myth, 107–8, 123; pregnancy of, 107–8; reviews of, 107, 110; telekinetic powers of, 107–10; white hair and blue eyes of, 17, 96, 108–9
"structures of feeling," 156
stump speech, 65, 194n48
submarines, 121, 133, 137–39
subversive messages, 16–17; and Catwoman, 79; and Martha Washington, 17; and Ormes, 31, 37–38, 54, 60
Sudan, 96, 109
Suez Crisis, 107, 203n23
Suicide Squad (comic book), 23–24, 86, 96, 114–15, 117*fig.*, 181, 200n47; "Blood and Snow," 117*fig.*
Super Black: American Pop Culture and Black Superheroes (Nama), 10–11
Super Friends (comic book), 98
Super Girl (comic book), 98
Superman: in *Final Crisis*, 103, *plate8*; and Nubia, 103, *plate8*; Obama as, 98–99; and Vixen, 114, 116, 118
supremacist ideology, 100; and comix, 176; culturally supremacist minds, 176; and Gargoyle (in *Nadia: The Secret of Blue Water*), 122, 138; and Nubia, 100–101; white-supremacist-capitalist patriarchy, 77, 198n23; white supremacists, 17, 40
surfing, 67, *plate3*
surveillance, culture of, 19, 22; and Childress, 46; and comix, 157; and McGruder, 31; and Ormes, 22, 31, 35, 45, 48, 54–57, 55*fig.*, 61, 63, 192n4; and witch hunt, 54, 55*fig.* *See also* FBI (Federal Bureau of Investigation)

working classes, 45, 81, 92, 151, 183.
    See also working-class women
working-class women, 32, 38, 40–41,
    44–45, 53; and Brinkley Girl, 34;
    and Catwoman, 70, 79, 83, 90, 92.
    See also domestic workers, Black
Works Progress Administration, 47
world expositions, 122, 124, 128–29,
    132–33, 135–36
World War II, 34; and cigarettes,
    52–53, 52*fig.*; Hiroshima bombing,
    9; Nagasaki bombing, 9; and
    Ormes, 45, 47, 50–53, 51*fig.*, 52*fig.*;
    and patriotism, 196nn3–4; V-E
    Day, 51; Victory Gardens, 51–52,
    51*fig.*
World War II, post, 37, 71, 197n7

X

xenophobia, 130
"X-er-cise your ballot, weather or
    not" (Ormes), 60, 61*fig.*
X-Men (comic book), 17, 21, 23–24, 93,
    96–97, 104, 106–10, 122, 177, 183;
    and comix, 159, 166; *X-Men I*, 84;
    X-Men II, 84
X-Men (films), 104, 106–7; *X-Men*
    United: The Last Stand (2006 film),
    104, 106

Y

Yang, Jeff, 9, 11
Yardin, David, *plate9, plate10*
Yoruba religious lore, 99
"You'll be GLAD we came as
    witches—wait an' see!" (Ormes),
    54, 55*fig.*
"You're stocked pretty heavy, Leo"
    (Ormes), 61
YouTube, 124

Z

Zambesi, 116, 118
Zambia, 116
zines, xi, 7, 13
Zione Cole Tempest (in *Songbirds*),
    164
Zonjic, Tonci, 26, *plate22*
Zoot Cat, 37